NO PURCHASE, NO PAY
Privateers and Pirates
1665-1715

NO PURCHASE, NO PAY

Sir Henry Morgan, Captain William Kidd,
Captain Woodes Rogers in the Great Age of
Privateers and Pirates
1665-1715

Alexander Winston

Eyre & Spottiswoode·London.

First published in Great Britain 1970
© *1969 Alexander Winston*
Printed in Great Britain for
Eyre & Spottiswoode (Publishers) Ltd
11 New Fetter Lane E.C.4
by Ebenezer Baylis & Son Ltd
The Trinity Press, Worcester
SBN 413 27170 6

ACKNOWLEDGMENTS

SCHOLARLY DEBTS are pleasurable both in the incurring and the confessing, and none more so than those assumed in the preparation of this book. The guidance of editors at Eyre and Spottiswoode in London and at Houghton Mifflin in Boston has been unfailingly patient and perceptive. Leonard W. Labaree, Farnam Professor of History, Yale University, now editor of the *Papers of Benjamin Franklin,* and his assistant, Miss Helen C. Boatfield, were generous in counsel; Dunbar Maury Hinrichs, a Connecticut neighbor, lent valuable aid concerning Kidd material; Miss Helen Rose Cline, Recorder of Trinity Church, New York, clarified present evidences of Kidd's membership there; Kenneth C. McGuffie, Registrar of the Admiralty, gave needed advice on the validity of Kidd's passes; John P. Burnham, Librarian of Yale's Numismatic Collection, supplied information on the relative value of old coins; and John P. Ferris of the History of Parliament Trust was a rich mine of lore in all aspects of seventeenth-century England.

I am equally indebted to those who assisted me in the many institutions where research was pursued: John F. Leavitt and John B. Briley at the Mystic Seaport, Mystic, Connecticut; Yale cartographer Robert Lee Williams; Mrs. Marget Kaye of the Yale Map Collection staff; Norman Evans at the London Public Records Office; Michael Sanderson, Librarian of the National Maritime Museum, Greenwich, England; and the many unknown who supplied books and manuscripts at Yale libraries, the Admiralty Library, the New York Historical Society, London's Guildhall, and the British Museum. Squash-partner and fellow-jogger Leo Silverstein demonstrated one more of his many talents by snapping the dust-jacket picture.

An old professor of mine used to beam on us and say that literary scholarship was the common endeavor of gentlemen and ladies in search of the truth. To all these gentlemen and ladies who have made the labors of that search easier for me, my grateful thanks.

New Haven, Connecticut

ALEXANDER WINSTON

AUTHOR'S NOTE

THE FIRST AIM of the present book has been historical accuracy so far as the evidence allows. All salient facts known about Morgan and Kidd have been included, and those concerning Rogers up to his Bahama governorship. Matters of conjecture are dealt with in footnotes. The reader is directed to Sources for the identification of quotations, and to the Bibliography for works referred to in Sources. Words and phrases taken from the arcane world of seamanship are explained in the Glossary of Sea Terms.

CONTENTS

ILLUSTRATIONS

MAPS

by Samuel H. Bryant

Morgan's West Indies
Kidd's Voyage
Rogers' Voyage

PROLOGUE

THE KING'S LEFT HAND

"All men love to take what belongs to others;
it is a universal desire;
only the manner of doing it differs."
Lesage, *Gil Blas*, Book I, Chapter 5

THE PIRATE was a dirty violent fellow, fathered by the devil and mothered by a sow; the privateer might be a gentleman born, an earl, the Lord Admiral himself. Pirates were the enemies of all and friends of none; privateers sailed with their country's blessing and returned to her cheers. The pirate's end was quick by noose or bullet if he was caught; the privateer was banqueted and decked with honors. The pirate was as empty of legality as the honest privateer was full. Both, however, shared one corrupting aim — plunder — and starved without it. No purchase (prize), no pay.

Piracy was as old as boats, as old as Cain; only the Ark was safe from it. But privateering, as far as the record goes, was born and died at precise dates. In 1243 Henry III of England, unable to grieve the French in any other way, licensed a trio of private sea captains to do it for him; in 1863 a rusty tugboat, authorized by the Confederate States to attack Union shipping during the American Civil War, staggered into Nassau harbor and was sold for junk. Between these two events lie a thousand sea battles, heroisms and betrayals without number, gallantries, cruelties, fame, ruin — the history, in short, of private fighting ships.

These ships answered to many names — privateers, corsairs, buccaneers, "sea-beggars," freebooters, "water-thieves," pirates — and wore many shades of respectability. All the vessels were privately owned, all preyed on ships at sea or towns accessible to the sea, and all took their pay in booty. To distinguish privateer from pirate can be done quite easily in theory: the pirate was a seagoing robber who recognized no government, obeyed no law, and deserved no mercy; whereas the privateer was the king's left hand by sea, legally commissioned as a naval auxiliary by a belligerent government and, in event of capture, could claim the courtesies of war.[1] But the anomalies of practice blurred these neat lines of definition as lawful privateering shaded into lawless piracy; Captain William Kidd, for example, has been equally defended as a privateer and damned as a pirate. The king's right hand was seldom sure what the left was doing, and suspected the worst. "The conduct of all privateers," grumped Lord Nelson in 1804, "is, as far as I have seen, so near piracy that I only wonder any civilized nation can allow them." [2]

They were allowed for one persuasive reason: they were needed. As we shall see, Jamaica needed Henry Morgan in 1665, King William needed Captain Kidd in 1695, and in 1708 Queen Anne welcomed Woodes Rogers and others against the French-Spanish alliance. If any European nation at war lacked a navy sufficiently powerful to sweep enemy shipping from the seas, but possessed a merchant marine easily convertible to armed service, and would surrender to merchant owners a share of plunder commensurate with their risk, privateers were sure to sail.[3]

---

[1] Privateering commissions were popularly referred to as "letters of marque" or "letters of marque and reprisal." The use of the word marque in this context is disputed; it may derive from the Latin *marcare* (to seize), the French *lettre de marque* (stamped), or the German *mark* (boundary). All three meanings contain a measure of truth, since the privateer carried an official letter patent authorizing him to cross foreign boundaries and seize foreign goods. The term "privateer" did not come into common use until the end of the seventeenth century, its first recorded instance being in 1660.

[2] Naval vessels also took prizes, plunder being a chief incentive to enter royal service, since salaries were meager. Among other reasons, naval officers disliked privateers for thinning out their opportunities to capture enemy merchantmen.

[3] The government served was not always the privateer's own nor, necessarily, an established one. English ships sometimes carried Portuguese commissions, or French; and exiled James II of England authorized English and Irish ships against his countrymen. In 1582, when the King of Spain, by invitation of Portugal, was also in occupation of the Portuguese throne, eleven English ships privateered against Spain under commission from Dom Antonio, pretender to the Portuguese throne.

For centuries England fulfilled these conditions heaped up and running over. Before the Tudors little that could be called a naval force was in being. Henry III had none; transports for his knights were supplied as feudal dues by Channel towns. The handful of vessels acquired by later kings were their personal property, often rented out in peacetime to swell the royal coffers, and at Henry VI's death, by order of his will, the Council sold off the navy of England to pay his debts. It was left to Elizabeth to mark the island's frontiers upon the sea and defend them with walls of wood, but she was too parsimonious to maintain a royal navy of any size. England's sea power had to be, and was, built on the hulls of her merchant marine.

By converting private ships to royal use, and lending out her own to freebooters, Elizabeth further obscured the shadowy line between legal vessels and lawless ones. The distinction became momentary, almost capricious, a matter of politics rather than law. The same vessel that piratically snatched neutral cargo on one cruise might sail under the queen's commission on another and fight the Armada as a naval vessel on the third. The Lord Admiral owned privateers, the Treasurer of the Navy sailed them; south coast gentry openly invested in them and, if their ships were accused in court, sat on the bench that handed down a tender verdict. Piracy "almost attained the dignity of a recognized profession" as hundreds of freebooters scoured the seas and brought in their booty unmolested. Though a few obscure sea rovers were strung up for appearance's sake, not a single captain suffered more than a petty fine. If Elizabeth had hanged every seaman guilty of illegal seizure she would have depopulated her ports and destroyed the island's only defense by sea.

In this lusty, felonious age, the great adversary was Spain, who cast her immense shadow over all Europe, over the Channel, and over England's last western isle. The world had never seen her like, nor ever would again. By assumption of the Por-

tuguese throne in 1580 Spain ruled four of the world's six conti-
nents and every sea save those of northern Europe and Africa's
Mediterranean coast. In Europe she held the strategic Low-
lands, the southern dependencies of Naples, Sicily, Sardinia,
and the Duchy of Milan. Her Hapsburg connections spun a
web of alliances over the rest of the continent. Her conscripted
infantry was without peer; her brilliant action against the Turk
at Lepanto in 1571 had given her the reputation of a foremost
power at sea. Through the port of Seville poured silver from
Peru, gold from Chile, emeralds from New Granada, the pearls
of Margarita, spices, silks, jade and lacquer-ware mule-packed
across Mexico, and such homelier products as tobacco, leather,
indigo and cocoa. Spain gave all the appearance of a colossus
between whose legs the little nations of Europe could only
crawl and peep.

Much of this grandeur was hollow, as the seventeenth century would prove. Time and again foreign wars and revolt in
her European dependencies emptied Spain's treasury. Oppressive and inequitable taxes stifled her few industries; agriculture
suffered as small farms vanished into the large domains of the
nobles and clergy; poverty increased and population in Castile
declined. Spain could not defend her overseas possessions nor,
in many cases, could they defend themselves. The *hidalgo*'s contempt for commerce and menial labor, his exaggerated sense of
personal honor, and apathy under a royal authority that was
near to absolute, dampened the native audacity that had carved
out an American empire. Where the conquistadors slept, their
toughness slept with them. The colonies were rich and vulnerable, too far from Spain to be protected by the homeland and
too widely scattered for mutual aid. Seafaring nations in northern Europe regarded them with understandable greed.

Attacks on Spain's American colonies were justified by her
policy of exclusion, which other maritime nations viewed as an
act of hostility. Spain was determined that no foreign ship
should enter her colonial ports, nor should, indeed, even sail

those waters.[4] In treaties made with the seafaring nations, she was unwilling to accord them the same trading rights in the colonies that she offered with herself. This became explicit when the peace treaty of Cateau-Cambrésis (1559) restored normal commercial relations between Spain and France, but ignored the Americas. By oral agreement the colonies were unaffected, their waters still closed to alien trade south of a "Line" generally recognized by Spain and her northern rivals as the Tropic of Cancer. This cut through the Florida Straits just north of the homeward route of the treasure fleets. Such an arbitrary barrier was tenable, of course, only to the extent that Spain could enforce it.

Her American colonists pleaded for forts and garrisons, but Spain chose to concentrate on guarding the homebound treasure galleons. A report to the Spanish king predicted that no colonial town could defend itself from the attack of 300 resolute men. The French soon showed this to be entirely accurate. In 1537 they raided Honduras and captured nine ships of the treasure fleet, in 1543 burned the settlement and Cubagua, off the Venezuela coast. François le Clerc pillaged Santiago de Cuba in 1554 with a squadron of royal vessels, and the next year his lieutenant, Jacques Sores, razed Havana.

Spain met the threat to her sea lanes by instituting armed convoys in 1543. Two fleets left Seville each spring, their

---

[4] Mercantilism, as this policy came to be called, was in no sense peculiar to Spain. In its various forms it was, and is, the economic expression of the national state. The aim of every seventeenth-century nation in Europe was to accumulate hard money by an excess of exports over imports, to increase population density for the uses of industry and defense, and to wrap a cocoon of exclusion acts around herself and her colonial possessions. Spain's edicts to this end were hotly protested by the northern sea powers, and promptly duplicated, though less rigidly, as soon as they gained colonies of their own. The Dutch succeeded best in the early seventeenth century, envied and emulated by the Commonwealth and later Stuarts in England, and by Colbert in France. Cromwell's Navigation Acts of 1651 seriously weakened the Dutch carrying trade by fastening British colonial commerce to English ports and English ships. The policy was disadvantageous to the colonies and worked only so long as they were submissive; in England's case it drove the North Americans to revolt in 1776.

routes, makeup and sailing dates minutely fixed. One made for the Caribbean coast of South America to gather the produce of New Granada at Cartagena, and that of Peru at Darien. Called the *galeones,* this fleet bore home the richest treasure in gold, silver and precious stones, and was guarded by six or eight warships. Parting from the *galeones* in the Leewards, the *flota* made course through the West Indies to Veracruz, on the Mexican coast. It picked up the produce of Mexico and that of the Philippines, which had been brought into the Pacific port of Acapulco by the Manila galleon and transported overland to Veracruz. Two guard ships convoyed the *flota.* Both fleets wintered in snug harbor and rendezvoused at Havana the following March. At its peak in 1600, as many as ninety vessels and ten men-of-war sailed up the Florida passage from Havana bound for Spain. The convoys posted an excellent record of safe crossings, while the colonies themselves, weak, indolent, ill-garrisoned, lay open to attack.

Boasting only twenty-five capital ships, Elizabethan England treated the Spanish giant with deference. John Hawkins of Plymouth tested the true steel of Spain's embargo with a peaceful trading voyage into the closed waters of the Caribbean in 1563. He carried four shiploads of African slaves to Hispaniola's[5] northern shore, sold half of them outright, and deposited the rest with planters pleased to get them on credit. To cover up this illicit deal, Hispaniola officials reported to Seville that they feared harm from Hawkins, and did business with him only to escape injury.

Encouraged by his first venture, Hawkins was soon back again, this time on the mainland, at Rio de la Hacha. He was scrupulously polite. He paid the harbor dues like an honest merchant, and received from town authorities a quite illegal license to conduct future business on their coast. Once more

[5] The island of the Greater Antilles now shared by Haiti and the Dominican Republic.

the report to Seville said that he blustered and roared at the innocent townsmen, bullying them into dealings which they abhorred. Spain hurried to end this clandestine commerce. Her ambassador in London protested so vehemently that Elizabeth forbade Hawkins to trespass again in Caribbean waters. She must have given him the wink, for she had money in the voyage, and knighted Hawkins for his success. Next year, when the ships went out, Hawkins prudently stayed home, but the Spanish now began to show their teeth. The voyage met sharp opposition in mainland ports, and some of its black cargo had to be released ashore lest they die of thirst.

Sir John resolved to put pressure on the Spanish; if they would not deal amicably with him, a few well-directed threats might teach them to be more cordial. He headed westward in 1567 with a command of nine ships, ranging in bulk from the heavily armed 700-ton *Jesus of Lübeck* (owned by Elizabeth) down to the 32-ton *Angel*.[6] They met with courtesy in defenseless anchorages along the Main. Rio de la Hacha, however, gave them a chill welcome — a hundred harquebusiers sheltered behind new fortifications. But a storming party produced in the town fathers what could pass for more friendly warmth, and under cover of night they rowed out to the ships to buy 200 slaves.

Off Cuba, August gales ripped into the fleet and it staggered westward under bare poles toward Mexico. Intermittent lulls enabled Hawkins to seize three Spanish vessels carrying a hundred passengers. The possession of these, he thought, might win provisions and a quiet haven wherever they fetched up.

Mauled and storm-drenched, they put into the treasure port

[6] Calculation of ship size was based on cubic capacity, not on weight of the hull. Tonnage (or, as it was originally spelled, tunnage) indicated the number of tuns (wine casks) that a ship could carry. This had its variations; a shipwright's method of measure might differ from a merchant's and gross tonnage (all space) was not the same as underdeck tonnage (equipment and living quarters subtracted).

of Veracruz. Town officials came out in boats, mistaking so large a fleet for an expected *flota*. Hawkins made no attempt to disabuse them of this error until they were prisoners on his deck. Then he requested permission (and very naturally got it) to repair ship under the lee of San Juan de Ulúa, a stony island in the bay. Dawn next day showed the tardy *flota*, thirteen great ships in all, riding outside the harbor. While the Spanish tossed uncomfortably under the lash of the northern gale, the two fleet commanders made a pact of amity between them, that neither one "should violate the peace upon pain of death." Hawkins did not know that the flagship concealed in its cabin two angry men — the new viceroy of Mexico, and one of his captains-general.

Once snugged safely into port, these two came out of hiding and carried on in a way that aroused Hawkins' suspicion. A horde of men appeared from shore, shifted the *flota*'s guns, dug in on the island, and vanished into the flagship's hold. The master of the *Jesus,* who spoke some Spanish, demanded the meaning of this warlike bustle. The viceroy assured him "that he, in the faith of a Viceroy, would be our defence from all villainies." It was a grand deception. On the morning of the third day the *flota* attacked without warning. Armed men poured from holds onto the Spanish decks, guns flamed, fire ships drifted down on the surprised English. Seamen tented ashore were slaughtered. Only two small barques escaped, overloaded with men from the doomed ships. Hawkins on the 50-ton *Minion* had 200 packed between her narrow gunwales, and had to put half ashore, where the Spaniards hunted them down. The ship's company suffered starvation and disease on the sad trip home, reaching England in January, 1569, with only fifteen gaunt-eyed survivors.

The other barque, the *Judith,* had limped into Plymouth a few days before. Her commander never forgave the Spaniards for San Juan de Ulúa. Tribalism in all its forms perverts justice, and this young man found it convenient to forget the assault on

Rio de la Hacha and the seized Spanish ships, while he brooded on the act of Spanish treachery. A likable fellow, too, ruddy and square-built, a cousin of Hawkins, named Francis Drake

Greed for the wealth of the Indies, lurid tales of cruelty to native peoples, and now the outrage at Veracruz turned England's gnawing resentment into passion. Soon there was more wood to the fire. Religious differences between Catholic Spain and Protestant England were violent enough without special provocation — each was anti-Christ to the other — but in 1570 the Pope excommunicated Elizabeth, and the Holy Office promised cleansing of guilt to anyone, "cook, brewer, baker, vintner, physician, grocer, surgeon or other" who would do away with her. In 1571 the Ridolfi plot to assassinate Elizabeth implicated the very throne of Spain. To the Bishop of Salisbury the divine message was clear, and it was favorable: "God would be pleased to see the Spanish plundered."

After San Juan de Ulúa, Drake not only loathed the Spanish; he set out to destroy them. In 1572 he was back in the Caribbean with a fighting force thin as a sword point, and as deadly. His two ships were puny in size but fitted for action, his seventy-three men and boys itched to pluck the lion's beard. They rushed Nombre de Dios by night, retreating only when Drake was wounded in the first encounter; they ran down the coast like a consuming fire; in the Darien hills they ambushed a fat packtrain loaded with silver. And from a tree high on Mount San Pablo, Drake stared westward at a pale bluish strip — the far Pacific.

Perched in his tree Drake vowed to sail those waters that no Englishman had ever touched.[7] Profitable, too; while the

---

[7] Drake's lieutenant, John Oxenham, beat him to the honor. In 1575 he led seventy men to the heights of Darien. At the headwaters of a river they built a forty-five-foot pinnace which floated them down to the Gulf of St. Miguel, on the Pacific side. Oxenham captured two barques stacked with gold and silver from Peru. Returning upstream with his loot he dallied too long, either because his men were mutinous, as Hakluyt reports or, in the more romantic tale of Kingsley's *Westward Ho!*, for the sake of a lovely lady. A Spanish posse pursued, tracing the invaders at one point by chicken feathers carelessly tossed on the stream. Oxenham was caught, and hanged in Lima.

Spanish mounted guard at the front door of their treasure house, he would slip in at the back. Who would look for a ship through the terrors of Magellan's passage? It was narrow, baffling, without anchorage or food, 300 miles of icy storms that froze seamen at their posts. Spain had even spread the rumor that an irresistible east-west current would prevent any return that way. Yet in 1578 Drake took three small ships through the straits and raided up the coast of Peru. He sailed faster than news of him. Spanish America dozed in the tropic sun while he sacked towns and captured rich prizes at sea. He lifted 4000 ducats[8] from a man sleeping under a tree; the man slept on. There was no need to kill a single Spaniard, and Drake did not. At the end of three years, home around the world, he brought the *Golden Hind* up the Thames in triumph. The voyage paid his backers a handsome forty-seven to one. Queen Elizabeth, who secretly had money in the venture, called Drake her "deare Pyrat" and knighted him on the deck of his ship.

The Spanish ambassador fumed that Elizabeth honored "the master thief of the known world," which was true. In a countermove Philip II of Spain seized all English ships and goods in his ports. He threw the seamen into prison where, Elizabeth charged, they were "flogged, tortured, famished, murdered, and buried like dogs in dung-heaps." Philip released them, but undeclared war was on.

For the next ten years Drake was the hammer, Spain the iron.

---

[8] The standard Spanish coin was the silver peso, or piaster, from which the American dollar was derived. It was also called the piece of eight, having the value of eight Spanish reals (12½¢); and two of these eight "bits" (25¢) has produced the American colloquialism of "two bits" for the quarter-dollar coin. The peso was worth 4s. 6d. in the seventeenth century, or 100¢ American, rating the shilling at 22¢ and the penny at 2¢. The Dutch guilder valued at 1s. 8d. or 38¢, the Indian rupee at 2s. 4d. or 52¢, the English crown and French *écu* at 5s. or $1.10. The ducat varied, according to its country of origin, from 83¢ to $2.32. All coins derived their value from their weight of precious metal; they were therefore clipped, scraped, filed and plugged, as well as suffering wear from long usage. Estimating the comparative purchasing power of money then and now is a matter of rough guesswork; students of the subject put it at ten to twenty times greater in the seventeenth century than in the mid-twentieth.

In 1585 he massed a fleet of twenty-eight privateers and two royal warships, burned Santiago in the Cape Verdes (where he lost 300 men by plague) and wheeled west to pounce on Caribbean ports. At Santo Domingo he bombarded the town by sea while a landing party circled to take it from the rear. At Cartagena he methodically burned one building after another until the citizens dug up the 110,000 ducat ransom. Illness reduced his 2300 men to only 800 able to haul a rope or heft a cutlass, but he made home with plunder worth half a million pounds.

In a dazzling raid in 1587 Drake littered Cadiz Harbor with the wreckage of Spanish ships. Next year his fast squadron was one of those that harried the Armada up the Channel and battered it off Gravelines as it fled into the North Sea. From that pinnacle, Drake's fortunes fell away. In 1595 he and Hawkins aimed their last blow at the jugular of the Spanish empire. They marshaled twenty-seven ships and 5000 fighting men, force enough to sweep the West Indies into a basket and snap the lid. Instead, they suffered repulse everywhere: the Canaries, Puerto Rico, Cuba, Darien. Disease, Spain's silent and subtle ally, carried off both commanders in their hour of disappointment — Hawkins at Havana, Drake on the coast of Darien.

Other Elizabethans risked their necks in exploits dimmed only by Drake's luster. Thomas Cavendish circumnavigated the globe in 1586, took nineteen Spanish ships in all, including the Manila galleon, and sailed up the Thames with China silk for sails. The Earl of Cumberland, who wore the queen's glove for an emblem on his hat, sent out nearly a dozen expeditions and went on four of them himself. In 1595 Raleigh attacked Trinidad, and in 1601 Captain William Parker sacked Porto Bello, the Caribbean outlet for the Gold Road from Panama.

Attacks that were baldly admitted beyond the "Line" had to be more covert on the European side. "Water-thieves," masked and smeared with soot, snatched Spanish ships out of the Thames estuary. Swift, maneuverable three-masters preyed on the Don's shipping all up the Channel coast. "Your mariners rob my master's ships on the sea, and trade where they are forbidden to go," the Spanish ambassador accused Elizabeth; "they plunder our people in the streets of your towns; they attack our vessels in your very harbors, and take out prisoners from them; your preachers insult my master from their pulpits, and when we apply for justice, we are answered with threats."

Or with duplicity, one could add. When the most flagrant of the "water-thieves" was caught, the Spanish ambassador urged that his manner of death fit his villainy. By all means, cried Elizabeth, let the wretch be a warning to those who prey on our good friends of Spain! We shall spraddle him naked on the stone floor of his dungeon with a cannon on his chest, and feed him raw grains of corn and sips of foul water until he dies! The ambassador was overjoyed. While he reported home that justice had been restored, Elizabeth quietly set the prisoner free.

At last the feverish Elizabethan age ended. Philip II of Spain died in his bare chamber in the Escorial, his gaze fixed steadfast on the distant altar. In 1603 the obstreperous Virgin of England was laid to rest, and amiable James Stuart came to the throne anxious for a tranquil reign. Under the early Stuarts youthful England, so gusty, wanton and muscular, began to take on a paunch. The new king quickly made peace with Spain and called in all privateering commissions.

"James was made up of two men," in Macaulay's opinion; "a witty well-read scholar who wrote, disputed and harangued, and a nervous, drivelling idiot who acted." Still, his actions suited the times. The flow of precious metals to Europe from American mines had vastly increased coinage. Ready money provided mobile capital, and capital in negotiable form rapidly expanded the possibilities of commerce. Stuart England saw that sticking *bandilleras* into the Spanish bull might be exciting sport, but would hardly do as long-term policy. The rising merchants were ready to let the glory go if their ships came safe to harbor with cargoes that turned a neat profit. Beyond the gray towns of little Europe opened the new-discovered world in its immensity and promise, redolent of spice, rustling with silk, roofed with silver, blazoned with gold. The seventeenth century became a race between the maritime powers — England, Holland, France — to dominate the New World's marts and seaways.[9]

The Dutch outran their rivals at the start. "Their North Pole is their traffic, measuring all things by that," grumbled the English. Holland built the best ships, manned them with the best crews, and loaded cargoes with the most efficiency. More French and British goods were carried in Dutch bottoms than in those of their own countries. In 1602 the Dutch East India Company began its spectacular career. Its powers were enormous: the right, east of the Cape of Good Hope, to colonize, maintain armed forces, set up courts, sign treaties and wage war. At its height in 1669 the Company owned 150 merchantmen, forty warships, and could put 10,000 soldiers in the field. When the Company was cheerful, all Holland wagged. In 1641 it forced the Portuguese out of Malacca, and a 1667 treaty with native princes gained it special privileges in Sumatra. By cornering the spice market the Dutch tripled the price of pepper in Europe. Where a little bloodshed was needed they did

---

[9] The instrument of commercial expansion was the private stock company, formed to explore and exploit a stated segment of the world market. Charters rewarded stockholders for their high risk by granting them monopolies, which the companies jealously guarded from interlopers. The most successful venture in England was the East India Company, organized as the year 1600 opened, with the sole access to the "whole, entire, and only trade and traffic to the East Indies." Among more than a dozen others were the Merchant Adventurers, who controlled the cloth trade with Germany; the Levant Company in the eastern Mediterranean; the Massachusetts Bay Company, which did so much to found the American nation; and Canada's Hudson's Bay Company, the lone survivor to our own day. Many went under, and the collapse of the South Sea Company in 1720 brought down the British government with it. Dutch companies were fewer, and more closely knit into Holland's economy; French companies, on which lay the paternalistic hand of the king, never achieved the independence and strength of their British and Dutch rivals. Weak or strong, the company usually went first, and empire followed.

not hesitate; at Amboina in 1623 they executed a few overzealous factors of the English East India Company. The English retreated to their India stations, far from the Dutch ambit.

Nor did Holland neglect Spain, whose Lowland wars had aroused in the Dutch an abiding hatred. In the Caribbean the Dutch smuggled where they could, and attacked where they could not. A West India Company organized in 1621 set its aim to be "above all in humbling the pride and might of Spain." Under its auspices, ten ships a month, that collected salt in a Venezuela lagoon, also bought tobacco from shore plantations and went on to pick up hides in remote bays of Hispaniola. Spanish authorities reacted with customary shortsightedness. They forbade Venezuelans to grow tobacco, and cleared settlers out of the disobedient northwest of Hispaniola. Off Havana in 1628 a Dutch privateering squadron scored a rare victory over the Spanish treasure fleet. Its commander, Pieter Heyn, who had twice been chained to the oar in Spanish galleys, drove the treasure ships onto Matanzas Beach and took fifteen million guilders out of them. The Dutch West India Company declared a fifty percent dividend.

Planting colonies in the West Indies, however, fell largely to the English and French. These eyed the long chain of Lesser Antilles which the Spanish had bypassed in favor of larger islands westward and the gold of the continent. English settlers landed in the central part of St. Christopher (St. Kitts) in 1623; not to be outdone, the French took possession of both ends. Soon the English were on Barbados, Nevis, Antigua, Montserrat; the French on Guadeloupe and Martinique. The Dutch settled Curaçao, Saba and St. Eustatius, sharing St. Martin with the English. The islands were lovely to look on, fertile and, above all, strategic — they bottled up the inland sea like a cork. Spain's few efforts to dislodge the intruders did more harm than good. When a royal fleet captured Nevis and St. Christopher in 1629, footloose fugitives scattered through the empty hills of northwest Hispaniola. As the Spanish harried them from this refuge, they took to the sea. Spain found that she had sowed the wind, and reaped the buccaneers.

Of all the Spanish colonies, only Jamaica was wrested away by force. Cromwell, the hard-bitten Puritan, dismissed Spain as "a Colossus stuffed with clouts," and hoped to snatch a strong base in the Caribbean. He had in hand a memorial from Thomas Gage, a priest turned Presbyterian, who had traveled widely in the Americas before his conversion. The colonies, Gage reported, were wealthy and weak, ripe for the plucking. Why not Hispaniola? Its capital of Santo Domingo boasted the honor of being Spain's oldest colonial town, and clung to its decaying glory as an aged general to his medals. In 1655 Cromwell dispatched a fleet of thirty-eight ships and 2500 men, with Hispaniola as the prime target. The men were exceptionally poor in quality, and 4000 recruits from England's Leeward colonies rated no better. The invasion was ill-planned, ill-commanded and ill-executed. A small defending force at Santo Domingo drove them off in panic. Loath to go home empty-handed, they dropped down to Jamaica, and took possession of the island from 1500 poorly armed Spaniards. The conduct of the two commanders was so bumbling that on their return to England they were sent to the Tower for a month to shrive their souls. Jamaica was held, however, and became a haven for the buccaneers.

Slowly a set of customs and formal rules developed to regulate privateering. When England engaged in war the king authorized the Admiralty to issue commissions, and the Admiralty in turn empowered colonial governors, and other suitable officials, to do the same. The commission named the enemy and added a stern warning not to harm the ships of friendly nations. Often it required that a third or a half of the privateer crew be landsmen, so that hardened seamen would be spared for naval service. Above all, the privateer was forbidden to appropriate booty for his own use, prior to legal condemnation. Prize ships and their goods were not to be "sold, spoiled, wasted or diminished" in any degree until the Admiralty court had ruled, and the privateer posted bond as a guarantee of compliance. This avoided unjust seizure, and assured the king his tenth of the prize value, and the Admiralty its fifteenth.

The rest of the plunder went to the captor. The crew signed on "no purchase, no pay," without set wages; all aboard took the risks of combat and shared its rewards. Privateering captains, such as Rogers or Kidd, tacked up their articles on the waterfront, and though a third of the seamen could not read, they knew by custom what the articles would say. The ship-owner, supplier of the whole voyage, was entitled to 40 or 50 percent of the plunder. Of the rest, the captain received five or six shares, other officers scaled down by rank from three to one and a half shares, able seamen had a share apiece, boys and apprentices a half-share. Enthusiasm for the chase was sharpened by rewards to the first man to sight a prize, and the first to board her. The articles also fixed compensation for injury or disablement: if a seaman died in action, his heirs were paid 1000 pieces of eight from the booty; loss of a right arm drew 600; a left arm or right leg, 500; a left leg, 400; a finger or eye, 100.

Pirate articles were similar, but since the entire crew owned the ship, they paid no owner's share; and in other ways they could afford to be more generous to themselves. The articles of Captain Lowther promised that a crewman maimed in battle could stay in the ship's company as long as he wished. Those of Captain Roberts gave a wounded man an *écu* a day up to sixty days under the surgeon's care and, since artificial limbs were hard to come by, would pay the same compensation for the loss of a hook or wooden leg as for hand or foot.

If a privateer was caught by the enemy, his commission was security against the hangman's noose. To have one in hand, even a questionable one, was convenient. As a result, they were bought and sold, issued in blank, forged, altered, redated. In

Governments made some pretense at policing these narrow waters. Beyond them, where the clamor of European wars rang dimly, but still rang, control was a slippery matter. Caribbean privateering took on a far more ambiguous form — the buccaneers of America.

The buccaneers started, innocently enough, as hunters. Columbus had brought domesticated animals to Hispaniola, which had none: cattle, pigs, sheep, and dogs so different from the squat, mute Caribbean kind that the natives did not recognize them as such. Since the Spaniard was addicted to town life, the herds spread through the outskirts of Santo Domingo under the care of Indians. When the Indians died out, cultivated land returned to scrub and the animals wandered off on their own. They multiplied prodigiously. By 1600 ship's parties were landing on the northwest shore of the island to replenish their meat in mountains that teemed with wild cattle and wild pigs.

Hunters drifted in to make it a business. Shipwrecked seamen, deserters, runaway servants, fleeing criminals, political and religious refugees, jobless laborers, wanderers of every stripe — all found there the anonymity they cherished. Family names were ignored. For comradeship and safety they hunted in pairs or small bands, each man a *matelot* (mate) to the others, with all but personal belongings held in common. A man needed no more estate than a knife and gun; the earth was his pillow, the sky his coverlet; he could kill his own meat, and sell the rest to passing ships for clothing, powder and rum.

The hunters smoked clay pipes, drank their liquor neat. Their dress was a narrow-brimmed hat, peaked in front, a long shirt bloused up with a rawhide belt, short trousers (or none, the shirt sufficed), and leggings of hide. From the belt hung two or three knives to cut brush and carve up the kill. Since they washed as seldom as possible, their clothes stiffened and turned black with the caked blood of slaughtered beasts until

c

the cloth looked tarred. These grimy Spartans barred women
— known troublemakers, all — and any hunter who tried to
bring one in, native or white, was expelled from the brother-
hood. Affection that they might have shown for wife or child
went to their guns, long-barreled beauties from Nantes or
Dieppe, polished to a gloss and stored from the damp in hide
cases. A leather pouch at the waist held their gun charges
handy for use: small paper cylinders, with powder and a one-
ounce ball in each. The hunter would slip one from his pouch
in an instant, bite off the end, pour a thin stream of priming
powder into the pan, drop the remaining charge down the barrel, seat it with a thump of the gun butt on the ground, and be
ready for action. They were deadly shots, the best in all the
Americas.

At dawn, as the sun rose out of the sea, the hunters whetted
their knives and left camp for the range. They skinned their
quarry where it fell, breakfasting on marrow sucked from the
soft bones. Then they cut the meat into strips and spread these
on a rude grill tied together with green vines. The method had
been learned from the Carib Indians; the grill, a *bukan* in native tongue, gave the hunters the bizarre name by which history knows them. French hunters (who predominated in number) called the meat *viande boucanée*, to dry it was *boucaner*,
and the man who did it was, perforce, a *boucanier*.[10] On a fire
of coals under the grill the hunters threw bones, fat and scraps
of hide from the slaughtered animals. Thick, odorous smoke
billowed up from this grisly heap; the meat took on a rich, red
color, a delectable flavor, and dried hard as kindling. Tied in
convenient bundles, a hundred pounds sold to ship crews for
three pieces of eight.

---

[10] Though the French invented the term, only the English applied it to the
freebooters of the Caribbean. The French called them *flibustiers* (from which
we derive "filibuster"), a word of debatable origin, probably connected with
the light, open "fly-boats" used by the early buccaneers. In Dutch they were
zee-rovers; the Spanish, with more emotion, called them *corsarios luteranos*
(lutheran corsairs), *demonios,* or *ladrones* (thieves).

Innocent enough, one would say, not doing anybody harm, but to the Spanish on the island the buccaneers were dangerous intruders. The city fathers of Santo Domingo took steps to get rid of them. Their first tactic was simple and pleasantly safe — to fan out from the south coast, slaughtering the wild cattle as they went, and so deprive the villains of their livelihood. The hunters retreated to the offshore island of Tortuga, and when Spanish soldiers routed them from there, slipped across the channel to Hispaniola again. The game of hide-and-seek was back where it started, but with a significant difference: the hunters had lost their great herds of wild cattle, and acquired a very sour view of the Spaniards. The 300 survivors requested the French at St. Christopher to put them under the protection of a governor.

In 1641 the governor-general at St. Christopher sent them a Huguenot named Levasseur, and bundled along with him forty or fifty other Protestants who had been an embarrassment to his Catholic settlers. Levasseur set up headquarters on Tortuga, an island humped like a turtle, with a steep sea cliff northward and a single harbor on the south. Under his rule Tortuga prospered. Population grew; plantings of tobacco and sugar were begun on the level land. Trading ships of the ubiquitous Dutch stopped by to pick up meat, hides and tallow. As time went on, however, Levasseur assumed the airs of a petty king. High on the rock above the harbor he built a fort and residence impregnable to direct assault, reached only by stone steps and iron ladders. Genially dubbed the "Dovecote," it nevertheless contained a dungeon known as "Purgatory," and a cagelike prison that was "Hell." In 1653 a couple of wastrels removed the governor's heavy hand by murdering him in a quarrel over a mistress.

His successor arrived bearing the generous title: Governor of Tortuga and Western Hispaniola. The Spanish offered instant disproof of this inflated claim by storming the island and deporting the settlers. The attacking force withdrew shortly to

meet the threat of Cromwell's 1655 expedition, but the Tortu-
gans no longer felt the island solid under their feet. They
began to call themselves Brethren of the Coast, and took to sea-
raiding as a livelihood. In dugout canoes and open boats,
oared, with a single sail, they launched tentative forays along
the Spanish shore. Soon a French rover, deservedly remembered as Pierre le Grand, made a discovery which the Spanish
long regretted. In a native *piragua,* with only twenty-eight
men weakened by hunger and exposure, Pierre sighted a Spanish *flota.* It sailed by in majesty, splendid with arms, while the
men quietly cursed it. Presently, however, the vice admiral's
ship came lagging along, quite alone. After nightfall, the
piragua slid under her stern. Pierre knocked a hole in the bottom of his boat to prevent all thought of return. The men
scrambled up the poop and seized the great ship without a
shot, surprising the officers over brandy and cards in the cabin.
Pierre's prudence matched his audacity, for he sailed his prize
straight to Dieppe and retired on the spoils.

In the time that it took to raise a sail, the buccaneers had
converted Pierre's exploit into a risky but profitable business.
They cruised the Caribbean waters jammed into little barques
that gave them no cover from wind and rain, raiding pig yards
ashore or catching turtles for food, cinching their belts, careless, foolhardy and brutish. Their single-masters of cedar,[11]
shallow-drafted to run into creeks and lagoons, mounted six to
ten light cannon, but the buccaneers relied on boarding. Every

[11] Cedarwood resisted shipworms, the curse of the old sailing vessel. Most
common of these borers were the soft-bodied teredos, not true worms but
mollusks, the shell reduced to a pair of curved plates equipped with fine teeth.
While young they entered a ship's planking through almost invisible holes,
then bored parallel to the surface as they grew to be adults four to six inches
long. Able to lay a million eggs a year, they could honeycomb a hull on a
long voyage. Other borers consumed the wood from the outside, layer by
layer. As protection, ships were double-planked, with a layer of felt and tar
between, and careened as often as possible. Bottoms were cleaned by scraping
off seaweed and barnacles, and applying a coat of wax, pitch and tar (sometimes mixed with sulphur or arsenic) to the planks. Brief experiments in sheath-
ing ships with lead failed when the galvanic action of lead on iron ate the
metal away. Until metal ships came into use, worms sent many a stout hull
either to the bottom or to the junkdealer.

man carried his own musket, pistol and heavy cutlass with its double guard and great curving blade. They learned to approach bow-on to a ship's quarter, where none of her stationary guns could fire, to pick off her men on deck with musketry and raking cannon, jam her rudder, and go up her sides agile as monkeys. It was a terrible sight. The Spanish studded their bulwarks with nails to discourage attacks over the side; they smeared their decks with grease, peas and tacks; they erected "closed quarters" from which to repel boarders after they had gained the deck — all to little avail. Yelling, wild-eyed buccaneers who clambered aboard with cutlasses gleaming and pistols spouting fire struck terror to the Spaniard's heart and unnerved his hand.

Buccaneers expected no quarter from the Spanish and gave none. From the early years (1655–1665) survive a few names to shudder at: Montbars, Portugues, Brasiliano, Lolonois — half-legendary brutes capable of chilling cruelty. Montbars, at least, claimed a moral sanction: he was so enraged by Spanish wrongs to the Indians that he dedicated his sword to the God of Vengeance, and won the nickname of "The Exterminator." Montbars enjoyed slitting a Spaniard's belly and hauling out his intestines, which he then nailed to the mast, and by putting firebrands to the victim's buttocks, drove him in a jog of death until he dropped. But Lolonois bears off the dark laurels as the worst of these madmen. In his bloody career he roasted prisoners alive, hacked them to pieces and licked the blade with relish, once sliced out a stubborn fellow's heart and gnawed it, warm and dripping, in his fury. He met his just due at the hands of Darien Indians who tore him, slowly, limb from limb. Most of the buccaneers stooped to the most callous barbarity if it would wring coin from a hapless town. When Panama was slow to ransom prisoners held by Captain Grogniet in 1685, he cut off twenty heads at random and sent them to the city in a sack, with the promise of twenty more daily until the money was paid.

Yet these rogues could show queer dashes of piety. After

seizing a town the French habitually repaired to church, while the dead still sprawled in the streets, to celebrate their victory with a solemn Te Deum. They pillaged ecclesiastical buildings first, as the wealthiest depositories of treasure, but carefully removed all images before burning a town. Sometimes sacred vessels and vestments stolen from the Spanish would be bestowed as votive offerings on clergy of a friendlier port. A Captain Daniel, as Père Labat tells it, went to extreme lengths to preserve an attitude of religious reverence in his crew. Anchored — fittingly — off the Îles des Saints, he haled a priest aboard to celebrate Mass, which was carried on with seamanly pomp: salvos of cannon at the Sanctus, Elevation, Benedictus and Exaudiat. When one of the crew showed frank indifference, Captain Daniel reproved him by shooting him through the head. The body was tossed overboard at once, lest the service be disturbed. An effective way, observed Père Labat dryly, to prevent the fellow from repeating his offense.[12]

The buccaneers maintained a nervous alliance with their Caribbean colonies because it was, to some extent, expedient for both. The buccaneer had to dispose of his booty for cash or goods; he could not eat silver ingots nor drink indigo nor patch worm-riddled planks with damask. He needed a friendly port — the indispensable "fence" of every thief — or pilfering was no use. The colonies, on their part, harbored the freebooters as their sole sea arm against Spain and, incidentally, grew rich on the plunder.

French buccaneers gathered at Tortuga, which was reconstituted in 1665 under its most astute governor, Bertrand d'Ogéron. *"Corbleu!"* he exclaimed, after one look at his unwashed citizens, "I shall order chains from France for these rascals!" He imported 150 French brides, all of whom had lost the power to blush. The grooms, now washed up and crammed

---

[12] Cf. Père Jean Baptiste Labat, *Memoirs* (London: Constable and Co., 1931), p. 222.

with virtue, were cautious. "Your past is nothing to me," each recited at the marriage ceremony, "for I did not know you then. I acquit you of all evil, but you must pledge me your word for the future. This" — touching his musket — "will soon avenge me should you prove false."

Sobered by family responsibilities, and his wife wary of the musket, many a French rover settled down to a planter's life on Hispaniola. D'Ogéron confined his 1500 *flibustiers* to the island of Tortuga, giving them letters of marque when they cruised, handling their booty when they returned. The benefit was mutual. He was their legal protector and middleman, they were his suppliers and defense.

English buccaneers of Morgan's heyday (1665–1675) found Jamaica to their liking. At Port Royal, crowded on the tip of a great twisting sandspit, large ships could ride in the glassy waters close to the king's colonnaded warehouse, while small barques beached up the inlet of Chocolatta Hole. Jamaica was badly run, but that made no difference. Port Royal excelled in one respect: it was reputed to be the wickedest town in America; indeed, some ventured in awed tones, perhaps in the whole world. A shocked visitor reckoned the count of its grog shops at one for every ten men. Governor Modyford blamed the high mortality among the settlers more on intemperance than fever; even stolid old army men, he mourned, "from strict saints are turned to the most debauched devils." West Indians, who were at first appalled that the English died off so fast, choked down some of the Jamaica rum and wondered rather that the islanders lived so long.

The raffish crew planted on Jamaica from the invasion force soon made plunder the island's major industry. Hardly had the smoke of the 1655 assault faded when some of the ships were off again, under Vice Admiral Goodson, to sack towns on the Spanish mainland. In 1659 a party foraging in the Venezuela woods hit on forty-two chests of silver destined for the Spanish king, to the value of 200,000 to 300,000 pieces of eight. Bucca-

neer ships came in deep-laden from raids on Santa Marta, Rio
de la Hacha, Santiago de Cuba, Campeche (Yucatan). Port
Royal merchants rubbed their hands over booty that they
bought cheap on the quay and sold dear in England. Buccaneer crews doubled the port's profit by spending their money in
wild sprees that lasted until they were broke. One fellow with
a glistening eye laid out 500 Spanish dollars to a prostitute if she
would strip for him in a tavern taproom. She was shy, but willing. No true buccaneer would go cruising again so long as a
single coin clung to the lining of his pocket. He gambled it
away, drank it up, lost it in bawdy houses. However the manner of its departure, the money fell at last into the patient hands
of Port Royal merchants.

Profit from buccaneering was a bit too grimy to push with
London, though Jamaicans did not hide it. More plausibly,
they pointed out that Spanish hostility kept the colony in a
tremor of fear. Three raids by the Spaniards had been beaten
off between 1655 and 1660, but an overwhelming force might
appear at any moment on their shores. Further, in 1666 Jamaica faced foes in every corner of the Caribbean. The French
and Dutch, united in war against England, added their threat
to that of the ever present and ever vengeful Spanish. News of
disaster swept in from other islands. The Dutch bombarded
Barbados in 1665; the next year the French routed the St.
Christopher English and shipped 8000 of them away. What
chance had Jamaica without the privateers? Port Royal's moldering little fort offered scant protection; the seat of government at St. Jago had but a powder house with the roof fallen in;
and the few "trained bands" scattered throughout the island
were remarkable for their lack of training.

During the first decade of the Restoration (1660–1670) London's reply to these pleas was ambiguous because the situation
remained ambiguous. The "Line" still removed Spanish America from Europe's amities as well as its alarums. Spain refused
to recognize England's rightful possession of Caribbean islands,

and would seize them again at the first opportunity. London neatly straddled the issue by deploring the buccaneers publicly and tolerating them privately.

This double game kept Jamaica on edge. Governors who arrived with strict orders to keep the peace soon begged for authority to commission the privateers. They could expect little help from the royal navy; in the Dutch wars it was engaged against the enemy in home waters, and in peace lack of funds and administrative venality sapped its strength. If, then, King Charles could not protect the island, should it not be allowed to protect itself? Jamaicans insisted that without the auxiliary force of buccaneers the feeble colony might be snuffed out. Since the king conceded that grave danger called for grave measures, Jamaicans had only to keep London convinced that the danger was indeed grave.

As long as European governments were irresolute, Caribbean governors could be bold. Buccaneers continued to roam from the Leewards to the Pacific, their legality obscure but never wholly deserted. Since they attacked only the Spanish, and Spain's exclusion policy was regarded as a prolonged act of hostility toward the northern nations, West Indian officials slipped letters of marque to the marauders while distant governments looked the other way. Spain stiffened her defenses with armed convoys, fewer sailings, and stone forts that bristled cannon. By 1665 a single ship was as futile as a peashooter against this armament. The Brethren of the Coast resorted to large companies that sailed in fleets headed by an admiral. Ships under the joint command of Morgan, Morris and Jackman looted Campeche and New Granada (Honduras) in 1665; Mansfield took out ten ships the next year; and Morgan's assault on Panama drew nearly every buccaneer that was sober — thirty-six ships and 1800 men, an army with banners. Between 1655 and 1671 the buccaneers sacked eighteen Spanish American cities, four towns, thirty-five villages — some many times over — and captured unnumbered ships.

It was too much like war, and Spain was sick of it. In 1670

she concluded with England the Treaty of Madrid, which recognized all English-held islands in the West Indies, and agreed
to peace beyond the "Line" so emphatically that cynics called it
the Treaty of America. More important, Jamaica's planters and
merchants were gradually swinging around to the conviction
that buccaneering was, in the long run, intolerable. How could
they ever work up a stable trade with those fellows running
wild? How could they and their ladies take a quiet stroll
through Port Royal with those uncouth beggars reeling out of
every pothouse? It wouldn't do. Spain had her privateers on
the hunt, as well, and no one was safe. It was bad for business,
said a report to London: "People have not married, built or settled as they would in time of peace; some for fear of being destroyed, others have got much and suddenly by privateer
bargains and are gone."

Civilized order was slowly driving out savage disorder. Early
in 1671, King Charles ordered the arrest of Jamaica's governor,
Sir Thomas Modyford, and, a year later, summoned Henry Morgan to London to answer for his misdeeds. Into the post of deputy governor, by royal appointment, went a man of sound commercial instincts, Sir Thomas Lynch, a planter who had long
damned buccaneering as "the sickness of Jamaica."

Calm settled on the Caribbean, but the beast only slept. The
Earl of Carlisle, an old friend of Morgan, took office as governor
in 1678. He told London that Jamaica still lay open to attack
unless the mercenary force of privateers was kept in arms. A
new generation of buccaneers emerged from hiding, fired with
the old lust for Spanish gold. In the autumn of 1679 a band
1000-strong plundered the royal warehouses of Nicaragua, entered their booty at Port Royal and paid the customs tax, honest
men all.

Once loosed, buccaneer bands swept westward to terrorize
the Pacific slopes of Spanish America for eight years. Three
hundred of them sacked Porto Bello in February, 1680, and in
April plunged across Darien in seven companies, each with its

captain and its banner. A motley crew, they had nothing to lose but their lives, and held them cheap; but among the queer assortment of adventurers were William Dampier (more hydrographer than pirate, whose picture graces the National Portrait Gallery in London); Basil Ringrose, Gentleman; the amiable Lionel Wafer, surgeon; and Captain Bartholomew Sharp, a contentious fellow later voted out of his command — all of whom wrote up their experiences.[13] Plunder proved scanty. Cliques formed, quarreled, split off; captains fell in combat and were replaced. Dampier's party struggled back across Darien, another under Sharp rounded the Horn, and both found British authorities incensed at their misdeeds. In 1683 the Jamaica assembly passed a severe and comprehensive act against freebooting anywhere, anytime. King Charles heartily approved it, and circulated copies to all colonial governors, as a model.

This shut off Port Royal as a base, but did not prevent a second wave of buccaneers into the Pacific. In 1684 a thousand of them were back at Panama, as fractious and pigheaded as ever: Dampier and Wafer aboard one ship, Ringrose on another; Captain Peter Harris and 97 men in canoes from over the isthmus; sly Captain Grogniet commanding 280 French and English; and a band of 180 Englishmen under Captain Townley.

[13] Lancelot Blackburne was in the West Indies in 1681, immediately after his ordination, and enemies of the witty and worldly churchman never ceased to accuse him of buccaneering. The story had it that a hardened freebooter arrived in England years later and asked what thievery his old comrade was up to now. "Doing even better" was the reply; "he's the archbishop of York." Narratives of the Pacific buccaneers include those of Dampier, *A New Voyage round the World*, 1697; Sharp, *The Voyages and Adventures of Capt. Bartt. Sharp*, 1684; and Wafer, *A New Voyage and Description of the Isthmus of Darien*, 1699. The journal of Basil Ringrose, who was later killed in Mexico in 1686, appeared as *The Dangerous Voyage and Bold Attempts of Captain Bartholomew Sharp and Others*, in the second volume of Esquemeling, *Bucaniers of America*, 1684. The 1684–1688 buccaneer invasion into the Pacific was reported by a minor French nobleman, Raveneau de Lussan, who came out with 30,000 pesos' worth of gold and jewels, mostly won in gambling with his fellow brigands. Cf. the English translation of his journal by Marguerite Eyer Wilbur: *Raveneau de Lussan, Buccaneer of the Spanish Main* (Cleveland, Arthur H. Clark Co., 1930).

Without a strong leader to mold them into a single fighting
force, they suffered reversals by land and sea, and broke up.
Wafer returned by the Horn, Dampier got home around the
world; the French and Townley's men fought their way back
across Nicaragua, dogged by Spanish troops, to reach the Caribbean in March, 1688 — four long years of slaughter and pillage.

Yet the end of the buccaneers was in sight, and they went out
with a groan instead of a cheer. Seven ships and 650 *flibustiers*
joined a 1697 French privateering force aimed at Cartagena,
Spain's chief port in the Caribbean. Aggrieved at their small
share of booty from the captured city, the *flibustiers* lingered to
ransack it again; then, sailing out, lost their haul to a British
naval squadron. *Exeunt,* without *sennet.* At the peace concluded that year, Spain formally recognized all English and
French occupied territories in the West Indies. The islanders
no longer needed mercenaries as protection against Spanish retaliation, nor did they want them about, upsetting the normal
course of trade. They shut the door firmly on buccaneering,
and locked it.[14]

Freebooting in one form or another was a disease from which
few recovered. The sea robber gladly risked ending his days by
what he jocosely called "hempen fever," rather than die more
slowly in the dull monotony and stifling authority of a law-
abiding ship. Merchant seamen squirmed under the captain's
thumb; he lashed them raw and poured vinegar in their welts;
he put them on biscuits and water, keelhauled them, worked

---

[14] One need not starve, for there was always smuggling to be done. In the
Spanish colonies, illegal goods outranked by ten to one those lawfully regis-
tered. An alien ship would limp into a Caribbean port pleading distress, and
beg to clear its hold for repairs. Agreeable to the ruse, local authorities kept
up appearances by sealing the unladen cargo into a warehouse, but by night
it went out the back door while tobacco, cotton, sugar and indigo from the
plantations replaced it. His fictitious leak repaired and the illegal cargo
stowed, the smuggler sailed blithely on to his next customer. Cf. Labat,
Memoirs, p. 170.

them in irons. While food lasted the merchant sailor ate salt beef blue with mold and wormy bread washed down with water that stank like a cistern; and when the food ran out on a long voyage, as it always did, he ate rats and chewed leather to ease his growling stomach. For this he was paid a shilling a day, and was lucky if he lived out the voyage to collect it.

Aboard pirate ships the crew could eat their fill and drink the wine keg dry in full knowledge that they would replenish the larder from the next victim. They were blessedly democratic to the point of anarchy. Since their ships had usually been captured, and belonged to the whole company, pirate crews elected their commanders, voted them out if dissatisfied, and set their own course. "They only permit him to be captain," his crew told Captain Bartholomew Roberts, "so that they may be captain over him." Pirate seamen might fall into the hands of a commander as gruesome as Blackbeard, but some served with gentlemen gone astray: Roberts, who frowned on profanity, or Misson, the social idealist. True, they were hunted men, with all nations allied against them, yet not one in a hundred went to the gallows. They expected to make their fortune in plunder, and some did. When they had robbed, brawled, gambled and whored until tired of it, they could always plead the king's pardon next time it was offered.

So the Caribbean sea rovers only shrugged — all that they asked was a chance to make a dishonest living — God, or the devil, would provide. Were there not other seas, other ports, other booty? There were, and ampler, too. After 1690 they established comfortable bases in the North American colonies, and set out to rob the rich eastern trade of the Red Sea and Indian Ocean.

England's Navigation Acts gave the colonies an excuse for widespread connivance with these "Red Sea Men." By a series of Acts enacted between 1651 and 1696 Parliament sought to control colonial trade to England's benefit — the same mercantile policy that had horrified her when Spain initiated it. Certain colonial products could be shipped only to the English market, and almost all goods bound to or from the colonies had to unlade in England, paying customs duties and incidental costs that pushed up their price. The plantation economy of the south and the Caribbean islands fitted into this system without serious dislocation, but North Atlantic colonies competed with, rather than complemented, the role of the mother country. They offered little in the way of raw materials that England could use. Their enterprise was commercial, as was hers, and they wanted an unrestricted market in which they could buy as cheaply, and sell as dearly, as that market would bear. All the colonies showed resentment of the Acts by deceptions strongly touched with rebellion. If sea rovers brought in goods that undercut the legitimate market, and coin that put ready cash into colonial pockets, then let them! Parliament had not consulted the colonists when it made the law, and Parliament need not be consulted when they broke it.

The few royal officials appointed to supervise American commerce were helpless. Leading citizens financed the sea rovers, supplying them with arms, provisions, chandlery, and that sweet cheer of every piratical heart, rum. Governors sold them dubious letters of marque at $100 apiece, judges dozed off when charges were presented against them, bribes to customs officers were entered as a normal expense in their voyages, merchants entertained them at dinner. A report from Maryland estimated that no less than sixty freebooters were based in American ports, taking up so many seamen that a lawful ship could hardly muster a crew. The royal surveyor of customs, Edward Randolph, called Carolina Admiralty courts "sharpers' shops," and complained that Governor Phips of Massachusetts had received him in his coach house and threatened to drub him as a public nuisance. A Pennsylvania agent told London: "All the persons I have employed in searching for and apprehending these pirates, are abused and affronted, and called enemies of the country, for disturbing and hindering honest men, as they were

pleased to call the pirates, from bringing their money and settling amongst them." Enterprising Bostonians set up a mint to
stamp plundered metal into coin. Little Rhode Island refused
an Admiralty court altogether, as an infringement of its charter.
New York was worse; a syndicate of respected merchants maintained a resident agent at Madagascar to supply the freebooters' needs (at a stiff markup), and to ship home their plundered
goods. King William, his energies absorbed in the French war
(1689–1697), could offer little more than a palliative to this
general connivance. In 1695 he appointed an honest governor
to clean up New England's ports and, with less success, dispatched Captain Kidd to harry the pirates by sea.

Prevalent evasion of the Navigation Acts shifted the spec-
trum of privateering toward lawlessness. The years 1690–1720
marked the flamboyant era of the skull and crossbones, tales of
buried treasure and haunted graves, pirates real and fictive
with black eye-patch and smoking pistols. Few sea rovers
sailed with legal intentions under legal commissions. Vicious
outcasts prowled American waters: Blackbeard, Stede Bonnet
(the only one known to make his victims walk the plank), even
two women who fought like men, but were true enough to their
sex for one of them to escape the hangman's noose by being
pregnant.

Sea rovers of the Indian Ocean were a different breed. They
fitted into the scheme of things, as North American merchants
conceived that scheme. They had a sense of order; one could
do business with them. Men like Tew, Coates, Glover, Mace,
Hoare and Moston looted the Grand Mogul's shipping but
stayed out of the way of the English; they fetched in salable
goods, paid off the right people, behaved themselves ashore,
strengthened the colonial economy in general, and enriched
their New England backers in particular.

Other "Red Sea Men" were less sensible, but more fascinat-
ing. "Long Ben" Avery captured the Grand Mogul's daughter
homebound from a pilgrimage to Mecca. He forced her to the

marriage bed, dreaming that one day a son of his might sit on the throne of India. Neither this nor other of his dreams bore fruit. He slipped into England under cover of an alias, but had the ill luck to fall in with dishonest people who conned him of his hoard, and he died a pauper.[15]

Another eastern pirate, "Black Bart" Roberts, won renown for his personal austerities as well as for his unmatched record of 400 vessels looted. Scrupulous in attire, abstemious (he drank only tea), Roberts strictly guarded the chastity of women prisoners who fell to his care, and gave his fiddlers the Sabbath off to keep it holy. He once urged a captured clergyman to remain aboard as chaplain, assuring him that the duties would be light — say daily prayers and mix rum punch for the crew. When that worthy man looked the prospective parish over and decided that it had no future, Roberts reluctantly freed him, retaining from his possessions only some prayer books and a corkscrew. Roberts made it a point to don his best for battle: starched shirt, damask waistcoat, dress sword, a jeweled cross (stolen, of course) about his neck. In 1722 a British man-of-war cornered him and he was cut down by a blast of grapeshot. By instruction, his men threw the body overboard at once — sword, cross and all.

An eccentric freebooter named Misson took up piracy as a noble protest against the wrongs of organized society. A Dominican monk in Rome fired him with utopian zeal, and the two agreed that they would strike a blow at human avarice by destroying its foundation in private property. A gentle soul, Misson never killed anyone unless he had to. On one occasion, the master of a captured ship fell in the action, and Misson buried

[15] Avery's notoriety left a faint but legible mark on the literature of his time. Defoe wrote a long pamphlet about him, entitled *The King of the Pirates*, and later made his fictional Captain Singleton a comrade-in-arms of Avery at Madagascar. The Theatre Royal in Drury Lane played a poetic melodrama, "The Successful Pyrate," in 1712, drawing inspiration from the romantic episode of the Mogul's daughter. Its blend of true love and offstage bloodletting entranced the most delicate, for after its run the play returned for a benefit performance "at the Desire of several Ladies of Quality."

1. A buccaneer of Hispaniola. Buccaneers originated as hunters of wild cattle, and preyed on Spanish towns and shipping only after the Spanish had driven them from their hunting ground. (From Oexmelin *Histoires des Adventuriers Filbustiers*. 1775. Beinecke Library, Yale)

2. Sir Francis Drake, England's most illustrious privateer, is buried at sea with all honours; off the coast of Darien (Panama) 1596 as seen

him with full honors, inscribing on his stone: "Here lies a gallant English Man." At Madagascar, Misson set up a pirate colony called Libertatia, and its citizens Liberi; all goods were held in common, and no wall nor hedge shut off a householder from his fellows. The world's stubborn evil can break most harshly upon such muddled saints. Madagascar natives wrecked his colony while he cruised for prey and, soon after, a tropic hurricane sent Misson to the bottom.[16]

The opening stages of England's armed rivalry with France pinned her fleet to European waters and left the Red Sea men to plunder at their ease. Charles II had received regular financial aid from Louis XIV after 1670, and James II avoided a direct clash with French ambitions, but Dutch William ascended the throne in February, 1689 resolved to beat France to her knees. He ate and drank that one purpose, he nursed his crooked, asthmatic body toward that one purpose, he camped eight summers with his troops for that one purpose, and died bequeathing to Queen Anne the same purpose still burning with its old fire.

William III's League of Augsburg (1689–1697) ringed France with hostile states — England and Holland in command of the sea, German principalities to the north, Austria eastward and, later, Savoy and Spain on the south. Dutch-English naval forces sealed up French ports. With no one to plunder, English privateering ebbed, but French corsairs suffered from no such handicap. They darted out of Dunkerque or St. Malo and fetched home prizes by the hundreds. When the Allies resorted to convoys, the corsairs hunted them in packs, some ships closing with the guard ships, while others ravaged the fleet like wolves in the fold. Mounting Allied sea power reduced their

---

[16] Only one contemporary account mentions Misson: that catchall of pirate lore, *A General History of the Robberies and Murders of the Most Notorious Pirates* (1724). Of its author, given as "Capt. Charles Johnson," nothing is known. Scholars speculate that the book may have been one more from the prolific pen of Daniel Defoe.

depredations as the war advanced, and the 1697 Peace of Ryswick brought this most glittering era of the French corsairs to a
close.

William and Louis XIV of France patched up their fragile
truce at Ryswick in anticipation of a crisis that would engage
all their cunning: the approaching death of Spain's childless
king, Charles II. Three candidates had some rights to the succession: Archduke Charles, second son of Emperor Leopold of
Austria; Duke Philip of Anjou, grandson of Louis XIV; and the
child Joseph, heir to the Elector of Bavaria. Since a Frenchman
on the Spanish throne would bring Spain's vast possessions
under Louis's thumb, and convert all Europe into a French fief,
William and Louis entered into a secret pact designed to preserve the balance of power. This Partition Treaty supported
the most innocuous candidate, little Joseph of Bavaria, and
awarded some of Spain's continental possessions to rival states.
The death of Joseph in 1699 nullified all their labors, and in
1700 a second Partition Treaty forwarded the claim of Archduke Charles. Spain was affronted that foreign states would
meddle in her royal succession. Shortly before fuddled Charles
II died in November, 1700, the Gallic party at the Spanish court
persuaded him to name Philip of Anjou as his heir, with the
protective stipulation that the thrones of Spain and France
would never be joined in a single monarch. Delighted, Louis
tore up the Partition Treaty. By dominating Spain, France
could now hold the continent of Europe, and half the seas of the
world, in her clenched fist.

Louis chanced it that the insular Tories, critics of the last
war, would keep England out of another.[17] At first his guess

---

[17] Although Whigs and Tories were not yet formal parties, they had fastened
insulting names on each other (Whig: a Scottish outlaw; Tory: an Irish
robber), and had assumed recognizable groupings to which the government
responded. Of the seven Lords Justices who served as regents for King William while he was away fighting the French in the summer of 1695, six were
Whig and one Tory — a discernible foreshadowing of party government.
The Whigs were vaguely liberal and parliamentary; they supported the war,
tolerated William's Dutch courtiers, and took a broad view of religion. The
more conservative Tories defended royal prerogative, dragged their feet on

seemed correct. Parliaments in both England and Holland formally accepted Philip as the rightful ruler of Spain. Louis moved swiftly to assume control of Europe. Companies of French troops expelled the Dutch from border forts ceded to them by the 1697 Treaty of Ryswick; others marched into the Milanese to shut Austria out of Italy. Having gotten thus far without challenge, Louis's arrogance passed all bounds. He announced that Philip of Spain might, after all, ascend the French throne in due time. At the death of exiled James II, he proclaimed James's son the true king of England. As a final thrust, he laid heavy duties on English trade with France, and instructed Spain to do the same. Tories and Whigs alike rallied to King William, who once more gathered a Grand Alliance to dispute the French hegemony. By the time he died of a riding accident in 1702, the war was neither simply William's nor the Whigs', but all England's.

The War of the Spanish Succession contained French ambitions on the continent of Europe and laid the foundations of England's empire abroad. It closed a half-century that saw the decline of Spain, the fall of Holland to second rank, the opening clash with France in a struggle that would not end until Waterloo, and the emergence of England as mistress of the seas.

As the European nations grappled at each other's throats under the later Stuarts (1660–1714), private fighting ships, whether licit or lawless, cruised with unprecedented daring. Some of their captains basked in the warmth of royal favor, some felt the ungentle hand of that "finisher of the law," the hangman. Of the scant few whose exploits have been reliably documented, we shall examine the fates of three — Sir Henry

---

the war, hated Dutchmen at court, and extolled the Established Church. William cried plague on both their houses. All the difference that he could see between the two parties, he said, "was that the Tories would cut his throat in the morning, the Whigs in the afternoon." He tried to remain above party conflict, but in order to get ministers who would work smoothly together, he appointed Whigs during their 1693–1699 ascendancy, and was then forced to replace them with Tories in 1700.

Morgan, Captain William Kidd and Captain Woodes Rogers. Roughly contemporary to each other, they reflect broad aspects of the same Stuart era, yet sailed different seas, in different decades, and in the service of different English monarchs. Their temperaments, abilities, and respect for maritime law offer sharp contrasts. Each was, in his own way, both heroic and pitiable. Each enjoyed an hour of greatness, until fortune led him by unforeseen paths to an unknown grave.

SIR HENRY MORGAN

*"Barring that natural expression
of villainy which we all have,
the man looked honest enough."*
Mark Twain, *A Mysterious Visit*

Florida Strait

Havana···Matanzas

C U B A

Yucatan Channel

Isle of
Pines

Sancti-
·Spiritus

Ana Maria
Bay

Puerto
Principe

Great Bahama Bank

Old Bahama Channel

Crooked I.

Gre
Inag

Santiago de Cuba

G R E A T E R

Windwa

Nombre de Dios

Portobello
San
Lorenzo
Fort

Chagres River

GOLD

Venta ROAD

D A R I E N

Panama City
Bay of Panama

MILES
0 10 20 30 40

ISTHMUS OF DARIEN

An enlargement of the area below

JAMAICA

St Jago
Port Royal

E
Point
Morant

R

HONDURAS

NICARAGUA

MOSQUITO COAST

Granada

Lake of
Nicaragua

San Juan R.

Cartago

C O S T A   R I C A

Providence I.

C A R I

Santa Marta

Cartagena

Magdalena

Porto
Bello

San Lorenzo
Fort

Nombre de Dios

D A R I E N

Panama
CITY

GULF OF
PANAMA

Gulf of
Darien

P A C I F I C   O C E A N

85

75

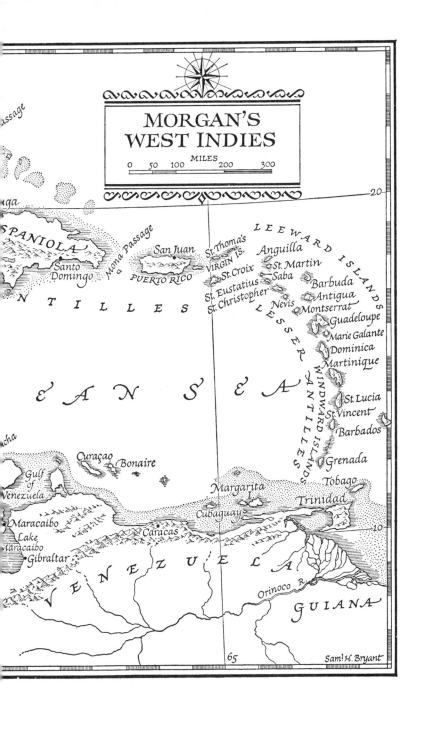

*T*HEIR TOPSAILS mounted the blue slope of sea south of Jamaica on an August afternoon, 1665. By dusk the ships were hull up, by dawn they lay off the spit of Port Royal, motionless in the early calm. The officer at Fort Charles, his elbows propped on the unfinished masonry of the rampart, kept them in his glass, while on either side of him the sleepy garrison swabbed cannon. To his relief, the strangers ran up English colors. Whitish puffs of smoke burst from their ports and vanished in the shrouds as the dull boom of a nine-gun salute rolled in across the still bay. The officer ordered his gunner to reply.

An east wind, so reliable that Jamaicans called it "the Doctor," soon darkened the great mirror of the sea. The ships glided close up to the quay and dropped anchor in the green, silt-laden waters. Their serried gunports, patched canvas, and tough, stringy-looking seamen marked them as buccaneers. The three captains rowed ashore and trudged down sandy Queen's Street to the governor's office at the King's House. One of them was a thick-shouldered, taciturn young Welshman named Henry Morgan.

Morgan's early life is a quagmire of conjecture.[1] Only two facts seem well-founded: he was born somewhere in Wales, sometime between December 21, 1634, and December 21, 1635. His birthplace may have been Llanrhymni in Glamorganshire, Pencarn in Monmouthshire, or Rymney, near Tredegar, in Monmouth; his father may have been Robert Morgan of Llanrhymni, Thomas Morgan of Pencarn or, to be sure, neither of

[1] For detailed discussions of Morgan's early life, cf. W. Adolphe Roberts, pp. 25–31; Lindsay, pp. 9–12.

them. Alexandre Esquemeling, who cruised with Morgan, and later wrote an eyewitness account of his voyages, said that Morgan's father "was a rich yeoman, or farmer, and of good quality in that country," ancestry which in our egalitarian times would reckon as praiseworthy, but Morgan thought it slanderous. In a crawling retraction, one of Esquemeling's English publishers raised Morgan's status to "a Gentleman's Son," and from what we know of Henry's kin this is more likely. Esquemeling also declared that Morgan came to Barbados as a bond servant. Statements that appear to originate with Morgan flatly deny this, but only one of them offers an alternative: he "went at first out of England with the Army commanded by General Venables for Hispaniola and Jamaica." Morgan was tight-mouthed, and the rest was as he preferred it — silence. After an obscure decade spent roaming the West Indies, he entered the history books at thirty years of age on that August day when the captains presented themselves before Jamaica's governor, Sir Thomas Modyford.

Henry was a stranger to Modyford, but the governor knew other island Morgans well, reputable men and a warlike breed. Henry's uncle, Sir Edward, had been his deputy governor. A portly, affectionate man, who arrived from England in the spring of 1664 with six motherless children at his coattails, Sir Edward did not enjoy his office for long. War broke out with Holland early in 1665 and Sir Edward, with Henry's cousin Thomas Morgan as his second in command, led a buccaneer assault on the Dutch island of St. Eustatius. "The good old Colonel," Modyford had written sadly to London, "leaping out of the boat, and being a corpulent man, got a strain, and his spirit being great he pursued over earnestly the enemy on a hot day, so that he surfeited and suddenly died." [2] At the King's

2 Despite Sir Edward's collapse early in the action, the assault force overcame feeble Dutch resistance and seized St. Eustatius. Lieutenant Colonel Thomas Morgan remained to make the conquest secure. In January of the next year (1666) France joined Holland in war against England. The French at both ends of St. Christopher (St. Kitts) overran the English settlement in the

House Modyford now studied Henry with a mixture of curiosity and calculating interest. If this younger and more sinewy Morgan was like the rest of the family, he would be useful.

The governor poured out wine to his visitors and settled back to hear their story. What had they been up to? They admitted as little as possible: a bit of raiding along the Campeche coast, then a sortie up the San Juan River to the Lake of Nicaragua, where they sacked Granada. And were they properly commissioned for such hostile acts? Yes, by Lord Windsor, then governor of Jamaica. Modyford reminded them that Windsor had been gone from office since October, 1662, and that their commissions were technically void after that date. The captains explained that since they were continuously at sea, they had no news of his departure from office. Modyford smiled into his glass and said nothing.

He had, in fact, little other choice. Although his royal instructions ordered him to maintain friendly relations with his Spanish neighbors, and withhold letters of marque against their ships or territories, he discovered soon after his arrival in 1664 that it would be dangerous to banish the buccaneers. Jamaica was a fist thrust deep into the vitals of Spanish America, and Spain had already made three descents upon the island, aimed at driving the English out. Only the buccaneering fleet and its 1500 brave men, he told London, stood between Jamaica and a Spanish attack in overwhelming force. So he played his double game: conciliation with the peace party in England, and covert aggression against Spain in the Caribbean.

---

center, and Thomas Morgan rushed reinforcements from St. Eustatius. He found the English governor at home in dressing gown and slippers, wringing his hands. Thomas stuck a pistol in his chest and threatened to put a bullet through him if he did not get out and rally his defenses. Better an uncertain death than a sure one, thought the governor, and put on his shoes. In the fighting Thomas Morgan was shot through both legs. Although we have no record that the wounds were fatal, he does not appear again in the story of Henry Morgan. Two other kinsmen do: Bledry, also a distant cousin, destined to be one of Henry's captains at Panama; and young Charles, son of Sir Edward, a riotous, incompetent crony of Henry's political years.

Henry Morgan soon proved as useful as Modyford hoped. Attacks on Spanish possessions might be touchy, but while war with Holland lasted, Jamaicans were duty-bound to mount an offensive against Dutch settlements in the Caribbean. Within a few weeks of Morgan's appearance at Port Royal, Modyford commissioned "the old privateer, Capt. Mansfield" against Curaçao, and that autumn Morgan sailed with the buccaneer expedition as Mansfield's vice admiral. Just as Modyford played a double game with London, the buccaneers played one with him. They had no intention of striking at either Dutch or French, who would give them hard knocks and little booty. Wily old Mansfield had a Portuguese letter of marque against Spain tucked in his pocket.[3] He and Morgan sacked the Cuban town of Sancti Spíritus, seized strategic but ill-garrisoned Providence Island, deep in Spanish American waters, and made an abortive march on the Costa Rican town of Cartago. In June, 1666, they were back to face Modyford's displeasure at Port Royal.

Modyford let them off with a mild rebuke, and bluffed it out as best he could with London. "There is no profitable employment for the privateers in the West Indies against the French or Dutch," the Jamaica Council declared, "and being a people that will not be brought to planting will prey on the Spanish whether countenanced at Jamaica or not." The governor accepted Providence Island into his jurisdiction and sent thirty-five men to hold it. He reminded London that the island was originally English, that Englishmen "first felled the trees and planted the land." In November, 1666, the Privy Council confirmed the conquest by appointing Modyford's brother, Sir James, as its governor.[4]

[3] Portugal's war of independence from Spain, begun in 1640, did not formally end until 1668.

[4] A tiny dot of land rising from the broad waters of the western Caribbean, Providence Island commanded the homeward route of ingot-laden *galeones* from Porto Bello and, in English hands, provided a handy springboard for mainland invasion. English Puritans occupied it in 1630; the Spanish drove them out in 1641; and when Mansfield's assault renewed the threat in 1666,

Meanwhile Mansfield, the elected head of the Caribbean buccaneers, had come home to a longer haven than Port Royal. He died, as many did in those troubled, careless times, under mysterious circumstances. Some said poison, others that the Spanish executed him in Havana. Whatever the nature of his end, all agreed that it was sudden and certain. Word passed from one buccaneer ship to another throughout the West Indies, and amid gruff nods and wiping of moustaches Henry Morgan succeeded to his command — Admiral of the Confederation of the Brethren of the Coast.

In the quiet interval before his next warlike departure, Morgan married his cousin, Mary Elizabeth, daughter of the late Sir Edward. Sir Edward had "died very poor," Modyford confided to Whitehall, and left little to support his "great family." But marriageable young ladies of quality were rare in the colonies, and the orphaned girls had not long to wait for husbands. The eldest married Colonel Robert Byndloss "of good estate," and a younger daughter became the wife of planter Henry Archbould, both prominent men and members of the Jamaica Council. Mary Elizabeth's life with her headstrong husband lies in absolute shadow. We have no hint of how she looked or what she thought, no word or gesture. Black mistresses were common in Jamaica, and mulatto bastards outnumbered children born in wedlock, but nothing points to unfaithfulness on Henry's part. At the end of twenty years of marriage, Mary Elizabeth was still his "very well and entirely beloved wife."

---

the Spanish hastened to counterattack. Sir James Modyford's November appointment as the island's governor was already too late; by August 10 a Spanish fleet, scratched up from mainland ports, had sailed into the harbor. The small band of defenders made valiant stand, in the end broke up the church organ pipes and fired off the fragments, but finally surrendered on condition that they be granted free passage back to Jamaica. This promise the Spaniards betrayed. They carried the survivors to Porto Bello and worked them as slaves; "having no clothes, their backs were blistered with the sun, their heads scorched, their necks, shoulders and hands raw with carrying stones and mortar, their feet chopped and their legs bruised and battered with irons," and some beaten until they died. English officers got better treatment — seventeen months in Panama dungeons before their release.

Meanwhile Modyford was busy excusing his aggressive policy to Whitehall. He frankly confessed that since March, 1666, he had been issuing letters of marque against Spain. "The Spanish look on us as intruders and trespassers wherever they find us in the Indies," he cried, "and use us accordingly; and were it in their power, as it is fixed in their wills, would soon turn us out of all our Plantations, and is it reasonable that we should quietly let them grow upon us, until they are able to do it?" He hammered home that the buccaneers were his only naval defense; they were his seawall, his bastion, his sharp sword, and they cared only for Spanish plunder. "Had my abilities suited so well with my wishes as the latter did with your Lordship's," he explained to the Secretary of State, "the privateers' attempts had only been practiced on the Dutch and French, and the Spaniards free of them, but I had no money to pay them nor frigates to force them; the former they could not get from our declared enemies, nothing could they expect but blows from them, and (as they often repeated to me) will that pay for new sails or rigging?" By their attacks on the Spaniards the buccaneers could cull vital information of Spain's intentions, while Spanish plunder kept their ships in repair and fattened the royal coffers with "15ths and 10ths." After all, were not the Spanish to blame? Were not smoking towns and pilfered ships repayment, in just measure, for Spanish cruelties too horrible to describe?

What thin sanction Modyford had, he laid out with the feigned boldness of a poker player who hopes that a weak hand will win. He recalled to the Secretary, Lord Arlington, that in November, 1664, his Lordship had advised "gentle usage" of the sea rovers. He took refuge in his cousin, the Duke of Albemarle,[5] "who upon serious consideration with his Majesty and

---

5 Although rusticated by broken health, George Monck, first Duke of Albemarle, was still one of the most powerful men in England. As military governor of Scotland he had brought his army down from the border and, by an astute secrecy about his final intentions, forced the disintegration of the Commonwealth government and the return of Charles Stuart in 1660. Two weeks after Charles landed at Dover he made Monck baron, earl, duke, and

the Lord Chancellor, by letter of June 1, 1665 gave Modyford latitude to grant or not commissions against the Spaniard, as he found it for the advantage of his Majesty's service and the good of this island." As a result of these encouragements, the Jamaica Council (neatly packed with Modyford adherents) had resolved on February 22, 1664, to issue letters of marque against Spain, and had set forth a round dozen excellent reasons for the decision.

Throughout 1667 Secretary Lord Arlington continued his mild remonstrance while Modyford persisted in stubborn, if evasive, disagreement. In January, 1668, the governor handed Morgan a commission "to draw together the English privateers, and take prisoners of the Spanish nation, whereby he might inform of the intentions of that enemy to invade Jamaica, of which Sir Thos. had frequent and strong advice."

Such an assignment to men greedy for spoil was a macabre piece of dishonesty, as Morgan well knew. He could have picked up prisoners in a rowboat. Instead, he assembled twelve ships and 700 men (200 of them French, contrary to his commission) among the cays south of Cuba. His captains gathered over rum punch in the flagship's cabin to discuss what placid town they would rifle. Havana? name of God, no! Havana had 30,000 people in it, and three forts grim as the gates of hell. Perhaps Puerto Principe, then; it lay fifty miles inland from the Cuban coast, and had never been pillaged. Its broad tobacco fields promised cupboards full of planters' gold. The decision made, they weighed anchor for Ana Maria Bay.

On board one of the ships a Spanish prisoner, hearing the news, slipped over the side by night and swam ashore to warn the town. Drums rolled in Puerto Principe's plaza. Carts loaded with valuables streamed past horse and foot coming in from the plantations. The mayor dispatched a hundred men

---

captain-general of the realm for life. A moderate in politics, a Presbyterian in religion, Monck's actions were marked at all times by courage and prudence of a high order. The Duke's death on January 3, 1670, deprived Mody- ford of his chief protector at court.

with axes and muskets to lay ambushes along the narrow track toward the bay, and billeted 700 militia in the town, with sentinels posted to give the alarm. Let the heretic dogs come; they were ready.

The buccaneers swarmed onto the beach at Ana Maria and took up the march — 500 hard-bitten, beggarly fellows who could sleep on their mothers' graves. That night they cinched their belts a notch and stretched out under the trees; next morning they spread into the woods and enveloped the annoying ambushes; by afternoon they were before the town, drums rolling and flags flying. They primed their guns and advanced in a half-moon across the grassy savanna.

With a shout the massed cavalry thundered down on them in an attempt to split the line and scatter the flanks. The buccaneers shot them out of their saddles and closed in on the Spanish foot. For four hours the militia defended the town, house by house. "If you surrender not voluntarily," the buccaneers warned them, "you shall see the town in a flame, and your wives and children torn in pieces before your faces," and the shattered militia finally surrendered. Morgan shut them into the churches while his men sacked the town. They tore up floors, dug in gardens, fished the bottom of wells; search parties scoured the woods for fugitives; prisoners screamed on the rack until they confessed to hidden wealth. When the last *peso* had been stowed in its bag, Morgan demanded ransom for the town or he would leave it a smoking ruin. Four prisoners allowed to comb the countryside for ransom money returned empty-handed. They begged for more time. But Morgan now had none to spare; a message taken from a captured courier had told him that a Spanish relief force was on the way. He quickly settled for a thousand head of cattle, to be delivered at once to his ships. Carrying with them six prisoners as hostages, the buccaneers hastened out of the stricken town toward the bay.

Eager to be rid of their tormentors, the townspeople rushed the cattle to Ana Maria. Morgan then gave the screw a last turn: he refused to surrender his hostages until the meat was dressed, salted and safely stowed in the ships. The crescent of white sand circling the bay turned into a vast slaughterhouse roofed by the sky.

The welcome meat, however, cost Morgan his French allies. One of them had laid aside some delectable marrowbones, and when an English buccaneer snatched a bone off the pile the Frenchman grappled with him in a fury. Nothing would salve the insult but to duel it out, pistol and cutlass. The Englishman did not wait for such formalities; without warning, he ran his opponent through. The French were mad with rage, and Morgan tried to settle the affair without open battle. To condone the murder would arouse the French to mortal passion; to hang the murderer on the spot would alienate the English. Morgan compromised by putting him in irons, with the promise of full punishment at Port Royal.[6] This restrained the French for the time being, without satisfying them. *Aux mains des Anglais, toujours la perfidie!* After the Puerto Principe spoil was divided, they deserted the fleet.

The shares of fifty pieces of eight apiece would not even pay the buccaneers' debts in Jamaica. They grumbled at so much labor for so little gain. "But Captain Morgan, who always communicated vigor with his words," reported his fellow buccaneer and biographer, Esquemeling, "infused such spirits into his men as were able to put every one of them instantly upon new designs; they being all persuaded by his reasons, that the sole execution of his orders would be a certain means of obtaining great riches. This persuasion had such influence upon their minds, that with inimitable courage they all resolved to follow him."[7] Concealing his plans, to prevent any leak to the Span-

[6] Morgan was true to his promise. The murderer was tried and hung in Port Royal after his return. Cf. Alexandre Esquemeling, *The Buccaneers of America*, p. 139.

[7] Alexandre Esquemeling was one of Morgan's men, very likely in the capacity of surgeon, and an eyewitness to the exploits which made Morgan famous. His detailed narrative in *Bucaniers of America* (1684) is our chief, and almost sole, source of information on Morgan's buccaneering career. If it

3. The other end of the scale : a common pirate is hanged on the gibbet at Wapping, on the Thames shore near the Tower of London. (National Maritime Museum, Greenwich)

4. Sir Henry Morgan. The only authentic likeness, this engraving appeared in a contemporary chronicle written by one of his men, Esquemeling's Bucaniers of America, 1684. (Beinecke Library, Yale)

iards, Morgan sailed south to the Darien shore where he announced his target: Porto Bello.

Morgan's captains were taken aback at this news, with good reason. Porto Bello's stout fortresses were surpassed only by Havana and Cartagena. Heavy guns covered both harbor and town, and the garrison of 300 regular troops could be strengthened on short notice by 900 armed militiamen. What chance had nine ships and 460 fighting men against those defenses? The captains might have saved their breath; it was like blowing on a mountain. "If our number is small, our hearts are great," Morgan replied. "And the fewer persons we are, the more union, and better shares we shall have in the spoil." The captains shook their heads but yielded. So let it be: Porto Bello.

Porto Bello lay on the Caribbean coast of Darien, sixty miles north from the city of Panama. In its ample harbor the *galeones* loaded the treasure of the entire South Pacific slope, from the isthmus to Chile. The town's permanent population numbered only 2000, counting slaves, but twice a year the sultry streets came to life when fairs were held. Then tall ships rode the bay, quays and plazas swarmed with merchants, silver ingots were stacked in the open for want of storage space, and rents shot to prodigious heights. Though called the Beautiful Port, the place was so unhealthy, sunk in the hills and flanked by fetid tidelands, that its creation was considered a joint enterprise: God made the harbor, and the devil made the climate.

Two cliffs guarded the entrance to the bay, which faced due west. On the northern summit rose Fort San Felipe, nicknamed the Iron Castle, its guns trained on the mile-wide stretch of water between the cliffs. Two miles from the entrance the town curved around the corner of the harbor, and at its seaward edge the fort of Santiago de la Gloria mounted the hill in tiers. Thirty brass cannon poked their tarnished snouts from its

---

caused Morgan embarrassment, it also gave him immortality as the greatest of Caribbean freebooters. Esquemeling may be suspected of some fictionizing, but in general his record bears the marks of reliability.

E

battlements, and beneath its cluster of guardhouses lay dungeons and the main storage chambers for powder and shot. Jutting from the middle of the waterfront stood the fort of San Jerónimo, surrounded by water on all sides and connected with land only by a causeway. To capture the town and bring in the ships, Morgan had to silence all these forts. It could not be done by sea, that was evident; only by land.[8]

Morgan sailed his fleet on a wide sweep around Porto Bello, to anchor in a river thirty miles west of the town. At nightfall tackles swung out and dropped twenty-three boats to the surface of the darkening stream. An attack force of 400 men slid down the ropes to row silently toward the sea.

The buccaneers manned the oars in relays through the night, with the dull white wash of surf on their right hand. At three o'clock, as the headland of the port loomed off their bow, they landed and dragged the boats to cover under the fringe of trees.

From here they would go on foot. Each man was a clanking arsenal: musket, cutlass swinging from a makeshift strap, powder and shot pouches at the belt, sacks of crude grenades over the shoulder. Their guide, a former prisoner at Porto Bello, had warned Morgan not to move a step toward the town until the headland watch was silenced. All right, said the admiral, close his mouth, and his eyes if you have to. A handful of picked men shed all arms but their knives and groped up the hillside.

---

[8] Names of the forts, their placement and Morgan's action against them are a tangle that only spirits from the vasty deep could unknot. Three professed eyewitness accounts of the action exist: Morgan's laconic "Information" delivered before Port Royal authorities after his return, and concurred in by six of his captains (*CSP, Colon.*, 1661–8, no. 1838); a letter accompanying the Spanish ambassador's protest to King Charles, and allegedly written by one of Morgan's captains (*CSP, Colon.*, 1669–74, no. 1); and Esquemeling's narrative (cf. *Buccaneers of America*, 1923, pp. 141–49). We have descriptions of the town in the brief remarks of Thomas Gage (who was there) and in more detail from Lionel Wafer (who was not). No one of these witnesses agrees with the others. The best secondary sources — Haring, Roberts, Lindsay and Masefield — are likewise at variance. Such diversity encourages fresh examination of the data. The order of events given here seems to the present writer most consistent with the imperfect evidence. The reader should be warned, however, that it maintains tradition by differing from everyone else.

The watch drowsed, with good reason. Porto Bello had lived untroubled for nearly seventy years. Any soldier who spent his lonely nights on the headland straining for the sound of a snapped twig would be a babbling madman before long. The buccaneers crept close; a sharp rush, a knife at the windpipe, and the watch was theirs. They dragged him quivering to the beach, where Morgan questioned him about forts, garrisons, guards. The Gloria fortress, stammered the captive, had 135 soldiers within its walls, the gates shut by night and a guard set. Any English prisoners there? Yes, ten or twelve, in a dungeon under the citadel.

The invaders took up their silent march, and before dawn looked down on the dim outlines of the Gloria fortress. Formidable to seaward, where the harbor waters lapped its great stones, the Gloria was poorly armed against land attack. Its upper walls were low; the hill above commanded its exposed platforms. The buccaneers loaded their muskets and took cover in a wide semicircle. At the first gray light of day the captive watch called out to the fort to surrender or the garrison would be slaughtered to a man. He was answered by a spurt of musket fire. In an instant the buccaneers were up with a wild yell, vaulted the walls, and cut down the defenders as they poured in confusion from their quarters. More than half the garrison, including its commanding officer, fell in the first onslaught, and the rest threw down their arms. Morgan shut them up in the citadel. Beneath it, in a moldy dungeon, eleven gaunt prisoners, awakened by the tumult, stared unbelieving at English faces.

Morgan had no desire to leave sixty Spanish soldiers at his back with the Gloria's guns at their disposal. He had promised no quarter and would give none. The buccaneers ran a powder train to the gate, touched a match to it and, while they marched off toward the town, blew up the citadel in a vast cloud of dust and death.

People in nightshirts fled before them through the streets of Porto Bello. A detachment of buccaneers ran for the churches and monasteries, where they cooped up the religious under guard. But the governor, a man of courage and energy, had already hurried his family to the fort of San Jerónimo. He ordered the cannon wheeled about to cover the town. Blasted by gunfire, the buccaneers scattered for shelter and sniped at the exposed gunners. All morning the running fire went on, costly in buccaneer dead. At noon the buccaneers assaulted the thick wooden doors of the fort with fire bombs. Stones and grenades from the overhanging barbican drove them off. Surrounded by water except for its narrow causeway, the San Jerónimo appeared impregnable.

In the early afternoon Morgan sounded a trumpet to cease fire. A truce party under a white flag made its wary way into the open to announce that unless the fort surrendered at once the buccaneers would scale its walls on ladders carried by the revered priests and nuns of the town. Do your worst, shouted the governor; we shall not give ourselves up alive. Morgan took the chance that this reply was a desperate bluff. His carpenters scratched up timbers to knock together broad scaling ladders capable of holding three or four men abreast. Eighty servants of God, both men and women, were driven at sword point through the town. Forced to pick up the ladders with threats of certain death if they did not, they staggered forward over the causeway, the buccaneers crouched low behind them with pistols cocked and earthen pots filled with gunpowder ready for the fuse. Their screams for mercy went unheard in the sudden burst of musketry. Many fell; the rest dragged on in terror, raised the ladders, and crawled against the gate for safety. Up swarmed the buccaneers. They threw their grenades at the fleeing defenders and leaped after them, cutlasses swinging.

Numb with fear, Spanish soldiers dropped their muskets in surrender, while the white-haired governor slashed at them for cowards. He alone was at bay now, backed up to the outermost parapet, his long rapier at the ready. The buccaneers held off a moment in grim admiration; his wife and daughter pleaded with him to give up. No, he shouted, he would rather die as a soldier than hang as a coward. The buccaneers shrugged, leveled their pistols, and shot him down.

The town was theirs, at the cost of eighteen English killed and thirty-five wounded. They locked the chief men of Porto Bello into a room of the fort, their ladies in another, and the Spanish wounded in a third, where they suffered without care. Next day the fleet, manned by its skeleton crews, appeared off the harbor entrance. A large contingent of buccaneers crossed the bay to subdue the fort of San Felipe. It proved not so iron as its nickname. Surrounded to landward, menaced from the sea, and Porto Bello already in enemy hands, the scant garrison voted for the white flag. English colors ran up in the place of Spanish, and with a boomed salute the fleet sailed in to anchor before the town.

Porto Bello was a plum ripe to the buccaneers' taste. They feasted in its kitchens, swilled the wine of its cellars, and raped Negro girls in the dank east end of town. They stripped homes and warehouses of everything that came loose. Search parties roamed the nearby hills; the plaza rang with screams of the tortured.[9] Two weeks of this prolonged debauchery, aided by

[9] Esquemeling makes but one reference of chilling brevity to torture at Porto Bello: "This they performed with such cruelty that many of them died upon the rack, or presently after." Independent evidence comes from John Styles, a sour Englishman who voyaged to Jamaica in search of fortune and landed in prison for debt. He told the secretary of state that cutting victims to pieces, burning fingers or toes with matches, and woolding (cinching a rope around the victim's head until his eyes stood out like eggs) were barbarisms practiced at Porto Bello; and that one woman was baked naked on a bed of hot stones. Though he was not himself one of Morgan's men, Styles claimed the buccaneers as his source. Many boasted of these atrocities, he told the secretary, "and one that was sick confessed with sorrow" that he had been party to them, for which God would exact sure justice. In his report, Morgan aimed to dull the edge of such accusations. The ladies of Porto Bello, he intimated, were treated with flawless gallantry. Though he offered them permission to join the Panama relief force, they preferred to stay under the protection of "a person of quality" (Morgan) rather than risk dishonor among the "rude Spanish soldiers." They remained, Morgan would have us believe, contentedly packed into one room of the fort until his departure, "when with many thanks and good wishes they repaired to their former houses."

the fatal climate, laid half of Morgan's men low with fever. When his ships were loaded and ready to depart, Morgan coolly demanded 100,000 pieces of eight as ransom or he would burn the town.

Porto Bello citizens protested that they had no money left. Then send to Panama, said Morgan; surely the governor is rich enough to redeem the second city of his province. A pair of Porto Bellans posted off to Panama found the governor there already collecting a force to relieve the town. Morgan was not surprised. At first news of the Spanish approach he marched a hundred of his best men to a narrow defile where a few could hold off an army. A short contest of arms was enough for the Spanish, who halted and pitched camp. The governor sent Morgan a blustering ultimatum "that in case he departed not suddenly with all his forces from Porto Bello, he ought to expect no quarter for himself nor his companions, when he should take them, as he hoped soon to do."

Morgan was contemptuous of the Spanish threat. The troops, he knew, would consist of a few braggart cavalry, the rest unreliable Negroes, Indians and vagabonds released from jail for the purpose. He could board his ships and sail off under fire, if he had to. He stepped up his demand: ransom the town or he would not only reduce it to ashes, but kill the prisoners as well. Since the Spanish troops had no stomach for fighting their way through, Morgan's threat left the Porto Bello emissaries without further choice — they brought in the money.

The Panama governor indulged in a last fatuous gesture. He expressed wonder that so few men could subdue fortresses bristling with cannon. What ingenious weapons had they used? In answer Morgan sent him a pistol, together with a few lead bullets, saying that "he desired him to accept that slender pattern of the arms wherewith he had taken Porto Bello, and keep them for a twelvemonth; after which time he promised to come to Panama and fetch them away."

In all, the buccaneers spent a riotous month in Porto Bello.

By mid-August they hauled aboard the best cannon from the forts, spiked the rest and sailed north for Cuba.[10] Among the cays they shared out 250,000 pieces of eight, besides silks, silver plate and 300 slaves — £60 in coin to each man. "Being arrived (in Port Royal)," sniffed Esquemeling, "they passed here some time in all sorts of vices and debauchery, according to their common manner of doing, spending with huge prodigality what others had gained with no small labour and toil."

Morgan's resounding exploits made Governor Modyford even bolder against Spain. His communications with London grew more shrill. Four years earlier a ship from Barbados had vanished with his son John aboard, and he had given the lad up as drowned; but on September 12 a captain's story indicated that John had fallen into Spanish hands, "questionless either murdered or sent into the South Seas in slavery by these our cruel neighbors." As a hint of what harsh fate his son might have suffered, Modyford listened on October 5 to the tale of three Englishmen from Providence Island, who had escaped their Porto Bello captivity. He hastened their tale of grief to Albermarle, with a warning note: "It is most certain that the Spaniards had full intention to attempt this island, but could not get the men; and they still hold the same minds, and therefore I cannot but presume to say, that it is very unequal that we should in any measure be restrained, while they are at liberty to act as they please upon us, from which we shall never be secure until the King of Spain acknowledges this island to be his Majesty's, and so includes it by name in the capitulations." The

---

[10] Cannon were fired from a touchhole at the base of the barrel. After tamping the charge down the nose of the gun, the gunner rammed a sharp rod through the touchhole to pierce the powder bag. He filled the hole with priming powder from his horn and sprinkled a train of it in the pan (to escape the blast up the hole when the gun fired), then touched the smoldering end of his rope match to the train, and the fire ran down the touchhole to set off the charge. A gun was "spiked" or "nailed" with a plug driven into the touchhole and broken off, putting the gun out of action until the plug was reamed or blown out.

best defense, thought Modyford, was to rock the Spanish back
on their heels so that they could never deal Jamaica a crushing
blow.

This strategy demanded successive attacks to keep the
enemy reeling. Morgan was in perfect accord, and by the early
days of 1669 had assembled 900 buccaneers for the next strike.
Most of the vessels that dropped anchor at the Île des Vaches[11]
were small, but two of them promised more firepower than he
had ever commanded. The thirty-four-gun royal frigate *Oxford*
sent by Modyford could be relied on. The other, a Frenchman
of equal strength, remained dubious — her captain had only
dropped by to look the situation over. Morgan tried persuasion
without effect. Greedy for the French ship's ranked guns and
stout hull, he decided to make up the wavering Frenchman's
mind for him. He learned that the ship had stopped an English
vessel earlier and, pleading distress, had taken off provisions.
The captain had paid with bills of exchange, but they might be
worthless. At any rate, it was an act of violence, perhaps piracy. Morgan invited the French officers to dine with him on
the *Oxford*; then, as they stepped aboard, he arrested them and
stowed them safely — he thought — below decks.

The invitation was a ruse, but the dinner was not. One by
one Morgan's fleet captains were piped over the side. Under a
sail stretched to shade the poop, surrounded by the untarnished
sea on which the sandy islands seemed to float, the buccaneers
toasted their new venture. They raised mugs to the king, the
queen, Modyford and Albemarle, and damnation to the Spanish. The party became boisterous; a few pistols were fired off at
improvised targets, a cannon was rolled out and blank rounds
echoed through the fleet. Suddenly, without warning, the *Oxford* blew up. The whole midships burst out of her; men, timbers and cables shot upward in a cloud of debris; the mainmast
rose from its seat, hung an instant, and crashed onto the poop,

[11] Cow Island, near Hispaniola's southwest coast. No linguists, the English
buccaneers called it Isle of Ash.

killing five of the captains. Morgan's luck held. When the shattered hulk went down, the only ones left alive were thirty men on his side of the dinner table.[12] For days sodden corpses, some grotesquely spread as though still clutching at air, bobbed on the tideless sea. The buccaneers stripped them of boots and swords, hacking off bloated fingers to get at rings, and left them to the ministry of the fish.

Morgan blamed the disaster on the Frenchmen, now conveniently dead and unable to deny it.[13] But he was shaken, stunned more in will than in body. He has always ruled the buccaneers by the very simplicity of his purposes; others might fret over details and weigh their risks, but Morgan marked out the large design and stuck to it. Now he seemed to have no design. He weakened his forces by sending the French ship to Modyford as replacement for the lost *Oxford* — politic, no doubt, but fatal to any move that he might make against a strong port. He frittered away a month in aimless cruising among the islands, picked up a few provisions here, feinted at Spanish defenses there. Half the fleet wandered off in search of prey. Not until February did Morgan's lax will revive. Reduced to eight ships and 500 men, he had to take firm action or see his whole venture disintegrate. He resolved to attack Maracaibo.

By March his fleet stood off the great triangular gulf which pierces Venezuela. The town lay on the western side of a shallow strait at the apex of the triangle, and beyond that the vast Lake of Maracaibo spread its tranquil length 150 miles to the

---

[12] Esquemeling says that 350 English buccaneers died in the explosion; surgeon Richard Browne, one of the few survivors, puts the death toll at 200. The latter figure appears more probable, since the normal crew of the *Oxford* numbered 160 men.

[13] Cartagena, a prime target for buccaneer attack, held a more elevated theory. People there saw the destruction of the frigate as a deliverance attributable to their patroness, Nuestra Señora de la Popa. Dampier heard later from Spaniards "that she was abroad that night the *Oxford* Man of War was blown up at the Isle of Vacca near Hispaniola, and that she came home all wet; as, belike, she often returns with her Cloathes dirty and torn with passing thro' Woods and bad ways . . ."

steep mountains southward. Maracaibo had 2500 inhabitants; Gibraltar, at the far end of the lake, another 1500 — a rich prize, taken together. A strong fort guarded the strait on the island of Palomas, west of the entrance, with lesser defenses on Virgilias to the east. The guns of Fort de la Barra, at Maracaibo itself, were trained on any enemy that broke through the first line of fire.

The buccaneer ships halted until nightfall beyond sight of the watchtower on Virgilias. After dark they spread single sails and coasted gently down on Palomas; at dawn they opened fire, and all day the light guns of the buccaneer fleet potted feebly at the stout walls of the fort, while its guns boomed reply. This would not do; nothing was left but hand-to-hand assault, cutlass in teeth. After sleeping the early night away, the buccaneers crowded into boats before dawn and slipped ashore. The first gray light found them crouched in the brush, pistols loaded, grenades in pouches, swords fresh-honed. The fort was strangely silent; not a defender appeared on the ramparts. They crept forward, showed themselves, stood up, shouted. No reply; the fort was empty. Beneath its floor the departing garrison had set a candle to the powder stores, which in another quarter-hour would have blown the buccaneers to the judgment seat. Morgan snatched away the flame. They carried a good haul of muskets and ammunition to the boats, spiked the cannon and returned aboard ship.

Next day they entered the straits and stormed into the Barra fort. It, too, was empty. All Maracaibo was deserted except for a few miserable wretches who had nothing to carry away and considered their lives not worth the effort. After searching the town for lurking snipers, the buccaneers settled comfortably into the best houses, with the church as their headquarters.

If they were to gain plunder, the countryside had to be combed for it. Families with women and children could not travel either fast or far. Search parties hastened out at the double, ranging farther each day through woods and plantations.

For three weeks patrols hauled in abject prisoners, and piled mule-loads of personal goods into the church. The prisoners were tortured with elaborate finesse: cords tightened about their heads until their eyes bulged from the sockets; flesh burned from fingers and toes, legs pulled with ropes until the joints cracked. When it appeared that Maracaibo had been stripped bare, and the last sufferer had shrieked the whereabouts of his hidden savings, the buccaneers packed up for Gibraltar.

Everything went on board, prisoners as well as booty, and Morgan dispatched a few of them ahead, in one of his ships, to warn Gibraltar of its fate if it did not surrender. Strengthened by soldiers from Maracaibo, the town decided to fight. Musketry and cannon fire greeted the invaders, whose response was, in Esquemeling's chaste rendering, "We must make one meal upon bitter things before we come to taste the sweetness of the sugar this place affords." The meal was not too bitter, after all. Early next morning they landed down the shore, broke off the main road into the woods, and approached the town from an unexpected quarter. The defenders nailed the cannon and fled.

Crammed into three large boats, the buccaneers swept up the rivers of Gibraltar on the hunt for fugitives. Rain poured down on them as though all the spigots of heaven had opened; the rivers boiled in flood, boats swamped, prisoners and men drowned, powder turned to mash. Fifty soldiers, thought Esquemeling, could have subdued them in their bedraggled condition, "but the fears which the Spaniards had conceived from the beginning were so great, that only hearing the leaves on the trees to stir, they often fancied them to be Pirates." After twelve days of this nightmare they came back, towing a train of boats piled high with abandoned booty.

Morgan had spent five weeks at Gibraltar and up its treacherous rivers. He demanded 5000 pieces of eight for the town, or he would put it to the torch. The distraught inhabitants, who had no means of paying, offered hostages until they could

Morgan took four of the citizens into custody, put all slaves aboard ship, and set sail for Maracaibo.

The town was as deserted as they had left it, but the gulf was not. From a sickly old gaffer taking the April sun they heard bad news — three Spanish men-of-war, lying at the entrance to the straits, blocked their escape. Morgan sent a boat to reconnoiter. It brought back word that was, if anything, worse: the ships — *Magdalena, La Marquesa* and *Luis* — mounted from twenty-six to forty large guns, and the Palomas fort, restored to action, was crowded with men. The Spanish had bottled up the buccaneers in the Lake of Maracaibo, and sealed the cork.

Morgan tried to bluff it out. Ignoring the blockade as not worthy of mention, he sent the Spanish squadron a demand to ransom Maracaibo. "My intent," replied Admiral del Campo, "is to dispute with you your passage out of the Lake, and follow and pursue you everywhere, to the end that you may see the performance of my duty." However, he offered to let the buccaneers pass if they would leave all captured booty behind and go out with empty ships.

Morgan assembled his men in the plaza and read them the Spanish reply. What will you do, he asked, give up the plunder or fight your way out? The buccaneers shouted with one voice that "they had rather fight, and spill the very last drop of blood they had in their veins, than surrender so easily the booty they had got with so much danger to their lives."

Bravely said, not so gently done. Morgan made del Campo a compromise offer: in return for free passage he would leave the town of Maracaibo untouched, releasing at the same time all white prisoners and half the slaves. Del Campo considered it an insult. He gave the buccaneers two days to submit, or he would bring his troops in after them.

Two days were enough for Morgan's men. They sawed down the bulwarks of a small ship captured at Gibraltar, ranged logs (blackened to the hue of iron) along her waist as cannon, and poked the painted ends of long Negro drums out of new-cut ports that represented a gundeck. Wooden skeletons draped with clothes, their stuffed heads topped with peasant caps, became gunners and crew. Pitch daubed on the rigging, brimstone poured in every corner, palm leaves dipped in tar strewed underfoot, a powder keg forward and a fuse run aft transformed the vessel into a floating bomb.

Morgan ordered the men prisoners securely bound in one ship, the women and most valuable plunder put into another, with a handful of crew to guard them. Twelve hardy volunteers manned the fire ship. All took oath to fight to the death, no quarter given; and at dusk on the last day of April they sailed down the straits toward the enemy.

Morgan signaled to drop anchor as night descended on the gulf. The Spanish lay close in, where the converging shores gave narrow passage, and behind them the great guns of Palomas Island once more commanded the channel to the sea. At dawn the buccaneers spread sail on the land breeze and steered for the enemy. The fire ship bore down on the *Magdalena* through a hail of musketry, grappled her shrouds with kedges, and fired the fuse. Behind the crew, now swimming away for their lives, the exploding powder blew a gaping hole in the *Magdalena*'s planks. As flames raced up her sides and into the rigging, she began to settle by the bow. Seeing this catastrophe, the *Luis* fled the battle, running so hard on the shore of Palomas that she stove her bottom and sank in shallow water. Only *La Marquesa* remained afloat. The buccaneers boarded and took her after a sharp, short fight.

Between them and open sea the Palomas fortress loomed more formidable than ever. Resolute men from Maracaibo had come back to restore its ordnance and breached walls; the Spanish squadron had added two massive eighteen-pounders to the sixteen guns which the fort already boasted; and now, with whole crews from the sunken ships massed on her ramparts, Palomas was a match for any fleet. All day the buccaneers ran up to the island and launched futile broadsides, fol-

lowed by a land attack at dusk that cost them thirty dead
without scratching the island's defenses.

Peril never dampened Morgan's zest for a profitable deal;
while other men's knees turned to water, he was thinking up
ways to wring a few coins from the foe. Now he repeated his
demand for ransom. Maracaibo citizens in the fort, anxious to
save their homes, paid him off this time with 20,000 pieces of
eight and 500 cattle. But Morgan still held the prisoners, who
begged del Campo to let the buccaneers pass in payment for
their release. He replied angrily that if they had worked as hard
to rout the invaders at first as they now did to get rid of them,
they would have forestalled all their grief.

By way of compensation for this retort, Morgan sent divers
into the chared hulk of the *Magdalena* and they brought up
15,000 pieces of eight in coin, besides melted plate, sword hilts,
and jewels whose luster the fire had not dulled. He now ordered a division of the whole treasure — 150,000 pieces of
eight, besides goods and slaves, each full share worth £30 —
so that any ship, lost in passage, took to the bottom its own
part of the booty, and no more.

Still, they had to get out of the gulf. All one day Morgan sent
boats loaded with men across the open water in full view of the
fort. They sat up very straight on their seats in martial array,
the sun glinting from their musket barrels, until they disappeared from sight at the back of the island. When a boat returned, apparently empty, the same men lay in its bottom, out
of sight below the thwarts, their muskets beside them. As fast
as the boats plied, the Spanish dug earthworks and wheeled the
great guns about, to meet the expected attack on their landward side.

Night fell, and with it the buccaneer ships weighed anchor.
Under bare poles the ships drifted seaward on the light breeze.
Opposite the fort they clapped on sail as the Spanish watch
cried alarm and the garrison rushed to wheel the guns about.
Only a few spent shot whistled through the rigging or bounced
off the hulls before the buccaneers were gone.

Beyond range, Morgan set the Maracaibo prisoners ashore by boat and, with a taunting salute to the fort, turned his fleet toward home. All ships survived a battering storm on the return, to brail up on the green waters of Port Royal on May 17, 1669.

After Maracaibo, Governor Modyford decided to proceed with caution. In a long letter to Lord Arlington he defended what the buccaneers had done, "not doubting but all sober and true Englishmen will not only absolve him but approve of his proceedings," and with the same pen he called in the privateers' commissions lest they do it again. A November letter assured the Duke of Albemarle that the buccaneers were settling meekly into the ways of peace. Some had taken small plantations, others dealt in hides, tallow, turtle-shell or logwood; and though a few unreclaimed rascals cruised at the old trade, "their ships will wear out, and then they must stay on shore or starve." Even Morgan had hung up his sword, and was building a house in the lovely Rio Minho Valley.

This pacific atmosphere in Jamaica soothed King Charles, who had problems enough. He secretly schemed with Louis of France to declare for the Roman church when the time seemed ripe, and rebellion in England was so sure to follow that Louis had promised French troops to crush it. Furthermore, the ambassador at Madrid was at the very moment concluding delicate treaty negotiations with Spain. No English raid must ruffle the fragile cordiality upon which the conversations rested. In June, 1670, Arlington flatly ordered Modyford to "absolutely and forthwith abstain and take strict care that no descents be made . . . upon any land or places possessed by the Spaniards to invade or plunder any of them."

In those days of laggard communication, national policy could take paradoxical turns. While Morgan was pillaging Maracaibo, the Spanish court was still groaning over Porto Bello; and while London was pressing hardest for peace in the

Caribbean, Spain launched open war. On April 20, 1669, the
queen-regent signed an order to assume the offensive against
the English settlements. She instructed her West Indian officers to "cause war to be published against that nation, and to
execute all the hostilities which are permitted in war, taking
possession of the ships, islands, places and ports which the English have in said Indies." Governor Modyford was gloomy at
the outlook. His brother Sir James talked of leaving while his
skin was whole. "The Spanish begin to take the right course to
ruin us," Sir James wrote to London; "this war, our making a
blind peace, no frigates, nor orders coming, gives us cruel appre-
hensions and makes many remiss."

Jamaicans habitually exaggerated the Spanish threat in order
to protect the buccaneers. Spain was in no position to mount a
full-scale attack; she had sent six men-of-war to the West Indies, and three of them had already been disposed of by Morgan's small force at Maracaibo. But the Spanish made the mistake of arousing Jamaica without injuring the island's power to
strike back. In June, 1670, an armed vessel from Santiago de
Cuba burned some houses on the north coast and carried off a
few prisoners. Some days later two warships repeated the raid.
The Jamaicans roared like stung lions. They were not going to
lose their lives or property for a bit of Whitehall diplomacy
carried on 3000 miles from the danger. The Council assembled
on June 29 and voted a state of emergency. It made Henry
Morgan commander of all the island forces by land or sea. On
July 2, it specifically commissioned him to subdue Santiago de
Cuba, but with wide powers to strike at any place that threatened Jamaica, and "to perform all manner of exploits which
may tend to the preservation and quiet of this Island." Modyford's instructions were more bloodthirsty. He ordered Morgan
to seize Santiago, and if he could not hold it, "then with all
expedition to destroy and burn and leave it a wilderness, putting
the male slaves to the sword." While so doing, Modyford
added, Morgan was somehow to show "loathness to spill the

blood of man," and in all things to convey true "moderation and good nature."

If Morgan had only to be gracious while he ran the Spaniard through, he would try to manage it. He smiled, no doubt, at the braggart challenge posted by a Spanish raider near Point Negril: "I, Captain Manuel Rivero Pardal, to the chief of the squadron of privateers in Jamaica. I am he who this year have done that which follows: — I went on shore at Caimanos, and burnt 20 houses, and fought with Captain Ary, and took from him a catch laden with provisions and a canoa. And I am he who took Captain Baines, and did carry the prize to Carthagena, and now am arrived to this coast, and have burnt it. And I am come to seek General Morgan, with two ships of 20 guns, and having seen this, I crave he would come out upon the coast and seek me, that he might see the valour of the Spaniards. And because I had no time I did not come to the mouth of Port Royal to speak by word of mouth in the name of my King, whom God preserve." Modyford, in well-simulated wrath, posted the piece of canvas to Secretary Arlington as clear proof of Spain's intransigence.[14]

All through the autumn of 1670 buccaneer ships sailed in to Morgan's rendezvous at the Île des Vaches. Modyford sent seven vessels, three of which had boldly presented themselves at Port Royal after plundering Granada without commissions. He forgave them this oversight, and hurried them off to Morgan. On the island beach the buccaneers careened ship, replanked, mended sails and rigging. Some provisioned the fleet from wild cattle on Hispaniola, smoking the flesh in the half-forgotten way of early *boucaniers*. Captain Collier scouted down to the mainland looking for grain. He exacted a ransom

[14] Next month one of Morgan's captains, John Morris, cornered this "vapouring Admiral of St. Jago" (as Jamaicans called him) in a Cuban bay. Driven to cover by a storm, Morris found Pardal already hauled up close to shore. Although the Spaniard was more heavily armed and carried twice his complement of men, Morris at once attacked. The Spanish musketeers fled at the first volley, and Pardal, trying vainly to rally them, fell dead with a musket ball in the neck. The captured ship was added to Morgan's fleet.

F

of 4000 bushels from Rio de la Hacha, as the price of departing peaceably, and had the good luck to capture a merchant ship loaded with more. In early December Morgan made a final round of inspection through the fleet. He had thirty-six ships, totaling 239 cannon and 1846 men, of whom 520 men in eight ships were French *flibustiers*. Most of the ships were small; twenty-five rated under fifty tons, and twenty-three mounted fewer than ten guns. Five of the smallest English craft had no guns at all, and the tiny *Prosperous*, at ten tons and a sixteen-man crew, was little more than a longboat. Morgan's *Satisfaction*, the confiscated French ship of the *Oxford* disaster, was the strongest at twenty-two guns.

Morgan assembled this attack force under a shield of maximum legality. He was commissioned by unanimous vote of the Jamaica Council and was backed, as never before, by public enthusiasm. Islanders enlisted with him as a patriotic duty — his cousin, Colonel Bledry Morgan, Major William Norman, Captain Edward Collier (formerly of the *Oxford*), Captain Robert Delander, and his old comrade John Morris. Richard Browne, who had been sitting at table when the *Oxford* blew up, and had floated from the wreckage on the mizzenmast, held the post of surgeon general. The fleet had some aspects of an official navy. Morgan made Edward Collier his vice-admiral, and appointed captains of troop. Orders from Modyford forbade ships to leave the fleet without surrendering their commissions, and no seaman could either leave or jump from ship to ship except by the Admiral's permission.

Modyford had instructed Morgan "to advise his fleet and soldiers that they were upon the old pleasing account of no purchase, no pay, and therefore that all which is got, shall be divided amongst them, according to the accustomed rules." The articles drawn up were generous to all but the seamen. The king got his usual tenth and the Admiralty its fifteenth. As admiral, Morgan was to receive one-hundredth of the spoil. Each captain drew five shares for himself and eight for his ship; besides their pay, surgeons were to have 200 pieces of eight for their medical chests, and carpenters could claim 100 pieces of eight for their tools. Recompense for injuries was slightly higher than usual: 600 pieces of eight for the loss of hand, arm or leg; for both arms, 1800; for both legs, 1500; an eye, 100; or the equivalent in slaves could be taken at the value of 100 pieces of eight each. The first man to enter a fort under fire, and the man who hauled down Spanish colors, would be rewarded with fifty pieces of eight. After these stated amounts were paid out, the seamen shared the rest. Aboard each ship the crew signed the articles, about two-thirds writing their names, the rest only able to put their marks.

Morgan's deliberate preparations at the Île des Vaches set Modyford's teeth on edge. Would the man never go? Before Morgan left Jamaica, wrote Modyford to London, the governor had exacted from him a solemn vow not to make any incursions on land. Morgan had pointed out that he must go ashore for wood, water and provisions, but would not trouble the Spanish colonists "unless he were assured of the enemy's embodying or laying up stores in their towns, for the destruction of this island" — an exception wide as a pasture gate. Rumors drifted in that the Madrid peace had been signed, that Modyford was to be recalled, that someone had already replaced his son Charles in the profitable post of secretary to the colony . . . Would Morgan never sail? The Dutch governor at Curaçao sent Modyford the treaty articles, and in December he posted them to Morgan, "intimating that though he had them from private hands and no orders to call him in, yet thought fit to let him see them, and to advise him to mind his Lordship's letter of 10th June, and do nothing that might prevent the accomplishment of his Majesty's peaceable intentions." Too late; the buccaneer fleet had vanished.[15]

---

[15] Lindsay and Roberts assume that, along with the treaty articles, the governor sent Morgan a private letter instructing him to return the treaty unopened, thus creating the deception that it never reached him. Such skullduggery was hardly necessary; until Modyford received specific instructions consequent to the Madrid pact, he was still empowered to commission the buccaneers against Spanish shipping.

If King Charles himself had descended to Morgan's deck in full panoply and forbade departure, Morgan might have given up. Nothing short of it would do. On December 2, 1670, he called his thirty-six captains aboard the *Satisfaction* to decide on their place of attack. They voted against Santiago de Cuba as too dangerous, although Morgan had ample force at his disposal to attempt any port in the Caribbean. The captains decided "for the good of Jamaica and the safety of all to take Panama, the President thereof having granted several Commissions against the English, to the great annoyance of Jamaica and our merchantmen." Obviously, Morgan's aim was less punishment than plunder. On December 8 the fleet hoisted sail and bore southwest toward its first landfall — Providence Island.

After Mansfield's brief conquest of Old Providence, Spain had studded the island with artillery. The twenty-gun Teresa Castle glowered from an islet close inshore at the harbor front, with two nearby forts situated so as to pour deadly crossfire into an enemy fleet. A half-dozen armed posts menaced invaders along the coast. But the parsimonious Spanish had garrisoned these elaborate defenses with a mere ninety regulars, backed by a rabble of slaves and some *bandidos* from Panama jails. Morgan resolved to reduce the island in order to protect his rear. On December 14 he dropped anchor in a shallow bay up the coast and put a thousand men ashore. They marched past a deserted battery, through countryside silent and empty, toward the harbor.

The Teresa's gunners were waiting for them with smoking matches, and poured such a cannonade on the vanguard that the men broke and scuttled for cover. The fort's drawbridge was up; the dry moat, twenty feet deep, was unassailable; musket balls would bounce off the battlements like pebbles from a sling. Against small arms the cursed rock could hold out for weeks.

With customary nonchalance the buccaneers had marched to

the assault stripped to their shirts and with no more food than they had in their bellies. That night, in a deluge of rain, some pulled down wooden huts to build sputtering fires, but most could only huddle under the dripping trees, and next morning were chilled to the bone and hungrier than ever. A lucky few gnawed the coarse flesh of a scabby old horse that they caught at pasture. The men were grumbling; they wanted to return to the ships.

Unless Morgan could contrive a miracle, he would have to retreat. At noon he rigged a canoe with a white shirt for a flag of truce, and sent it to the Teresa with a demand for immediate surrender or no quarter given. The governor replied that he was quite willing to surrender, but to save face, and possibly his neck as well, he hoped that Morgan would oblige with a respectable show of force. It could be simply done, he explained. Let the buccaneers ashore stage a noisy night attack, using powder but no shot. The Spanish would resist in the same bloodless manner. The fleet would come in with cannon blazing (but no shot) and secretly land a shore party. The brave governor, rushing to direct the fire of a nearby battery, would run plump into their arms, and they would force him, with a pistol in his ribs, to smuggle them into the Teresa. In return for the surrender, he asked only that all prisoners taken from the island be released unhurt on the mainland.

Morgan agreed to the pantomime, warning the governor that one hint of trickery by the defenders and he would cut all their throats. That night the buccaneers advanced with a fine din of harmless musketry. The fleet sailed up, its cannon belching only yellow flame, the captured governor led the attackers through the massive gates of the fortress, and the garrison ran obediently to shut itself in the guardhouse. Without a wound on either side, Morgan had carried Providence Island by storm.

Sham conquest can be heady business, and as Morgan now looked southward toward Darien his confidence outran his judgment. At the mouth of the Chagres — his river road over much of the isthmus — loomed the San Lorenzo fortress. He detached Captain Joseph Bradley and told him to subdue it, while Morgan stayed behind to destroy the Providence defenses. The rest of the fleet would coast into the Chagres River mouth in a week, after Bradley had accomplished his mission. Four hundred men would be enough.

Subduing the San Lorenzo, Bradley discovered, required more blood than bluff. The main fort crowned a steep cliff to seaward; behind it, a deep cleft spanned by a drawbridge formed a natural moat, and every other approach was guarded by double palisades, filled with earth and fronted by a twelve-foot ditch. A stout garrison of 350 soldiers manned these forbidding ramparts.

Ignorant of the fort's true strength, Bradley threw away any chance of surprise by sailing straight up to the river mouth. From its height the fort launched a barrage that sobered the invaders, and they drew off to anchor three miles eastward. All the next morning they hacked a path through the jungle. At the fort they were greeted with a thunderous volley that left the ground strewn with dead and wounded, and the attackers spent the rest of the day hidden in the dense foliage, ducking cannon balls that crashed through the trees. The dark of night permitted them to creep closer. One buccaneer, grazed by an arrow, wrapped the shaft in torn shirt cloth and shot it back into the fort. His powder charge ignited the wrapping, it in turn set fire to a thatched roof, an exploding powder keg spread the flames, and most of the garrison had to leave their posts to fight the blaze. This gave the buccaneers a chance to worm up to the palisades and set a match to them. The stockade burned away, the loose dirt cascaded down, and by daybreak the outer works lay in ruins. Now the attackers moved in through the breaches, picking off the exposed gunners. The Spanish began to leap down the cliff to escape the horrors of capture. Their captain fell in a last stand before the citadel, and by noon the sweat-stained buccaneers took full possession of the fort.

Morgan was not to remember the Chagres with pleasure. The buccaneers lost a hundred dead, and another seventy lay wounded, among them Captain Bradley, both his legs crushed by a cannon ball. Not a Spanish officer remained alive, and only thirty soldiers, most of them wounded, survived to surrender. When the ships sailed in from Old Providence a week later, and saw English colors floating from the fort, they recklessly crowded into the river mouth, where a half-dozen of them (including Morgan's flagship) ripped out their bottoms on a hidden reef. Moreover, information gathered from the Spanish soldiers was ominous. Panama, they learned, had been alerted for weeks by a renegade who deserted Captain Collier's foraging expedition to Rio de la Hacha. Ambushes lined the Chagres; 500 resolute men were concentrated at Venta de Cruz, where the invaders must leave their boats; and an army of 3600 confidently awaited their arrival on the plain before Panama City.

Having spilled blood to get that far, nothing could turn the buccaneers back. Morgan appointed Major William Norman commandant of the fort to replace Captain Bradley, who had died of his wounds, and put 300 men under him ashore and another 150 to guard the fleet. Providence Island prisoners began rebuilding the charred palisades. Morgan collected riverboats that lay under the protection of the fort, seven of them rating as sloops and mounting light guns. Putting his remaining 1400 men into the sloops and thirty-six shallow-draft riverboats, he was ready to push off against the Spaniard on January 9, 1671. He expected to cover the forty-eight miles to Panama in six days and, since provisions were short, to live off the countryside as he went. In both expectations he was to be painfully disappointed.

The first day they rowed eighteen miles up the low, placid river, but by late afternoon the men, crammed shoulder to shoulder in the boats, were stiff and hungry. Foraging the shore produced no food, and they lay down to unquiet sleep with only a pipe of tobacco to ease their growling stomachs. On the second day sandbars clogged with debris brought the boats almost to a standstill. On the third day they tried to hack a path along the shore, but the swampy footing, dense jungle growth knotted with vines, the mosquitoes, wood ticks and snakes thick as Pharaoh's plague, drove them back to the river. Upstream a few miles at Cedro Bueno, Morgan abandoned the heavy sloops, leaving 200 men to guard them.

On their fourth day without food, under the pitiless sun, the men staggered with weakness. At Torna Cavallos a large Spanish force had decamped at their approach, leaving behind only a few leather bags, not very tasty, but edible. The famished buccaneers cut the bags into strips. They beat the strips between stones, dipped them in the river to soften them, scraped off the hair, roasted them and chewed the morsels slowly, washing them down with plenty of water. On the fifth day, the vanguard hit on a grotto with some meal, plantains and two jars of wine tucked into its dark interior. Morgan gave this food to those most weakened with hunger. Some of the men could no longer walk, and even the strongest traded places from boat to land to equalize the rigors of the march.

On the sixth day they wove like drunkards, eyes staring from sunken cheekbones, stumbling, feebly champing with slack jaws on grass and leaves. The fate of Panama, that sumptuous city, now rested in the gnarled hands of an unknown farmer who tilled a plot just north of Venta de Cruz. Though he emptied his larder and drove off his stock, he left a barn full of maize, which the buccaneers found. They gnawed the dry ears, and revived. By late afternoon they had routed a band of Indians and made camp on the riverbank opposite Venta de Cruz. This was the end of the river route; from here the Gold Road ran down to Panama.

The Spanish were busy, after their fashion. Religious processions bore sacred images up and down the streets of Panama City. The Host was displayed in all churches day and night, and Governor Juan Perez de Guzmán gave to the Virgin a votive ring priced by the jewelers at 4000 pieces of eight. More practically, he sent a detachment of 250 men to retake San Lorenzo, and a 500-man force to halt the march of the buccaneers. Both ran for home without a shot.

On the seventh day the buccaneers cleaned their guns and crossed the river, delighted to see smoke rising from what they supposed to be the cookstoves of Venta de Cruz. Unfortunately, it was the town itself in flames, and when they charged up, sweaty and panting, nothing remained but the king's warehouse, which the Spanish had not had the nerve to fire. The buccaneers ate a few stray dogs and cats that wandered among the ruins, and made themselves thoroughly sick by gulping wine found in the royal warehouse.

From Venta, Morgan sent the boats back downstream to join the moored sloops. On the eighth day he posted a vanguard of 200 men ahead to meet any ambush, and the rest followed down the hilly Gold Road, swinging their cutlasses to clear the overhanging foliage. No Spaniard appeared, but in a narrow defile a thousand Indians launched a hail of arrows on them, inflicting some losses.

On the ninth day they were up at dawn, plodding along the road in the cool of early morning. By noon they could see the blue strip of Pacific waters on the far horizon and, below them, a broad vale teeming with livestock. They ran to slaughter the herds and eat the meat half-roasted, blood running down their beards and shirts. Restored, they marched on, until in the evening the spire of Panama's cathedral loomed above the plain. The buccaneers tossed their hats in the air, sounded bugles and beat drums. A troop of 200 Spanish horse that appeared on their flank shouted insults from a safe distance: "Dogs! we shall meet you!" The buccaneers paid no heed, and lay down to sleep eager for the next day's battle.

Don Juan Perez de Guzmán, His Most Catholic Majesty's governor at Panama, was ailing. He got out of bed to marshal his defenses in battle array on the plain three miles east of the city, facing the road from Venta. His 2300 foot and 600 horse were more than double the 1200 buccaneers marching to the assault, but two-thirds of the infantry were Negroes, Indians and slaves. Their handarms were clumsy, short-ranged pieces, and the three antiquated field cannon that formed the artillery were of wood covered with leather. As a desperate strategem, Guzmán had collected a herd of 1500 cattle which, at the auspicious moment, he would drive on the enemy's rear.

In numbers the Spanish array was impressive, and Morgan had no desire for a head-on attack. He led his men off the road into the scrub, circling eastward, to come in on the enemy flank. The approach proved much to the buccaneers' advantage; a hill on one side and marshy ground on the other forced the more numerous enemy to operate on a narrow front. Morgan formed up his men in a solid body, wedged at both ends, like a lozenge. Captain John Morris and Colonel Lawrence Prince commanded the vanguard of 300 marksmen; the main corps of 600 had Morgan on its left and Collier on its right; and Colonel Bledry Morgan, a tried soldier, brought up 300 men in the rear. Banners flying and bugles blaring, the buccaneers advanced at a trot.

The Spanish cavalry raised a glittering forest of swords and spurred to meet the vanguard. A single volley shattered them; men and horses crashed to the ground; the charge split on the point of the wedge and streamed down the sides under a hail of musketry. They wheeled, came bravely on again, until their captain fell and they scattered in retreat. The massed herd of cattle, now driven at the buccaneer rear by Indian cowboys, turned tail at the gunfire and lumbered away, snorting with panic. Only the Spanish foot remained, quavering the Magnificat and still drawn up to meet a frontal attack down the Venta road. The buccaneers struck their flank, and after a single wild fusillade, the Spanish fled for their lives toward the city. "The enemies' retreat came to plain running," commented Morgan.[16]

The buccaneers, too worn out to give chase, followed more slowly, rooting fugitives from the bushes along the shore and shooting them without mercy. They had no time for prisoners; some priests captured on the field of battle were pistoled at Morgan's command. Inside the city 200 fresh troops met the invaders with cannon fire of iron scraps. Before the streets were cleared of snipers the city was in flames, raging beyond control through the rows of wooden houses, and although buccaneers and Spanish worked side by side to stem the blaze blowing up buildings in its path, it burned all night and the next day, until Panama, the buccaneers' prize, was a smoldering ruin. Up in smoke went the gracious homes, the warehouses stocked with goods, the stables, shops, inns, cafés. Only a stone church or two, some miserable huts on the far outskirts, and government buildings on a peninsula jutting into the bay, remained intact. "Thus," said Morgan with grim eloquence, "was consumed that famous and antient city of Panama, which is the greatest mart for silver and gold in the whole world." [17]

[16] The capture of Panama was the most disgraceful defeat suffered by the Spanish in the New World. Very probably the buccaneers could have been turned back halfway across Darien, harried from tree to tree when so weak that they could hardly put one foot before the other, but Panama citizens wanted the main Spanish force held to protect the city. Too long at peace, robbed of local vigor by Madrid's autocratic rule, softened by the pervasive institution of slavery, Panama Spaniards showed themselves as inept before the hardy buccaneers as the Aztecs had been against Cortes. Nothing else explains how a populous province allowed a band of famished brigands to struggle for nine days across Darien virtually unchallenged, and rout Panama's defending army in two hours of fighting.

[17] "About noon," says Esquemeling, "he [Morgan] caused certain men privately to set fire to several great edifices of the city"—a charge patently absurd, since burning Panama would destroy the very plunder that Morgan came for. Morgan's report states that the Spanish in the city, "instead of fighting commanded it to be fired, and blew up the chief fort, which was done in such haste that 40 of their own soldiers were blown up." In Guzmán's apologia to Madrid, he plainly states that before he fled the city he gave order to destroy the powder magazines, and we may presume that these explosions began the fires.

Little was left to sack, but Morgan did his energetic best. His men burrowed for precious metal in the warm ashes and fished in well bottoms. Search parties that scouted the countryside for twenty miles round about the city fetched in 3000 prisoners with their valuables. To overtake the major wealth that had been dispatched away by sea, Morgan sent out the few small craft that remained in harbor, and while they failed to catch the treasure ships, they captured others that sailed innocently into port, ignorant of the city's fall.

One such prize, runs Esquemeling's romantic tale, carried a chaste and beauteous *señora.* She enchanted Morgan, who made a prolonged, though gentlemanly, assault on her virtue. He wooed her at first with favors, giving her a comfortable apartment in the government house and a Negro maid to care for her every wish. When these kindnesses failed to soften the lady's fidelity to her husband, Morgan tried the harsh approach — he shut her up in the cellar. Damp and dark though it was, she remained adamant to his advances. At last he gave up and sent her to the discomforts of the other prisoners, with a high ransom on her lovely head. At Venta, on the return across Darien, she complained to Morgan that two priests had used her ransom money to release someone else. Morgan freed her in a final flourish of gallantry, and sent her on muleback to Panama.[18]

Most of Panama's riches were gone beyond recall. Two great ships had made south with full cargo before the buccaneers marched in — one of them with a towering gold altar roped to its deck — and unnumbered packtrains had vanished into the highlands toward Mexico. To snare fleeing Spaniards who had

---

[18] Morgan called the whole episode sheer fiction on Esquemeling's part, and perhaps it was. Surgeon General Richard Browne, whose admiration for Morgan turned to distaste after the sharing out of the Panama booty, and who would have welcomed any opportunity to defame him, reported only that women prisoners at Panama were well-treated. Cf. *CSP, Colon.,* 1669–74, no. 608.

not run far or fast enough, strip them of their goods, torture more wealth out of them, and exact ransom for their release, was the buccaneers' only hope for gain. They plied this course relentlessly among the ashes of the dead city, and when the return journey over Darien began on February 14, 600 wailing prisoners plodded along, away from what once had been the stately plazas and cool patios of home. To their pleas Morgan replied that "he came not thither to hear lamentations and cries, but rather to seek money." Pay up, he warned, or be sold into slavery. As an added incentive, he saw to it that they got only scraps of food, and so little water that their tongues thickened and their voices croaked. He was, sighed Esquemeling, "a man little given to mercy." At Venta more ransom money came in, the prisoners were freed, and on February 24 the men jammed into the small boats for the swift descent down the Chagres.

As the time approached to share out, some buccaneers began to mutter that plunder had been concealed. Morgan ordered everyone out of the boats at Cedro Bueno, where they joined the sloops, and announced that to satisfy their suspicions, all would be searched. Bags were turned inside out, pockets emptied, muskets disassembled, powder poured from horns, noses and ears inspected for small gems. Morgan was examined as minutely as the others. The grumblers thus quieted, they sped on downstream. Within two days from Venta de Cruz they were back under the cliff at San Lorenzo. Here Morgan made a last try at increasing their haul. He sent a boatload of Providence Island prisoners to Porto Bello (as he had promised) with a demand to ransom the San Lorenzo fort or he would raze it to the ground. Not a piaster, dog of a heretic, replied Porto Bello; do what you will.

No matter, thought the buccaneers; their booty would pay well enough for the hardships and hunger, the crippling wounds and dead left along the way. But when they shared out, it came to only 200 pieces of eight per man, and they cried robbery. Morgan paid no attention, says Esquemeling, "having designed in his mind to cheat them as much as he could." He calmly dismantled the fortress, loading the best cannon into the Port Royal ships, and on March 6, 1671, spread sail for home.[19] On April 20 he dictated a brief narrative of the Panama exploit, which went to London, and on May 31 he reported verbally to the Jamaica Council, "who gave him many thanks for the execution of his last commission [read the minutes] and approve very well of his acting therein."

The Panama raid cast a cloud of gloom over the Spanish court. "It is impossible for me to describe the effect of this news upon Madrid," the English ambassador told London. All Spain went into mourning, the queen-regent spent hours on her knees, imploring God's vengeance, and the Spanish ambassador in London poured out his grievances to King Charles. Charles had already taken steps to rectify the situation. In September, 1670, he appointed Sir Thomas Lynch deputy governor of Jamaica. Lynch was a wealthy Jamaica landowner who had supported Modyford until they parted on the issue of the buccaneers. Gossip attributed his appointment to a large loan made to King Charles, but Lynch was able and articulate, and represented the peaceful policy toward Spain which was gathering adherents among leading Jamaicans. On January 4, 1671, the King revoked Modyford's commission as governor.

---

[19] Most commentators have condemned Morgan for rank dishonesty in the sharing out, but evidence supporting such an accusation is scant. It is probable that the resentful buccaneers were simply weak in arithmetic. Even if they had collected booty worth 500,000 pieces of eight (which is highly doubtful, and more than triples Morgan's official figure of 135,000), each share, after the agreed deductions had been made, would have come to no more than the 200 pieces of eight that they actually received. Further, all the captains, and most of the men, must have accepted the dividend as fair, while only a sullen minority shouted fraud. One man, even Morgan, could not swindle thirty-six captains and hundreds of greedy rogues willing to spit him on a cutlass. Surgeon General Richard Browne's statement, that anyone protesting would have been clapped in irons, implies that enough loyal men stood by Morgan to do the clapping.

"Whereas Sir Thos. Modyford, late Governor of Jamaica, hath contrary to the King's express commands, made many depredations and hostilities against the subjects of his Majesty's good brother the Catholic King," Lynch was ordered to arrest Modyford and send him to England under guard. Modyford's son Charles, his London agent, was imprisoned in the Tower as guarantee that Modyford's arrest would go smoothly.

Lynch approached the arrest of Sir Thomas with the utmost caution. Handsome, well-dressed, mannerly, Modyford was popular in the island — "the soule of Jamaica," his epitaph would read. A year before, when rumors of Modyford's imminent removal had drifted to Jamaica, fifty-four military officers (including Morgan as colonel) and 300 merchants and freeholders had petitioned London for his continuance in office. From such widespread support London foresaw a bloody uprising, and instructed Lynch to make the island secure before he took action. The captain of the royal frigate *Assistance,* on which Lynch arrived at Port Royal in June, 1671, was to remain aboard ship to give Lynch armed protection if needed. In case the privateers rose in rebellion, he was to sink, burn or otherwise destroy them, on orders from the king.

Lynch did not lack courage; he was simply discreet. He assumed the reins of government, made no mention of his intent to seize Modyford, suppressed news that the governor's son had been taken into custody, and split up the standing soldiery of the port under two commanders. He set spies to watch Modyford's movements, and to keep an eye on ships by which his escape might be effected. He lived as a guest in Modyford's house, ate his meat, drank his cherished port wine in perfect cordiality. Lynch despised sentiment; it was fitting that he should live under Modyford's roof as a royal officer, equally fitting that he should arrest him in the line of duty.

The occasion to act came with the arrival at Port Royal of a few Council members. Lynch invited them aboard the *Assistance* for punch, and over the fragrant mugs informed Modyford that he had no choice but to detain him there on the king's orders. It was amiable, if somewhat abrupt, and he assured Modyford "that his life and fortune were in no danger." Modyford only remarked that the caution had been a bit excessive. When the Council assembled, Lynch held his ground on the way he had gone about the business, pointing out that if it had been too open, a riot might easily have ensued; and indeed, irate citizens had already sworn to cut Lynch's throat. On August 22, 1671, the *Jamaica Merchant* (partly owned by Mody-ford) carried the former governor out of Port Royal Harbor under guard of a dozen soldiers and two officers. The long east-ward tack was slow, but not too slow for one whose fate was a prison cell. In mid-November the guard marched Modyford into the dread precincts of the Tower. Only then was his hos-tage son released.

Never one to fuss about other people's misery, Morgan lay low. He was, in fact, a sick man — the Panama trek had worn him thin. His stomach troubled him; he grumped around his Rio Minho estate, hawking and spitting, swilling rum, cursing the servants. With Modyford gone to the Tower, he could be next — and was. By mid-December he was summoned to London to "answer for his offences against the King, his crown and dignity." The king! Had not Morgan saved those islands that shone like pearls in the king's crown, and preserved the royal dignity, indeed that of every freedom-loving Englishman, from the ravages of Spain? Even Lynch, in the heat of triumph over his buccaneering rivals, had a generous word for the fallen admiral. "To speak the truth of him," Lynch confided to Lon-don, "he's an honest brave fellow, and had both Sir T.M. and the Council's commission and instructions" against the Span-iard. Still, duty was duty, and Lynch promised to get Morgan off to London as soon as a frigate was ready. He had no fear of insurrection in this instance. Many buccaneers nursed a fierce grudge against their old commander over the small shares of Panama spoil, and "they would take it for a great compliment to be severe with Morgan, whom they rail on horribly for starving, cheating and deserting them."

In April, 1672, Morgan's health improved a little. Lynch sent him aboard H.M.S. *Welcome*, a creaky old hulk that Lynch predicted, with some complacency, would break up in the first gale. It sailed on the 6th, and managed to make the voyage to England without going to the bottom. Morgan's fellow passenger was a buccaneering captain charged with piracy — hardly a reassuring companion. The three-months voyage tried them both, and from Spithead on July 4 the *Welcome*'s captain informed the Privy Council that his two prisoners were "very much tired with their long confinement, especially Colonel Morgan, who is very sickly."

The wheels of state ground exceeding slow. With Morgan out of the West Indies, and Spain placated on that score, Charles was in no hurry to push the matter further. Nor was Morgan; after all, the longer his case gathered dust, the less chance of punishment. He had not been arrested; he had not been jailed; on his personal cognizance he roamed the bawdy Restoration capital at will; he could tipple under the grimy beams of the Black Swan or Bottle of Hay, lay a bet at the Newmarket races, watch the skaters on St. James Pond, sample plays at the several theaters that were everyone's delight, or journey west to his native Wales. The hero of Panama was welcome at noble houses. Through Modyford he became an intimate of the Earl of Carlisle and the young rakehell Duke of Albemarle, both destined to be governors of Jamaica. John Evelyn noted in his diary that he met Morgan at the house of Lord Berkeley, together with Modyford, who had made his penance and was released from the Tower.

Morgan's hearing, when it finally took place, was an amiable tête-à-tête with the Board of Trade. Two years had passed; they had almost forgotten him. Morgan had brought along from Jamaica a letter of commendation from Major General James Banister, commander of the armed forces in the island,

and a member of its Council, which assured Secretary Lord Arlington that Morgan had received "a very high and honourable applause for his noble services," and his Lordship should know him to be "a very well deserving person, and one of great courage and conduct, who may, with his Majesty's pleasure, perform good public service at home, or be very advantageous to this island, if war should again break forth with the Spaniard." William Morgan of Tredegar, royal officer in Monmouthshire as well as kinsman, submitted that cousin Henry had conducted himself laudably in Jamaica, "and all good men would be troubled if a person of his loyalty and consideration as to his Majesty's affairs in those parts should fall for want of friends to assist him."

The Lords of Trade nodded sagely over these evidences of good will. Friends, in seventeenth-century jurisprudence, weighed more heavily than that tenuous thing, justice. Morgan's defense was airtight, at any rate. As long as he could maintain that he was legally commissioned, and had no subsequent orders to the contrary, it would be hard to build a case against him. King Charles veered like a weathercock in a fluky breeze. In November, 1673, he received Morgan in his chambers and presented him with a jeweled snuffbox bearing the royal portrait in miniature.[20] In January, 1674, he appointed Morgan deputy-governor of Jamaica, reposing "particular confidence in his loyalty, prudence and courage, and long experience in that Colony," and in June added the post of lieutenant general of all Jamaican armed forces. With a tap of the royal sword Charles created the despoiler of Spain Sir Henry Morgan, Knight. Modyford became chief justice, and Morgan's friend, the Earl of Carlisle, was named governor. The foe of buccaneering, Sir Thomas Lynch, was removed from office by order of November 20, 1674 and the master buccaneer, Mor-

[20] All trace of the box has been lost. The only proof of its existence is C. E. Long who, in an article in the *Gentleman's Magazine*, London, February–March, 1832, declared that he saw it in the possession of a descendant of Morgan's brother-in-law, Colonel Robert Byndloss.

gan, took his place — a staggering reversal of policy. Morgan's instructions were delivered to him by the hand of a wizened, hawk-nosed clerk of the Board of Trade, John Locke.[21]

Such unmarred perfection could hardly endure. Soon Carlisle postponed his appointment, and on April 3, 1674, his name was struck from the commission and that of Lord Vaughan inserted in its place. Pepys jotted into his diary the opinion of an esteemed friend that Vaughan was "one of the lewdest fellows of the age" — censure indeed, considering the age — but his bleak lechery was very different from Morgan's hearty roistering.[22] The two never hit it off. Vaughan suspected Morgan from the start, and when their ships weighed anchor from the Downs on January 8, 1675, Vaughan issued strict orders that they should stay together throughout the voyage.

Determined to beat Vaughan home, Morgan contrived to evade the orders. Somehow the *Jamaica Merchant*'s anchor fouled in the mud, and before they worked it loose Vaughan's ship was out of sight. Somehow their courses differed, and the *Jamaica*'s captain could never explain how he fetched up at Morgan's old rendezvous of the Île des Vaches. Mean minds,

[21] Locke became the most influential philosopher in English history. His *Treatise on Civil Government* (1690), basing William III's reign on the consent of the people, powerfully shaped the thinking of later revolutionists in America and France. The unhampered freshness of his experiential analysis of knowledge in the 1690 *Essay Concerning Human Understanding* began the fruitful stream of philosophic thought which flowed through Berkeley, Hume, Kant and on to our own day. In Locke, natural law, religious toleration, the appeal to experience, and the application of reason to all affairs, human and divine, rang the knell for whatever vestiges of medievalism remained in seventeenth-century England. As no one else, he summarized the fundamental concepts of the modern mind. A practical man, not given to flights of speculation, Locke engaged in public affairs during much of his life.

[22] No man is all bad, but Vaughan's detractors came close to picturing him so. "A person of as ill fame as ill face," growled the Duke of Clarendon. A letter quoted by the sober *Complete Peerage*, III, p. 8, accuses him of amassing wealth at the expense of Jamaica, selling fellow-Welshmen into slavery, and denying his daughter a fitting dowry. Vaughan had some literary pretensions, wrote a bit of poetry and enjoyed the smart conversation of London's Kit Kat Club. Dryden dedicated a play to him — the poet's bawdiest, laid in a brothel. More to his credit, the Royal Society elected him its president 1686–89.

like that of Vaughan, would attribute it to the fact that Sir
Thomas Modyford, who was also aboard, was part owner of the
Jamaica, and in an excellent position to issue commands. But
the manner of their fetching up at the Île des Vaches was certainly not according to plan. They came in driven by a storm so
furious that it wrecked their ship, and they would have perished to a man, Morgan was sure, if he had not known every
inch of the shore. By good chance an old buccaneering comrade was riding out the gale under the island's lee. He set the
castaways down at the Port Royal quay on the 5th day of
March.

Morgan had won the race, and until Vaughan's sail came
over the horizon he was acting governor of Jamaica. Two and a
half years after Lynch had sent him under guard to England, he
would have the pleasure of ousting Lynch from office. On the
second day after his arrival Morgan had assembled the Council
at the capital of St. Jago de la Vega, a sleepy town twelve miles
inland from the port. Lynch sat glumly by while Morgan announced his dismissal and took from him the authority of government. Four days later another Council meeting at Port
Royal placed the Great Seal of the island in Morgan's hands.
Who could be sure, in those precarious times of frail ships on
troubled seas, that Vaughan would ever arrive?

The triumph was sweet, but lasted only a week. When
Vaughan's frigate sailed in on March 14 he was bursting with
rage. "In the Downs I gave him orders in writing to keep me
company, and in no case to be separated from me but by stress
of weather," he fumed to London, "however he, God knows by
what fate, coveting to be here before me, wilfully lost me." Jamaicans soothed him with an eleven-course inaugural feast, "73
dishes of succulent spiced fishes, birds sweetely stuffed, fowles
roasted and so tender their flesh parted in the fingers, meate in
great quantity, pastries with sufficiency of herbes."

These blandishments salved Vaughan's vanity without sof-

tening his animosity toward Morgan. He allied himself with
Lynch to crush the buccaneers, but it was the wrong moment.
Alarmed by the appointment of her old enemies to high office
in Jamaica, Spain took strenuous measures to protect her American dominion. Early in 1674 she put out a fleet of fast open
boats, ninety feet long and armed with cannon, to range the
Caribbean against intruders. The more peaceable Jamaica
showed itself, the more bold Spanish aggression became. Soon
the swift Spanish *guardacostas* had snatched up thirty English
merchant vessels. Vaughan was caught in his chosen policy; if
he took a warlike stand now, he would put himself straight into
the hands of his hated rival, Morgan.

Morgan lolled in a shady hammock and let Vaughan stew in
his own juice. The governor vented his feelings in strident letters to London. "I am perfectly weary of him," he cried, "and I
frankly tell you that I think it is for his Majesty's service he
should be removed, and the charge of so useless an officer
saved." Worse, by his scandalous behavior Morgan "has made
himself and his authority so cheap at the Port, drinking and
gaming at the taverns, that I intend to remove thither speedily
myself for the reputation of the Island and the security of the
place." The Secretary of State gave Vaughan cold comfort —
regretted the disagreeable affair — suggested he make up the
quarrel as best he could — undercut the governor by requesting from Morgan a general report on conditions in the island.
Morgan replied in a grieved tone that he really knew nothing,
since Vaughan never confided in him.

Vaughan suspected Morgan of a secret liaison with the privateers. "What I most resent," he complained, "is . . . that I find
Sir Henry, contrary to his duty and trust, endeavours to set up
privateering, and has obstructed all my designs and purposes
for the reducing of those that do use this course of life." The
quarrel came to an open test over the trial of a privateer captain, John Deane. In April, 1676, an Admiralty court presided
over by Vaughan condemned him to death, but London legal

authorities voided the trial on the grounds that pirates must appear before special commissions and under common law. When Morgan made disparaging remarks about Vaughan's conduct of the affair, the governor could contain his wrath no longer. He summoned Morgan and Byndloss before the Council for a showdown.

At the meeting, behind the closed jalousies of Vaughan's dim parlor at St. Jago, Morgan was all innocence. Had they not encouraged the buccaneers? demanded Vaughan. Morgan was not aware of it, and Byndloss exclaimed that if the governor would give him a frigate he would bring in the buccaneers' heads on a pike, so great was his abhorrence of them. Had not Morgan written letters concerning buccaneers to the French governors at Hispaniola and St. Christopher? Morgan knew no law against that; if such an order existed, perhaps Vaughan would show it to him. But had not Morgan done so in the governor's name? Morgan expressed hurt surprise. He asked his secretary if such letters had been sent. No, declared the secretary, none; when Lord Vaughan withheld this authority, no letters were sent.

The Council declined action, other than to forward the minutes of the meeting to the king. Morgan posted off a stern defense: "If ever I err in one tittle, then let me ever be condemned for the greatest villain in the world . . . I sucked the milk of loyalty, and if I would have sold one little part of it I might have been richer than my enemies ever will be . . . My unhappiness is that I serve a superior here that is jealous of all my actions and puts himself to study my ruin." The Lords of Trade brushed the matter aside for a year, then informed Vaughan that nothing could be done without further investigation. Vaughan was, after all, an interim governor, and expendable. To the vast relief of the island, he was recalled at the end of 1677. King Charles's original choice, the Earl of Carlisle, accepted commission to the office on March 1, 1678.

During his few months as acting governor, Morgan devoted himself to strengthening Jamaica's defenses. Holland had been weakened by three maritime wars with England, and serious threat from Spain could be dismissed as negligible, but France now loomed as the great rival which she was to be for a century to come. Although Charles II was pensioner to the French king, and tied to him by the 1670 Treaty of Dover, ships that harbored at Port Royal kept reporting imminent war between the two. Rumor spread that Louis XIV had amassed a huge fleet capable of clamping French rule on any Caribbean colony.[23]

To repel attack from such powerful armament Port Royal had only Fort Charles behind the town, begun in 1660 to celebrate the coronation, and still unfinished. Morgan put the whole island on a war footing. It was work to his liking; he was at the fortifications early and late, until he had reduced himself to "a perishing condition." He put all ships under governmental control, conscripted infantry and appointed officers to drill them, doubled the port guard so that not a canoe could slip in unseen. Using one slave out of every ten from the plantations as laborers, he completed the red-brick triangle of Fort Charles and established two new forts, the Rupert and the Carlisle, on the harbor-front. By April 25 he reported the task done, and when Carlisle sailed in to assume office in July, a triple· salute from the ramparts greeted him.[24]

[23] Rumor was right, although the initial target was Dutch. More than thirty vessels, carrying in their crews 1200 *flibustiers* from Tortuga, made south for Holland's Caribbean stronghold of Curaçao on May 7, 1678. The French threat ended when a storm blew the 81-gun flagship and other vanguard frigates onto a jagged reef at the Isle of Aves. As they wallowed in the surf with the seas gushing through their split timbers, they fired warning cannon, but the rest of the flotilla took these as a signal to follow, and eleven more warships rode onto the reef, where their bottoms were knocked out. Five hundred seamen drowned.

[24] Charles Howard, Earl of Carlisle, had been suspected of Royalist sympathies even while he served with distinction as an officer in the Commonwealth army. Charles II made him an earl in 1661, and entrusted him with large duties as Privy Councillor and Lord Lieutenant of Cumberland and Westmorland. It is probable that Carlisle met Morgan during the latter's London sojourn, for he requested that Morgan continue as his deputy, and in Jamaica, during Vaughan's interim regime, Morgan toasted Carlisle's health and wished him early arrival as the island's governor. Carlisle, in return,

Under Carlisle, Morgan reached the apogee of his political power in Jamaica: deputy governor, senior member of the Council, lieutenant general of all armed forces, and judge-admiral of the Admiralty Court. But Carlisle brought bad news as well. He was charged by the Privy Council in London with the responsibility of fixing on the troublesome island a new and oppressive system of legislation. It provided that the governor in Council (which the king also appointed) should originate all bills and forward them direct to the king, who would then modify or reject them as he pleased. Only thereafter would the bills go to the Jamaica Assembly for its obedient approval.

Jamaicans denounced the proposed act as a death blow to their rights under the English constitution, and impractical as well, since every bill, however urgent, would have to cross the ocean twice and win the assent of three governing bodies before going into effect. Led by an able young lawyer and landowner, Samuel Long, the Assembly spurned the new order in its entirety. Carlisle raged at their obstinacy, called them fools, cowards, asses and traitors. Long replied calmly that "he asked nor desired nothing but his right and privileges as an Englishman, and that he ought to have and would not be contented with less."

The deadlock put Morgan into a quandary. As a Crown officer he could hardly oppose the king's commands, and as Carlisle's friend he hesitated to join the opposition. It would have taken a bigger man than Morgan to resign office and declare himself for the parliamentary party. Vague principles of basic rights and natural law moved his cagey mind not at all. He did the only thing left open to him — stayed out of the quarrel entirely.

This decision was eased by Morgan's need to look after the large holdings that he had acquired. Besides his land on the

---

maintained a warm affection for Morgan, commending his diligence in office, and when he left his duties on Morgan's shoulders in 1680 Carlisle added £600 of his own to Morgan's salary. Otherwise, in Carlisle's revealing comment, "with his generous humor, I know that he will be a beggar."

Rio Minho he now had "pens" in St. Mary Parish on the north side of the island, and in St. George Parish eastward. On the rich coastal plains he grew sugar, cocoa, indigo, cotton and ginger. The tobacco was only fair, but good enough for his pipe. Grapes, apples and pimientos flourished in the unfailing sunshine and heavy night dew; citrus fruit and vegetables supplied his table, which groaned with food like any planter's. If he inclined he could hunt game fowl in the hills or hook fish that swarmed the rivers. More likely, he would stretch out in a hammock where the breeze fanned him, with a cool glass nestled on his stomach.

A crisis in Carlisle's struggle with the Assembly broke this rural peace. In a wild flare of temper the governor threw Samuel Long into jail and dissolved the stubborn Assembly. Nothing was left but an appeal to London. The Assembly chose Long and Colonel William Beeston to present its case before the Privy Council, and Carlisle sailed in May, 1680, to defend his interests in the matter. Morgan revealed his true sentiments by signing a Council petition that urged modification of the "new model" government. As Carlisle's ship disappeared over the horizon he took the helm of Jamaican affairs for his final, and longest, period.

Early in his term of office Carlisle had shared Morgan's tolerance for the "sweet trade" of buccaneering. He revived Modyford's tactics by expressing dismay that Jamaica had "not above four thousand whites able to bear arms, a secret not fit to be made public." Word spread in buccaneer lairs that Jamaica would be soft on them, and there was some evidence for it. Raiders who snatched indigo, coin and plate out of Honduran warehouses in the autumn of 1679 brought their plunder to Port Royal without harm. Made bold by this new cordiality, six captains combined forces off Point Morant, and in February, 1680, went ashore on the Darien coast. They marched four days toward Porto Bello, and though "many of them were weak, being three days without food, and their feet cut with the rocks for want of shoes," they took the town easily. Others joined them by April, and they crossed Darien to harry the Pacific coast of Spanish America for eighteen months.

Morgan had to calculate how this news would affect forces playing upon his personal security. He sensed, as much as saw, that the day of brash attacks on Spanish territory was past. The climate of opinion had subtly changed since Morgan's men had taken the same path across Darien ten years before. If trade was the coming thing, Jamaicans saw, the buccaneers would soon be more nuisance than benefit. Morgan's enemies, however, were not at home; they were in London. Sir Thomas Lynch, resolute foe of all freebooters, was there, and Lord Vaughan, spiteful as ever. A cantankerous captain named Mingham, whose ship Morgan had confiscated, was howling for justice at Whitehall. Long and Beeston, nor quite his bitter antagonists, would do him no good. All were in London at the ear of the king.

His calculations made, Morgan quickly turned into the fiercest persecutor of buccaneers that the Caribbean would ever see. He warned them to come in, apply for pardon, and take up Crown land like honest fellows, or he would have their bones clacking in the breeze at Gallows Point. In his zeal he lumped privateers and pirates together as a "dangerous pestilence" from which Jamaica must be forever cleansed; although, with a sly thrust, he reminded London that "privateers in the West Indies can be no less easily extirpated than robbers on the King's highway in England." [25] He had been diligent, however: "I have put to death, imprisoned and transported to the Spaniard for execution all English and Spanish pirates that I could get within this government." He had been stern justice itself:

[25] Morgan himself, we must recall, cannot be convicted of piracy. On all five of his recorded voyages, from the one which opens our narrative to the climax at Panama, he sailed with legitimate privateering commissions from the governors of Jamaica. Although he invariably overreached his authority, his legal base was sufficiently secure to protect him.

"When any of the pirates are brought to me I use the utmost severity of the law against them"; yet his heart was grieved, for "I abhor bloodshed, and I am greatly dissatisfied that in my short government I have been so often compelled to punish criminals with death." But he would suffer with a good will if the king's pleasure could be furthered and friendly trade with Spain established, since "nothing can be more fatal to the prosperity of this Colony than the temptingly alluring boldness and success of the privateers." Toward those who spoke evil of him or doubted his sincerity, he had only compassion: "God forgive 'em. I do." [26]

King Charles had something more important in mind for Jamaica than a handful of unkempt pirates. Eager to salvage what he could from his concession on the governmental system, he chose the moment to impose a perpetual revenue on the island. It was Morgan's task to gain the Assembly's consent. Charles did not care how he did it; he could wheedle, finesse, bribe, threaten, or ram the bill down their ungrateful throats, but get it through he must. The Assembly fought this annual grant to the Crown as stubbornly as it had the "new-model" government. While Charles chafed at the delay, they wrangled all through the spring and summer of 1681. Morgan met with "an absolute averseness to a perpetual revenue," said his plaintive report in May, and the king could only hope for a compromise.

In April the king in council severely censured Morgan for his handling of the Mingham case. His action on that occasion was quite unwarranted, they ruled, "contemptuous toward your Majesty's Council Board and throughout oppressive and unjust." In June the king had to order the execution of some pirates that Morgan had reprieved. By August the ax was raised and Morgan felt its shadow. "I wonder that notwithstanding

[26] Private letters (now lost) written by Morgan and seen by Bryan Edwards, historian of the West Indies, dripped such pious sentiments that he wondered if Morgan was a great soul, much maligned, or an odious hypocrite — a question still unanswered. Cf. Lindsay, p. 222.

my diligence and care," he wrote to the Secretary of State, "I should have been evilly represented to the King by people who are causelessly prejudiced against me, but I hope you have too good an opinion of me to believe them." Evidently not, for in September the ax fell; Charles revoked Morgan's commission as deputy governor and lieutenant general of armed forces. To cap the humiliation, he appointed Morgan's old opponent, Sir Thomas Lynch, as governor of Jamaica.

Lynch was a businessman, prepared at any time to swallow pride if it would get some trade, but Morgan's contempt for him was a mistake. For all his drab commercialism, he was able and astute. Morgan's hostility to the Lynch regime took the form of an obstructive clique of political cronies which he called the Loyal Club. It claimed to represent true toryism in the island, the only sure support of the Crown and, by implication, put Lynch's adherents into the camp of whiggish dissent. "A little drunken, silly party," Lynch described it to London, made up of Robert Byndloss ("one of the worst men I know"); attorney Roger Elletson ("an ill man; he was driven here by his crimes and necessities"); Henry's nephew, Colonel Charles Morgan, who habitually beat up his soldiers at the fort in a drunken rage; a henchman of Byndloss, named Cradock; and a bibulous parson of Port Royal, one Longworth. On the whole a turbulent, insolent lot, said Lynch, but capable of giving him "more trouble than I ever had in my life." He would certainly seize the first opportunity to get rid of them.

The opportunity was occasioned by an explosive pair — the same truculent Mingham who had brought London's censure on Morgan, and Captain Churchill of the naval brig *Falcon*, an arrogant protégé of Lord High Admiral the Duke of York. At the Port Royal quay in the summer of 1683 the two got into a squabble. Mingham became abusive, and Churchill retaliated by hoisting Mingham's mate, naked and kicking, from the *Falcon*'s yardarm. When the mate of a nearby ship, one William

Flood, rowed over to the *Falcon* to rescue his friend, Churchill ducked Flood in the bay and laid twenty lashes on his back.

Mingham rushed to Lynch for justice. No one wished to affront the Duke of York's favorite for the sake of "a virulent, base-natured fellow," as Lynch called Mingham. They passed the issue about like a hot coal, from Lynch to the Admiralty court to the Assembly to the Council to the courts-martial in England. But in a few days matters took a more serious turn: Flood was feverish, Flood was deathly sick from his ducking and the welts that seamed his back, Flood died. Crews of the ships brawled in Port Royal streets until the jail was jammed with rioters.

Flood's captain hastened to report his mate's death to Lynch, who was ill at home. "Do you say your mate was murdered?" cried Lynch. No, the captain would not say that — yet. He wanted Churchill detained in port until the case was judicially settled. "By chance," Lynch recalled, "Sir Henry Morgan was with me. I told him to go down and, commanding the regiments and forts, I bade him do what was reasonable and legal."

In a contest between the detested Mingham and a friend of the Duke of York, Morgan would not bother with either reason or legality. In seven hours of deliberation he wheedled and bullied the jury to a verdict of death by natural causes. Mingham at once raised the cry that Morgan had manipulated the choice of jurors, had been biased and dishonest in his conduct of the inquest, and had countenanced, indeed encouraged, the browbeating of witnesses and rejection of evidence by the attorney-general. The foreman and seven jury members backed up his accusation.

The affair simmered until early October, when rioting broke out between naval seamen and the merchant crews. Charges and countercharges flew; royalists were inflamed against Whigs and Dissenters against Anglicans; heads were broken, treasonable speeches made, while frightened householders sat behind locked doors, their pistols loaded and cocked. In all the disorder Lynch thought he saw the Loyal Club at work, stirring things up in an attempt to discredit his administration. He was sick of the Club's disruptive activities, and so were most level-headed Jamaicans. The hour had come to strike.

Always the prudent politician, Lynch polled his Council before going into action. They were as vexed as he, and stood by him to a man. Within a week of the Port Royal disorders he called his full government together at St. Jago, where the Assembly presented its assurance of "loyalty to him, and their willingness to support him in all measures for the preservation of the peace." On October 9, the first day of sessions, Lynch charged Robert Byndloss with disrespect toward the Council, with striking the receiver-general of Jamaica, and arguing the riots with Henders Molesworth (Lynch's nominee for lieutenant governor) in a profane and violent manner. The Council suspended Byndloss from its membership and ordered him out of town in an hour's time.

On October 12 Lynch accused Sir Henry Morgan of "disorders, passions and miscarriage at Port Royal on various occasions, and for countenancing sundry men in disloyalty to the Governor." Worse, a woman had sworn under oath that Sir Henry, reeling past her door one night, had shouted, "God damn the Assembly!" Very likely. Morgan made lame reply that he hoped not to be blamed for the faults of others. The Council proceeded to strip him of every public office that he still held.

On October 16 affidavits were read against Charles Morgan, who was then removed as Captain of the Fort. On the 17th the Council ruled that attorney Roger Elletson was guilty of "malicious disturbances of the justices at sessions," and of "consorting with lewd fellows." After disbarring him from the practice of law in island courts, the Council demanded £2000 security for his good behavior.

There was no use fighting it, and none of Morgan's men tried. Clear proof of guilt troubled the seventeenth-century mind very little when its passions were stirred. The island was aroused against Morgan's irksome clique, that was all; the government intended to get rid of them, and rid of them it would be, no matter what they or anyone else testified. Their last lonely hope was to appeal over Lynch's head to London.

Charles Morgan took ship for that purpose, while Lynch's reports to the Board of Trade painted the malefactors in blackest colors. Byndloss, he snorted, was simply contemptible — "I would not live if my credit came into the scale with such a man." Charles Morgan was "so haughty, passionate and given to drink, that it is impossible either to serve him or use him." As for Sir Henry, "in his drink (he) reflects on the Government, swears, damns and curses most extravagantly . . . Had you full knowledge of his behavior while Lieut-Govr., of his excesses, passions and incapacity, you would marvel rather how he ever came to be employed, than why he is now turned out." Altogether, "these men are of great violence and no sense," Lynch summed them up. The London hearing pitted incompetent Charles Morgan against an imposing team, Sir Charles Lyttleton and Colonel William Beeston, who defended the government action.[27] On June 18, 1684 the Lords of Trade upheld all the dismissals.

Morgan's tarnished reputation risked further damage from one of his own buccaneers, an obscure Dutchman whose sonorous name of Alexandre Olivier Exquemeling suffered a sea change to John or Alexandre Esquemeling among the English. In 1678, he had published *De Americaensche Zeeroovers*, a detailed narrative of Morgan's murderous assaults on the Spanish colonies.[28] Early in January, 1684, William Crooke, a London

[27] Sir Charles was acting governor of Jamaica 1662–1664, founded the town of Port Royal, convened the first elected Assembly and, after his return to England, was a member of Parliament. Beeston had been a leading figure in Jamaica since 1660. He was Speaker of the Assembly during the conflict with Carlisle, and represented the colony in its successful effort to retain its right of self-government. Knighted in 1692, he became lieutenant-governor of Jamaica the next year, its governor 1700–1702.
[28] In the book's opening pages, Esquemeling tells us that as a lad of fifteen years he indentured himself to the Dutch West India Company, never a

bookseller, brought out an English translation entitled *Bucaniers of America; . . . especially the exploits of Sir Henry Morgan.* Within a few days Thomas Malthus of London published a bowdlerized version, *The History of the Bucaniers; . . . More especially the unparalleled achievements of Sir Henry Morgan,* which whitewashed Morgan of many faults attributed to him in Crooke's more faithful rendering of the original work.

It was difficult for Morgan to refute particulars related by Esquemeling, but he took steps to cast a veil of doubt over the whole book. Through a London solicitor he threatened both publishers with a libel suit for £10,000 each. Crooke hastened to make peace with so redoubtable an opponent. In a subsequent edition — which printed the alleged falsehoods exactly as before — he denounced Esquemeling for wilfully distorting the truth, and Morgan's case against him was dropped.[29]

---

prosperous concern, and when the Company withdrew from Tortuga his indenture was sold to a new master who treated him cruelly. He sickened under the harsh usage, and fearing that the boy would die and lose him his investment, this master sold him in turn to a kindly surgeon. It is supposed that young Esquemeling picked up enough medical knowledge from the surgeon to serve in that capacity among the buccaneers. Some scholars contend that behind the pseudonymous pen name was Hendrik Barentson Smeeks, later surgeon-apothecary of Zwolle, Holland, an occasional writer of romances, and author of *Krinki Kesmes* (1715), a predecessor, and possible source, of Defoe's *Robinson Crusoe.* Whoever was author of the *Buccaneers of America,* it remains to this day the chief, and almost only, source of information on Caribbean freebooters prior to 1670.

[29] Later in 1684 "P.A. Esq." (Philip Ayres) issued a hodgepodge little volume of Spanish American oddments which included Morgan's official report on the Panama foray. His preface was devoted to exonerating Morgan from evil deeds narrated by Esquemeling. "All those Cruelties, contrary to the nature and temper of an Englishman, I have heard absolutely contradicted by persons of infallible credit." Cadiz Spanish back from Panama acknowledged that Morgan treated the women of that city with courtesy, the preface declared, and the episode of the lovely lady was dismissed as "altogether a Romance." In fact, "never Man behaved himself with more true valour and resolution of mind to accomplish what he had undertaken, shewed more prudent and soldierly Conduct, nor took more care of preventing all irregularities amongst his Men, by his own example, than the renowned Sir Henry Morgan, who has been thus scandalously affronted by these Scurrilous Pens . . ." P.A. Esq.'s motives are indecipherable, but there are grounds for wonder if Morgan arranged, and paid for, this defense from an unlikely quarter.

5. Morgan's men attacking the San Lorenzo Fort at the mouth of the Chagres River. It was a bloody but necessary assault, opening the way over Darien to Panama City. (Esquemeling Bucaneers of America : Rare Book Division, New York Public Library)

6. The battle between the Spanish and Morgan's men before the city of Panama. (National Maritime Museum, Greenwich)

Malthus refused to cave in so easily. He would not retract, but he did not contest the suit. The libel brief presented by Morgan's lawyer in May, 1685, was more curious for what it left out than for what it put in. It did indeed maintain that Sir Henry had never regarded piracy with anything but abhorrence; "and whereas also in the West Indies and other parts of America there are certain thiefs and a kind of pirates called Bucaniers who subsist and maintain themselves by piracy, burning houses and town, and depredations, and the subjects of the King of Spain and others professing the Christian religion pillaged and caused injury without any lawful authority, against Divine and human laws, for which kind of men called Bucaniers the aforesaid Henry always had and still has hatred, Nevertheless the aforesaid Thomas Malthus not unacquainted with the premises but cunningly contriving and intending to draw the aforesaid Henry into it to the great displeasure of the Lord the King who now is, to injure his good name and fame and to the great peril of life that is laid upon a pirate . . . falsely and of his malice caused to be printed, spread abroad and published . . . ," etc.

Then followed a patchy recital of Esquemeling's errors: Morgan's arrival as an indentured servant at Barbados, his early apprenticeship with the buccaneers, Mansfield's voyage, the Puerto Principe raid, ending with confused reference to an assault on an unidentifiable fort. No mention made of the attacks on Porto Bello, Maracaibo or Panama, no denial of atrocities, no refutation of fictitious ladies or seamen duped at the Chagres or commissions overstepped.

Still, by the matters cited in the libel plea "the aforesaid Henry, to the grave displeasure of the Lord the King who now is, to the prejudice of his good name and fame and to the peril of losing his life, was brought into great dishonour with other persons, subjects of the said Lord the King, so that they have wholly withdrawn themselves from the society and acquaintance of the same Henry." Though the word of a knight against that of

H

a lowly bookseller would have left the king's court in little
doubt as to its decision, Malthus' absence defaulted the case,
and Morgan was awarded £210 damages. Malthus was ordered to make public retraction. His groveling apology concluded with some doggerel that must have been tossed off before breakfast:

> Let the great Morgan, our fam'd Bucanier,
> In his late Enterprise make this appear,
> Who with a handfull of brave Englishmen,
> Frighted the whole America of Spain
> And when he was upon the Indian Shore,
> Had he from England's King derived his power,
> Charles had been crowned the Indies' Emperour.
> Though the Poles brag of their last year's campaign,
> And the French King boast of what he's done to Spain,
> Great Morgan's fame shall last as long as there
> Is beat of Drum or any sound of War.

For the moment Morgan had achieved his purpose. After the
court decision, remarked an observer, the "History of ye Buccaneers was looked upon as fabulous and sold for noe more than
waste paper."

Now death, the implacable meddler, remedied Morgan's
grievances against Lynch. The governor died in August, 1684,
and his appointed successor, Sir Philip Howard, died before
taking office. This opened the way for Christopher Monck, second Duke of Albemarle, wastrel son of the great Duke, and a
friend of Morgan. Young Christopher was one of those Restoration lords who took on the burdens of maturity too early for
their small shoulders to bear. At thirteen he was in Parliament,
where his advocacy of Clarendon's downfall must have brought
a grim shake of the head from the veteran statesman. At sixteen he married Elizabeth, daughter of the Duke of Newcastle,
by the bedside of his dying father, while his mother lay dying
in a nearby room. The girl, whom he had scarcely seen before

the hasty ceremony, was so eccentric that she earned the nickname of "the mad Duchess." Not really mad, mused her father,
just foolish. Christopher succeeded to the dukedom, with its
many honors, when he was but seventeen. His wild extrava-
gances during the next fifteen years dimmed the title's luster
and drained its fortune. Though young Albemarle had taken
up arms in defense of the royal succession during Monmouth's
uprising ("he is said to have shown neither capacity nor courage"), and bore the Sceptre and Dove at James's coronation in
1685, the stodgy king was offended at his excesses. It was popularly supposed that the Jamaica appointment was granted to
get rid of him. On the contrary, he sought the office, being obsessed with the expectation of repairing his shattered finances
from sunken Spanish galleons. In 1686 he had organized a two-
ship expedition commanded by a Massachusetts adventurer,
William Phips, who brought home more than £300,000 from
the waters of Hispaniola — a haul so breathtaking that James
II struck a medal in its honor. Albemarle's appetite for precious metals was insatiable. He pried out of James II the right
to any sunken treasure found over half of the West Indies and,
in addition, mining concessions for fifty-one years throughout
all of England's American colonies. Jamaica was the vantage
point from which he could exploit these privileges.

From the day that his appointment was assured, Albemarle
besieged the king to return Morgan and his cronies to office. In
October, 1686, he proposed Morgan, Byndloss, Colonel Ballard
and Sir Francis White for his Council. King James rejected the
list. In November he again suggested Morgan's name, without
success. When he tried once more in April, 1687, James told
him that only if Morgan presented himself at Court would his
case be reviewed. And on Albemarle's arrival at Port Royal on
December 19, 1687, while still aboard ship, he postscripted to
the Lords of Trade: "One thing I have omitted to mention to
your Lordships, as you will find by the minutes of the Council
concerning Sir Henry Morgan, where the whole Council have

desired me that I would favourably recommend him to his Majestie for readmission into the Council, which I earnestly do, and desire your Lordships will please to move it to his Majestie." Such persistence may not have deserved reward, but got it. On April 10, 1688, the King agreed to lift Morgan's suspension from the Jamaica Council.

Pudgy Christopher Monck was the greatest personage ever to set foot on Jamaican soil, and he proceeded to act the part. The frigate *Assistance* had provided him space for 500 tons of luggage and a retinue of 100, with special cabins built on deck to house the ladies. To be sure of spiritual respite, he had brought along furniture for a whole chapel, with books of homilies, and enough copies of the Thirty-nine Articles of faith for every church in the island. Three days of entertainment graced his arrival. The local orator announced that the harum-scarum Duchess's presence "was an honour which the opulent kingdoms of Peru and Mexico would never arrive at, and Columbus's ghost would be appeased for all the indignities he suffered from the Spaniards, could he but know that his beloved soil was hallowed by such footsteps."

Many Jamaicans soon wished Albemarle well gone. He dismissed the attorney-general and marshal, appointed new justices of the peace, arrested an Assembly member for the treasonable remark, *"Salus populi suprema lex"* — the welfare of the people is the highest law — and fined anyone who spoke slightingly of his actions. He dissolved the Assembly and called for new elections, in which rival candidates accused each other of dishonesty at the polls. When he announced to the Council his intention of making Roger Elletson his chief justice, three of the four Supreme Court justices resigned in heated protest. Wherever Lynch's henchmen went out, Morgan's came in. The island was "utterly undone," said planters and merchants in a petition to the king, the best men "turned out of all authority and command, and their places, as well civil as military, filled up with needy and mechanic men, such as tapsters, barbers and the like."

When the Assembly met in July, 1688, Roger Elletson, its speaker, lauded Morgan and roundly denounced poor Lynch, now in his grave. "But the name of the wicked shall rot," he promised. On July 18 Morgan was reinstated as a member of the Council. Albemarle doubted if he would have a chance to enjoy it. "I am afraid he will not live long," the Duke confided to the Lords of Trade, "being extraordinarily ill."

This was indeed true. Hans Sloane, Albemarle's private physician, regarded Morgan with alarm.[30] At fifty-three Sir Henry was disintegrating physically, as so many did in the Indies, where they died simply "of the climate." He was "Lean, sallow-coloured," Sloane carefully noted down, "his Eyes a little yellowish, and Belly a little jutting out and prominent." He lacked appetite, retched violently in the morning, suffered from swollen legs. Sloane's counsel to abstain from drink and get more rest did Morgan good while he briefly observed it, but he would sooner go to an early grave than give up his midnight bouts with the bottle, so "falling afterwards into his old Course of life, and not taking well any Advice to the contrary, his Belly swelled so as not to be contained in his Coat." Morgan was ready to try any doctor who might cure him without reforming his habits. One Negro medicine man gave him enemas of urine and plastered him with mud packs. Sloane scoffed at these crude remedies, but his own were no more sensible: eat juniper berries and rub with scorpion oil. They would do as well as any. Morgan was not dying of natural causes, he was gradually killing himself.

Against the evil day, he made his last will and testament.

[30] Twenty-eight-year old Hans Sloane had already shown the scientific curiosity that would later make him London's most skilled practitioner of medicine. Queen Anne consulted him, and George II appointed him court physician. During his fifteen months in Jamaica he took copious notes on the island's flora and fauna, collecting 800 specimens of plants. His two-volume *A Voyage to the Island* (vol. I: 1707, vol. II: 1725), containing these observations, won him election to learned societies in France, Russia and Spain. Sloane's will offered his collection (which he had augmented with that of William Courten) to the British Government. It was bought at the low price he specified, Montagu House obtained for its display, the Cottonian and Harleian collections added, and so began the British Museum, in 1754.

The bulk of his estate went for her lifetime to "my very well and entirely beloved wife, Dame Mary Elizabeth Morgan." It would then pass to any of several young kinsmen, listed in order of precedence, who would take his name.[31] Robert Elletson was to have his blue saddle, a brace of silver-handled pistols, and the choice of a horse from his stables; Colonel Ballard his green saddle. To St. Mary Parish went £100 for a school (which never got it), and to a married sister in England "sixty pounds per annum for life, to be paid yearly at the hands of my honourable cousin Mr. Thomas Morgan of Tredegar."

Morgan's cough racked him more severely as August progressed; he fought for breath, his swollen legs would no longer support him, and on the 25th he died. Albemarle proclaimed for his friend all the honors of a state funeral. The cortege moved at solemn pace along the bayside, draped carriages joining it on the way, and many on foot walking beside it, "having black ribbands, being very seemly dressed in black." The captain of the frigate *Assistance* penned in his log: "This day about 11 hours morn'g, Sir Harry Morgan dies & on the 26th was brought over from Passage Fort to the King's House at Port Royall, from thence to the church & after a sermon was carried to the Pallisadoes & there buried. All the forts fired an equal number of guns, wee fired two & twenty, & after wee & the *Drake* had fired, all the merchantmen fired."[32]

---

[31] After Mary Elizabeth's death, Robert Byndloss's second son succeeded to the estate as Charles Morgan-Byndloss. His son, Henry Morgan-Byndloss, served as attorney-general of Jamaica 1754–1755.

[32] Legend persisted that Morgan saw his last days in a London prison, at the instigation of Spain. Leslie (1739) lamented that due to this confinement there "he was seized with a slow and lingering distemper, which at once robbed him of Life, and the World of a truly great Man." Gardner (1873) said that "he died soon after his removal to England," pining for the seas and skies of Jamaica; Bancroft (1883) left him behind bars without killing him off, but wished to, for "he was a ruffian whose hell-born depravity of heart was relieved by no gleam of a better nature;" Howard Pyle (1897) declared him dead "in the tower of London for the very deeds for which he was knighted"; another old wives' tale had him acquitted, only to perish in a Houndsditch brawl; and in the preface to *Raveneau de Lussan* (1930) the translator topped all by putting Morgan to death at the hands of Caribbean Indians.

So the pest of Spain, the troubler of so many quiet men, was safely stowed beneath the hot sands of the spit. But not for long. On a sultry, windless morning of June, 1692, the sky turned red over the island and a sound like thunder rolled down from the mountains. The parson of Port Royal, about to have a bit of wormwood wine with the governor, never got the glass to his lips. Beneath the bay the earth heaved and split, the whole waterfront of the port slid into the sea, St. Paul's church tower collapsed, its bells jangling; a towering wave, in the wake of the shock, carried a frigate over the ruined housetops and floated it down Queen's Street. The burial ground vanished into the gulf. Now Morgan had a sea grave both wide and deep, and no man knows the place of it.

CAPTAIN WILLIAM KIDD

*"Brother, brother —
we are both in the wrong —
we shall be both losers in the dispute —."*
John Gay, *Beggar's Opera*, Act II, Scene 2

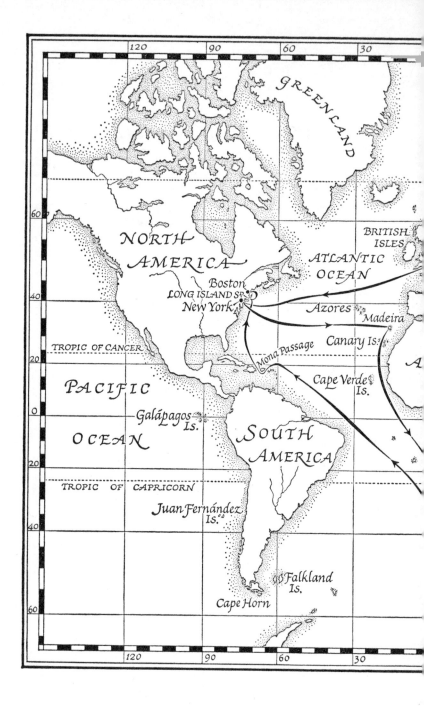

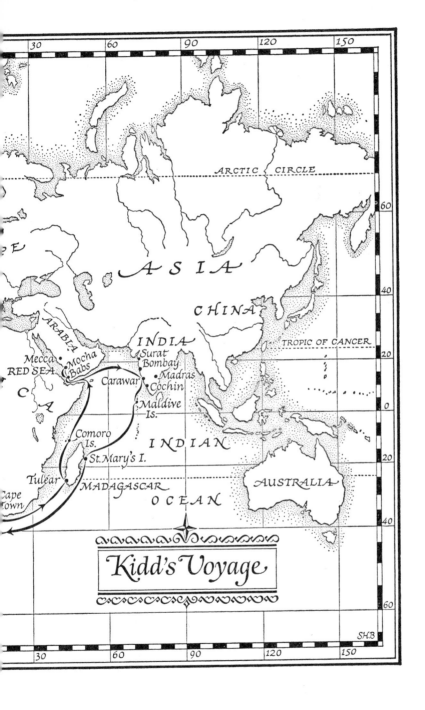

Kidd's Voyage

In August, 1695, it seemed to Londoners that they were having more than their share of bad news. A mad soldier rode through the city shouting that King William was dead in Flanders, and threatening to shoot anyone who denied it. During the month Parliament managed to dig up more corruption than usual; a key witness in an East India Company scandal discreetly vanished; forged Bank of England notes in circulation made every shopkeeper nervous; and unseasonable weather — wet, chill, even frosty — nipped early crops and shortened tempers. A stranger in London, William Kidd of New York, had his bad luck, too. He chanced to meet a fellow New Yorker named Robert Livingston.

Livingston's clenched jaw and misshapen nose gave him the look of a coal-heaver's helper, but the mind behind them was shrewd and tenacious. "Never disbursing six pence but with the expectation of twelve," sneered Governor Fletcher of New York, "his beginning being but a little Book keeper, he has screwed himself into one of the most considerable estates in the province." Fletcher had blocked payment for provincial offices that he held, and Livingston was in London to appeal the matter. By blackening Fletcher's whole administration, he hoped to lend plausibility to his own case. He persuaded Kidd, and Kidd's young brother-in-law, Samuel Bradley, to appear as witnesses before the Board of Trade. On August 28 Kidd testified that Fletcher had rigged a recent provincial election by bringing illegal voters off the ships.

Beyond question Kidd was a respectable witness — man of property, family head, member of Trinity Church, New York, and generally honored in the colonies. At the outset of war with France in 1689 he had joined his armed sloop to the English fleet mustered in the West Indies, where he saw action at Marie Galante and St. Martin. "He was a mighty man there," recalled fleet commander Thomas Hewson; "he was with me in two engagements against the French, and fought as well as any man I ever saw, according to the proportion of his men." When Kidd's crew ran off with his ship to go pirating, the grateful governor of the British Leewards gave him a captured barkentine to replace it.[1]

Back in New York by February, 1691, Kidd had thrown his support to the king's cause in the unhappy affair of Jacob Leisler, who had seized control of the port during the confusion that followed the 1688 revolution in England.[2] In gratitude, the New York Assembly voted Kidd a £150 purse for "the many good services done to this province," and Massachusetts engaged him to fend off a French privateer that threatened its coast. "On the whole a gentlemanly and clever man," thought the New York Council; "neither in his domestic relations nor in his personal history . . . could ought be said against him."

Kidd had been born in Scotland, his parentage now unknown

---

[1] An example of how easily common seamen turned pirate. The leader of Kidd's crew in this robbery of his vessel was Robert Culliford, whom he would meet years later and half a world away, under even more unpleasant circumstances. Two other of his men, Burgess and Mason, had careers notorious enough to be recorded in the annals of piracy.

[2] A sincere but bullheaded New York merchant, Jacob Leisler represented the Dutch, the common people and, he thought, the true Protestant cause. He surrendered power, but with some reluctance, to the authority of King William's new governor, Colonel Henry Sloughter. Landowners and merchants (Livingston among them) who had suffered under Leisler's rule wanted his scalp, and got it. A court stacked with his enemies condemned him and his son-in-law, Jacob Milbourne, to death. Few thought that Governor Sloughter would go so far as to sign the death warrant, but a merchant whom Leisler had jailed got the governor in his cups and guided his unsteady hand to the fatal signature. Livingston and Kidd went together to enjoy the hanging on May 16, 1691. At the sight of Livingston in the throng, Milbourne called out to him, "You have caused the king that I must now die, but before God's tribunal I will implead you for the same!" A 1698 Act of Parliament canceled the court decision. The bodies of the two victims, once even denied Christian burial, were now exhumed and lay in state at City Hall. Kidd failed to reckon that he who condones injustice to others should beware: he may be next.

and his birthplace only surmised.[3] No record exists of his life prior to 1688, when he purchased a house from his future wife, then the widowed Sarah Bradley Cox. "Lovely and accomplished," but illiterate, Sarah could not stay long out of wedlock. Alderman William Cox, whom she married at fifteen, died three years later, and her second husband, shipmaster-merchant John Oort, died May 5, 1691. With unseemly haste she and Kidd took out a marriage license on May 16, a day further graced by the hanging of Jacob Leisler.

Through marriage Kidd acquired a comfortable estate.[4] The scrolled dormers and fluted chimneys of his tall house were landmarks for ships bound in to New York moorage. Glossy pewter filled his sideboard; that rare thing in the colonies, a Turkish carpet, covered his parlor floor; casks of Madeira wine stocked his celler. In summer heat he could take his wife and small daughter, Elizabeth, up the East River to the cool shade of their Saw Kill farm.

At fifty years of age, and enviably well off, Kidd might have been content. He was not. When he met Livingston in London he carried a letter from James Graham, attorney-general of

[3] Kidd's birth date is variously conjectured from 1645 to 1660. The only statement with some faint ring of authority is that of the Newgate chaplain, Paul Lorrain, who in 1701 reported him "about 56 years old." Fond tradition makes him the son of the Reverend John Kidd, Calvinist minister of Greenock, Scotland, on the theory, no doubt, that only a clergyman's son could come to such a bad end. Researches by Harold Wilkins reveal that no John Kidd is known to have ministered there, and that another shepherd, famed for hitting the bottle, was in charge at the time. Moreover, the Greenock birthplace emerges tardily, in that graveyard of criminal folklore, *The Newgate Calendar*. We know that Kidd was Scot by birth, had enough education to write a competent letter, and followed the sea to a captain's rating; we have no exact data on where he was born or when, who his parents were, nor a single fact about the first four decades of his life.

[4] In 1695 the entire town occupied only the lower tip of Manhattan below Wall Street, where a sod barrier protected the settlement on its landward side. Kidd owned what is now some of the most valuable property in the world — 56 Wall Street, 86–90 and 119–21 Pearl Street, 52–56 Water Street, and 25, 27 and 29 Pine Street. Cox, we know, left Sarah the handsome house on Pearl Street, the Saw Kill farm (now 74th Street on the East River) and £1900. Cf. pamphlet, *New York's Land-holding Sea Rover*, New York Title and Guarantee Co. (New York: Lotus Press, 1901).

New York, and former speaker of its Assembly, addressed to William Blathwayt, a busy politician who was well-known for dispensing favors. "He is a Stranger at home" (London), read the letter, "which gives birth to this earnestly recommending him to yor Honors favor in procuring him a Command of one of his Majty's Ships of warr." Graham assured Blathwayt that Kidd "has been very prudent & successful in his Conduct here & doubt not but his fame has reached yor Parts, and whatever favor or Countenance yor Honor shews him I do assure yor Honor he will be very grateful, being a person of good ability amongst us here." Unfortunately, Blathwayt was in Flanders with the king. That left Kidd as far as ever from mounting the quarterdeck of a royal frigate.

However, Livingston's subtle hand was already spinning for Kidd an alternative to the naval command. The London government was exasperated at colonial evasion of the Navigation Acts, which forbade the development of manufacturing in the colonies, and confined their trade to English ports and English ships. These restrictions had put such a damper on American commerce that the colonists had worked illegal shipping into a major, and quite respectable, business. North Atlantic ports were the worst offenders; in New York a privateering commission could be picked up for £100, and half-a-dozen known freebooters might harbor there at once, while their men swaggered in the streets. The Madagascar trade was doubly attractive, for it paid off at both ends: powder, shot, biscuits and rum fetched huge prices east of Africa, while tea, spices, jewels and cloth plundered from eastern merchantmen were snapped up in colonial shops. "We have a parcel of pirates called the Red Sea men, in these parts, who get great booty of Arabian gold," confided a New Yorker to the Board of Trade. "The Governor encourages them, since they make due acknowledgement."

Everyone in "wild worldly" New York benefited from the illicit traffic. Its women dressed gaily in pilfered damask; its prosperous merchants drank deep, smoked like bonfires, raced their horses on the Strand, and put money into any under-handed deal that offered profit. Greasing palms became a fixed habit: the governor got his doubloons, the customs officer his pounds, the river boy his pence. Governor Fletcher made a favorite of pirate captain Thomas Tew, dining him at home and parading him abroad in his coach. He explained suavely to London that he only wished to cure Tew of swearing, and convert him to the Church.

The chief sufferer from Red Sea pirates, England's East India Company, rained protests on the Board of Trade. No one could ignore the Company for long; its dignity was immense, its dividends unfailing, its value to the nation's economy incalculable. The dozen round-bellied East India ships that voyaged beyond the Cape were the pride of England's merchant fleet, and their captains were princes among seamen. The Company's corporate prayer exhorted God to "be always present with thy servants the English Company Trading to the East Indies," and so far He always had. Now, said the directors, American pirates put their very existence in jeopardy. Enraged by staggering losses at sea, native rulers had shut down Company stations and nearly massacred the factors. England must destroy piracy in eastern seas or the stations would be banished from Indian soil entirely.

King William moved to suppress the Red Sea men by replacing Fletcher with Richard Coote, Earl of Bellomont. Bellomont's flighty young wife handicapped him, and he had a tendency to gout, but his honesty was proven, and his sense of duty rock-hard. In the summer of 1695 William designated him governor of New York and Massachusetts, binding him by instruction to enforce the Navigation Acts and stifle piracy from Jersey to the point of Maine. "I send you, my Lord, to New York," said the king, "because an honest and intrepid man is wanted to put these abuses down, and because I believe you to be such a man."

Over tea at East India House the directors approved of Bel-

7. Morgan outmanouvers the Spanish squadron at Maracaibo. One Spanish warship was fired, another one run aground and the third captured (Mansell Collection, London)

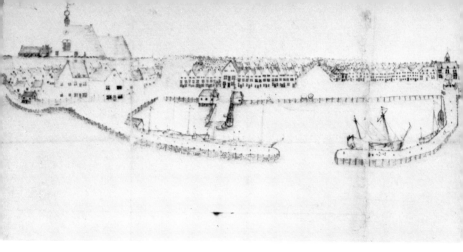

8. A view of New York Harbour from Brooklyn Heights, 1679. (Long Island Historical Society)

9. William Kidd's house near the sod wall which at the time marked Wall Street. Painting by Edward L. Henry (Title Guarantee Coy, New York)

lomont's appointment — in the long run. The "long run" made
them shudder. Pirates prowled at the instant; while a director
raised his cup and put it down again they could snatch a prize
so rich that the Mogul would lock up every station in India.
The Company petitioned for a man-of-war to sail immediately
for patrol duty in eastern seas. The Admiralty's response was
regretful but obdurate; England's war with France engaged
every ship of the line. Then why not a well-armed privateer, at
least? he could take his reward from pirate plunder that he captured. Harassed by Company plaints, King William warmed to
the idea. "We can make it a private undertaking," he remarked
to some of his Council; "I will give £3000 and you can furnish
the balance."

Privy Councillors were obliged to support the king's proposal
if anyone took it up, but no one did. The idea languished until
August 10 when Livingston knocked at Bellomont's door in
London to make the acquaintance of his future governor. As
the two put their heads together over colonial affairs, all interests converged. The East India Company wanted immediate
action against piracy, the government wanted to placate the
Company, Bellomont wanted success in his future New York
office, Livingston wanted to ingratiate himself with the Privy
Council (which would pass upon his plea for compensation),
and Kidd wanted service with the king. Livingston simply
drew these strands of desire together, and knotted them.

Since King William was now in Flanders with the army, he
never contributed his promised share. As financial backers for
the proposed voyage Bellomont enlisted four of England's leading men: Lord Keeper of the Great Seal Sir John Somers, Secretary of State the Duke of Shrewsbury, First Lord of the Admiralty Sir Edward Russell, and Master General of Ordnance the
Earl of Romney. He persuaded a London merchant, Edmund
Harrison, to bring ready cash into the venture.[5]

[5] John Somers was a man of great probity, the best head of government that
England had seen, or was to see, in decades. Shrewsbury possessed such charm
that William called him "the King of Hearts," but his neurotic temperament
and delicate conscience unfit him for politics, and he soon retired from public

Now they lacked only a stout commander of known courage and integrity. Livingston had just the man — Captain William Kidd of New York, a brave seaman who knew the pirate lairs like the back of his hand. Above temptation, too, "liv'd regularly and had a competent Estate of his own and had mary'd at New York a Wife with considerable fortune, by whom he had a child." But at first approach Kidd was reluctant. He temporized, he excused himself. "I was without my knowledge, pitched upon to be the commander," he later complained. Meeting an old comrade of West Indian days, Captain Hewson, Kidd sought his opinion on the matter. Hewson "told him he had enough already, and might be content with what he had." That, sighed Kidd, "was his own inclination."

Driving with single-minded tenacity, Livingston kept after Kidd to accept. Bellomont wondered aloud how any man who wished to be thought loyal could refuse so clear a call to serve his king. The refusal would stamp Kidd as politically suspect, in Bellomont's opinion, so that he might well encounter trouble getting his barkentine free of customs. The pressure on Kidd was overpowering. If he hoped to command a royal frigate some day, he had better not stickle at this patriotic mission proposed by the king himself, backed by influential ministers, and urged by the governor-designate of his home province. In the end, he accepted. Livingston rushed him from one lordly house to another, but left the blunt captain to cool his heels in the hall while he consulted the great men in their chambers.

---

life. Macaulay thought Russell "emphatically a bad man, insolent, malignant, greedy, faithless." The least of the four, Romney, had held high posts with singular lack of distinction before settling into his present sinecure. All, however, were men of influence. Shrewsbury, Romney and Russell numbered three of the Immortal Seven who had risked their necks to invite William to England in 1688. This seated them firmly in the king's affections. He had made Shrewsbury a duke and Romney an earl; by 1698 Somers was Lord Somers and Russell became the Earl of Orford. That year the king knighted Edmund Harrison. Harrison paid all of Bellomont's share in the proposed voyage and half of Shrewsbury's on strict terms. "He gave me a terrible hard Presbyterian grip in the articles," said Bellomont resentfully, and never forgave him.

Things were shaping up nicely, Livingston jotted in his diary on October 3: "I hope by this my affairs may have a happy ending." On October 10 Livingston, Bellomont and Kidd signed the Articles of Agreement.

The articles held between "the Earl of Bellomont of the one part, and Robert Levingston Esq and Capt William Kid of the other." [6] They made Bellomont accountable for four-fifths of the costs, the remaining fifth falling upon Livingston and Kidd jointly. Kidd was to sign his men "no prize, no pay," and their share of captured booty was not to exceed a quarter of the total. No division of spoil could be made until properly condemned in an Admiralty court. Kidd must report to Bellomont in Boston by March 20, 1697 without breaking or diminishing cargo in any way. If the enterprise failed to gain booty, Kidd and Livingston agreed to repay the entire investment of the other backers, keeping the ship as their recompense. Good conduct bonds were set high for both: £10,000 from Livingston, £20,000 from Kidd.

The Agreement, indeed the whole situation, was clearly disadvantageous to Kidd. He was forced to sell his barkentine in London and, still pressed for cash, dispose of a third of his interest to a city merchant willing to take the long chance. With a hundred hands, half of them raw landsmen, he was expected to fight ships better armed than himself, and crews made up of the most desperate seamen afloat. Time was against him; it was highly improbable that he could round the Cape, capture elusive freebooters laden with spoil, put prize crews aboard out of his own small complement, and bring his flotilla safe to Boston in fourteen months. Moreover, the whole venture was senseless. No one needed permission to chase pirates, and if

---

[6] Even official papers in the seventeenth century spelled names with an abandon that staggers our prosaic minds. Livingston was severally Leviston, Leviton and Lillington; Kidd became Kid, Cidd, Kidde and Keede; and his prize ship was called the *Quedagh, Quedaw, Quetta, Quitta, Quidah, Kedah, Cara, Karra, Karry* and, the boldest stroke, *Scudee.*

Kidd had wanted to privateer, he could have gotten a New York commission at the snap of his fingers. His acceptance of the London Agreement was a hopeless gesture — he dared not refuse.

Five more documents flowed from the scribe's pen before the voyage was in order. The Admiralty grasped at this opportunity to add another hardy privateer to its naval arm. On December 11, 1695, it commissioned Kidd "to apprehend seize and take the Ships Vessels and Goods belonging to the French King or his Subjects or Inhabitants within the Dominions of the said French King; and such other Ships Vessels and Goods as are or shall be liable to confiscation." Although this authority had played little part in the elaborate plans that preceded Kidd's voyage, we shall see that it became the one under which he actually cruised. On January 26, 1696, Sir John Somers issued the king's special commission to hunt down pirates. "To our Trusty and well-beloved Captain Kidd," it began, and instructed him to seize pirates wherever he found them, but warned that "we do hereby jointly charge and command you, as you will answer the same at your utmost Peril, That you do not, in any manner, offend or molest any of our Friends or Allies, their Ships or Subjects."

So far the documents promised Kidd plenty of hardship, but no reward. In April, 1696, King William got around to signing the grant of all captured ships and goods to the London backers. Plunder became thereby the property of Bellomont, Harrison and, curiously enough, not the government ministers by name, but four aliases in their place. Booty would go to these six "as far as the said Premises, or any of them, do, shall or may belong to Us, or can or may be granted or grantable by Us, or is or are in our Power to dispose of." In a final document, Bellomont assigned to Livingston and Kidd, severally, one-tenth of the distributable booty.

Kidd had long since sailed on his voyage. In the autumn of 1695 he found a pretty, trim-lined ship still on the stocks at Castle's Yard, Deptford. He named her the *Adventure Galley*, and busied himself for the next three months rigging her out. She was 287 tons burden, flush-decked, carried thirty-four guns, and had ports for twenty-three sweeps on a side to row in calm weather. Seventy men of dubious quality signed on. Bellomont's sailing orders of February 25, 1696, bade Kidd execute his mission where it could best be done, and permitted him to return to England rather than Boston if he hit upon a strong convoy. In the last days of February the *Adventure* cast moorings to drop down the Thames.

Though Kidd had missed command of a royal frigate, he preened himself that the king's orders gave him authority as great. Down the Thames he neglected to dip his colors to a naval yacht, and when it fired a warning gun his men slapped their backsides in derision. The yacht's officers quickly haled Kidd into Sheerness to answer for the insult. The incident taught him nothing. At the Nore he boldly anchored alongside H.M.S. *Duchess of Queensborough*, and in no time a lieutenant was aboard to press some of his men. In vain Kidd brandished his commissions, in vain protested that he was on the king's business and could not be molested. Unruffled by these claims, the lieutenant carried off twenty of his ablest hands. Kidd hurried to tell Lord Admiral Russell at Sittingbourne that he now had hardly enough men to work the ship, let alone fight pirates. Russell ordered the men returned. The same number came back, but not the same men; the *Duchess* took Kidd's best, and gave him its worst. After nineteen days' delay he sailed from Plymouth on April 23 in gloomy mood, his destination not Madagascar and the Red Sea pirates, but New York.

On the crossing, Kidd overhauled a French banker bound for Newfoundland with salt and fishing gear in her hold. He convoyed her into New York, where she was condemned and sold as a legitimate prize of war under his Admiralty commission.

The king got his tenth, the governor his fifteenth, and with the remaining prize money Kidd bought provisions for the voyage.

New York seems an odd port of call for a ship bound east of Africa. Bellomont certainly thought so. He declared later that Kidd "broke articles with us at the first dash, for instead of sailing to those seas which pyrat ships frequent, he came directly to New York and loyter'd away severall moneths." Kidd loitered, in part, because he enjoyed it. After unquiet London it was good to go out on his railed stoop and watch the blue smoke rising from farm chimneys on the Brooklyn hills. In the cool of morning he could take Elizabeth through the town gate to play in the little stream where servant girls washed clothes and spread them on the bank to dry. If the day turned sultry, Sarah packed a lunch and he rowed the family upriver to the shade trees of Saw Kill. Trinity Church borrowed his tackle to hoist stones for its new house of worship; he strolled by, every day or so, to see how the work progressed.[7]

Kidd was also in New York for the more practical purpose of bringing his crew to fighting strength. The few men he had could hardly fire a proper broadside, and none would be left to shift sails. To get new hands he ignored the Articles of Agreement by reserving only forty shares for the ship, and surrendering the rest to the crew. Eighty-five seamen who signed on were as bad as his Londoners — drifters, wharf rats, pirates on the loose, ship jumpers, men contemptuous of discipline and greedy for loot. Governor Fletcher took a sour view of them. "Many flocked to him from all parts, men of desperate fortunes and necessities, in expectation of getting vast treasure," he wrote to the Board of Trade. "It is generally believed here,

---

[7] This was Trinity's first house of worship — small, square, with a tall spire. The great fire of 1776 gutted it, leaving only the stone shell. Nothing was saved from the interior, but church records have preserved the names of twenty communicants whose pews ranged the sides and back. Kidd held pew sixteen. The vestry meeting room in the present parish house was designed to follow the manner of chapter houses abroad, with single seats for vestrymen against the walls. Over each of these was placed the name of an original pewholder. Number sixteen carries the discreet inscription: "Captain William Kidd. Commanded 'Adventure Galley.'"

they will have money *per fas aut nefas*, that if he misses the design named in his commission, he will not be able to govern such a herd of men under no pay." [8] In Albany, Livingston got wind of the change in articles. Though the news worried him privately, he made the best of it. He wrote Shrewsbury that he regretted Kidd's London men were "so few and many of them mutinous," but he still hoped for a good voyage.

On September 6, 1696, the *Adventure* shook out sails for her 9000-mile run to the Indian Ocean. October saw her at Madeira and the Cape Verdes, where Kidd took on wood, water and provisions, gave some gear to a Barbados brigantine in distress, and bore south for the Cape. Early in December he fell in with a squadron of four English warships. They were, as usual, shorthanded. Their commander thought Kidd's resounding commissions a bit too impressive to seize men off the *Adventure* by force, and made the mistake of merely requesting them. Kidd had learned his lesson at the Nore. He pretended to agree; he downed quantities of the commander's excellent wine to seal the bargain, then, in the night calm, ordered out the *Adventure*'s sweeps and slipped silently over the horizon.

Beyond the Cape, in fighting waters at last, Kidd showed no inclination to fight Red Sea men. The *Adventure* stood at the jutting south tip of Madagascar, the fork in the sea road, the point of decision. Go east to the fifteen pirate ships and forty-gun shore battery of St. Mary's, go west to the quiet Mozambique Channel. Kidd went west. In the bay of Tuléar the owner of a Barbados sloop staggered aboard in the last stages of cholera and promptly died. Kidd expressed his displeasure at the sloop, its crew and its dead owner. When the *Adventure* set sail up the Channel, the sloop fell in behind. It dogged them 150 miles north to Johanna in the Comoros, and east to Mahilla

8 An exception: Sarah Kidd's younger brother, Samuel Bradley. He owned some New York property and, as we have seen, was of sufficient stature to appear before the Board of Trade in the Livingston case. He signed on as crewman with the starboard watch for the Indian Ocean voyage.

Island, where the *Adventure* careened ship. Kidd angrily ordered the sloop off, but she clung to his wake, watchful, expectant, an ill omen. She stuck with him until plague hit his crew at Mahilla and fifty men died in a week; then she departed, satisfied. Back at Johanna Kidd picked up thirty replacements off the beach. They were of all nations, more raffish and malingering then those he had lost.

With this ragged crew, Kidd made his first strike that brought on the charge of piracy. North of the Comoros lay the Babs, in the mouth of the Red Sea, and beyond them on the barren Arabian coast, the port of Mocha, southern terminus for caravans to the Levant. Besides coffee, dyewood, ivory and ostrich feathers, Mocha did a flourishing business in Moslem pilgrims bound to and from Mecca. On July 25, 1697, much in the fashion of the Red Sea men that he had come to hunt, Kidd took his station among the Babs. Boats dispatched up the straits brought back word that fifteen ships were in port, preparing to sail. "Come boys," gloated Kidd, "I will make money out of that fleet." They loaded shot, swabbed cannon, filled powder baskets, spread sand and passed out small arms. On August 15 lookouts on a small peak ashore frantically waved a signal flag. The fleet was coming down.

It came down to Kidd's liking, slow and ponderous, on a breath of wind. He set topsails and manned the sweeps. Aloft went the broad red pennant that announced surrender or no quarter given. As the first ship emerged beyond the islands the sweeps stroked and the *Adventure* moved out in search of quarry. Kidd picked a fat Moorish merchantman and struck in to intercept her.

Luck was against him, he soon discovered. The Mogul fleet was convoyed by three well-armed guard ships, two Dutchmen behind to shield the stragglers, and the English East Indiaman *Sceptre* running well forward. As the *Sceptre* fired her bow gun, other scattered shots sounded from the fleet. Kidd brought the *Adventure* about and let go a broadside at the quarry. She took shot in hull and rigging, but kept her course.

The *Sceptre* now hoisted English colors, sailing and towing for the intruder, her seamen shouting. This was more than Kidd counted on. He had little stomach for fighting guard ships, and none for firing on his country's flag. The *Adventure* sheered away and made south, her sweeps churning the still waters to foam. Next day she was out of sight, but by no means forgotten.

She veered eastward for the coast of India. The sands were running out for William Kidd, New York gentleman and servant of the king. He had been a year and a half from London with nothing to show for it, was six months overdue on the agreement with Bellomont, and now had met galling failure at the Babs. The ship was beginning to leak, the men to grumble. He must get plunder soon, or face mutiny.

Early in September Kidd hailed a small Moorish barque in the broad waters of the Arabian Sea. An Englishman named Parker captained her, and she had a Portuguese mate. Nothing qualified her as a prize. The boarding party brought back a bale of pepper and another of coffee, for the mess. Kidd let them keep it; it would quiet the men. They found a few coins, and slapped some of the crew with the flat of their cutlasses to see if there was more. Being in strange waters and among strange people, Kidd forced Parker to go along with him as pilot, and the Portuguese as interpreter. The barque's frightened crew turned tail for Carawar, where they poured out their story to the East India Company factors.

When the *Adventure* dropped anchor at Carawar two weeks later for wood and water, the factors were justly suspicious. Two of them came aboard to demand the immediate release of Parker and the Portuguese. Kidd had his prisoners shut away in the hold, out of sight, and he denied having them at all. He was reluctant to allow any of his men to go ashore lest they reveal this falsehood, or even desert. At least two succeeded, however, made depositions at the Bombay station, and were shipped from there to London to render account personally at the East India home office.

To get rid of Kidd, the Carawar factors warned him that Portuguese warships were on the prowl nearby — he had better clear out or be bottled up in port. He took this for truth, and it proved to be; next day two Portuguese gave chase near Goa. One of them never made firing range. Kidd fought the other most of a day before she drew off, leaving him eleven men wounded, and the *Adventure,* her hull splintered and rigging torn, more unseaworthy than ever. They limped south to the Maldives, only to run into more trouble — natives ashore cut the cooper's throat. In angry retaliation Kidd shot one of them and burned a few huts. The *Adventure* wandered away on the empty sea as the breeze drove her, the sun cruelly hot, cramped quarters stifling, worms in the food, the men lousy, and no plunder in sight.

Weeks passed before the *Adventure* overhauled a merchantman off the tip of India. Unfortunately, the *Loyal Captain* was English, all her papers in order, and Kidd refused to molest her. Near the end of their patience, a few of his men brought out their small arms and threatened to take her on their own. "I am not come to take any Englishman or lawful traders," Kidd reminded them. "I have no commission to take any but the King's enemies and pirates. If you attempt to do any such thing, you will never come on board the *Galley* again. I will attack you and drive you into Bombay, and will carry you before the council there."

The brief uprising sputtered out, but the men were disgusted at losing a pretty haul. No need for it, either, gunner Moore told them; he knew how he would go about it. Just show an amiable face to the *Loyal Captain's* officers, get them to sign a statement that the *Adventure* had done them no harm, and then loot her to the keel. Easy as that; only their weak-kneed captain stood in the way. The men's resentment went deep. It flared up again two weeks later when Moore, who had been sick, sat grinding a chisel on deck. A knot of sullen hands gathered about him.

Kidd glowered at them. "How could you have put me in the way to take this ship and been clear?" he demanded of Moore.

"We would get the captain and men aboard," replied the gunner. "Then we would plunder her, and have it under their hands that we did not take her."

"This is Judas-like!" exclaimed Kidd. "I dare not do such a thing."

"We may do it," said Moore calmly. "We are beggars already."

"Why," cried Kidd, "may we take this ship because we are poor, you lousy dog?"

"If I am a lousy dog, you have made me so. You have brought me to ruin, and many more."

"Have I ruined you, you dog?" shouted Kidd, in a fury. "You are a saucy fellow to give me those words." He walked down the deck and back again, fuming. Suddenly he caught up a wooden bucket by its strap and cracked Moore on the side of the head. The gunner pitched off his stool into the scuppers. "You have given me my last blow," he gasped.

His maties carried Moore below to the surgeon. "Damn him, he is a villain," growled Kidd after them. When the gunner died next day, Kidd shrugged. There were worse things than killing a mutinous crewman at sea. "I do not care so much for the death of my gunner, as for other passages of my voyage," he remarked later to his surgeon, "for I have good friends in England that will bring me off that." [9]

With mutiny in the air and Moore's death on his hands, Kidd's luck hit bottom. It could go nowhere but up. In a few days he put a shot across the bow of a small ship bearing up the Malabar coast. The *Adventure* raised French colors; the stranger did the same. To make the ruse more credible, Kidd

[9] While the main outlines of Moore's death are clear, details vary with the bias of the narrator. For coherence, the above version of the incident has been pieced together from the fragmentary testimony of several who were present.

dressed a French crewman in officer's garb and had him hail the ship in French. Her Dutch skipper came aboard and presented to the bogus captain a pass issued by the French East India Company director at Surat. This was enough for Kidd. "By God, have I catched you?" he roared, when he had the pass in his hands. "You are a free prize to England!"

The *Rouparelle* was not much of a prize, to be sure. Her cargo consisted of baled cotton, some quilts and sugar, and two horses. She was Moorish owned, commanded by three Dutch officers. The Dutchmen elected to join Kidd. He sold the cargo ashore and shared out the proceeds to his men, renamed her the *November* for the month of her capture, and put a prize crew aboard.

Kidd's men had tasted blood, and liked it. Coasting west of India on December 28, Kidd stopped a fifty-ton Moorish ketch and relieved her of some sugar candy in tubs, and a bale of coffee. On January 9, 1698, he plundered a Portuguese vessel of wax, opium, rice, iron and butter. He stopped another Portuguese on January 20, kept her a week, but abandoned her when a Dutch squadron showed its sails on the horizon.

These were small game, looted to appease the crew. Kidd still looked for the big catch, the one that would satisfy his backers at a stroke, and even win recognition from the king. At the beginning of February, 1698, he sighted the *Quedah Merchant* wallowing north ten miles from Cochin on the Malabar coast. She flew an Armenian flag, but Kidd chased her and brought her to with a cannon shot. He broke out a French flag; to his delight, she did the same. Now it was the *Quedah's* turn to build up the ruse. A Frenchman employed by the French East India Company at Surat boarded the *Adventure,* posing as the *Quedah's* captain and armed with a pass issued by his company. That did the trick. Kidd ran up the English jack and claimed the *Quedah* as a lawful prize.

The only thing French about her was the pass. She was owned by Indians, cargoed by Armenians from Persia, manned by Moors, and captained by an Englishman. The pass put her under French protection, and even the French agent admitted that she was Kidd's prize by custom of the sea. Still, Kidd had his misgivings. He announced to his men that since the capture was questionable he was willing to let the *Quedah* go. They shouted him down. They were going to share the spoil; if there was guilt in it, they would share that, too.

The *Quedah* rode low with a princely cargo of silks, muslins, gold, jewels, sugar, iron, saltpeter and guns. Armenian merchants who were aboard overseeing their goods offered to ransom the ship for 20,000 rupees. Since the prize valued at many times that figure, Kidd refused. At last he had made his voyage. He sold off £10,000 of the merchandise ashore, shared to his crew, and sailed west.

By this time the *Adventure* was literally falling to pieces. She had been either badly built or badly treated, and all the shipmaker's art — keelson, strakes, rungs, beakhead — was breaking up. Cables cinched around her hull firmed up the leaky planks, but eight men still had to work the pumps continuously in hourly shifts. For all her creaky state, she outsailed her consorts to arrive April 1 at a most unlikely haven: St. Mary's, Madagascar. Kidd, the professed foe of all pirates, had taken refuge in the pirates' lair.

Only one ship was at anchor, the *Mocha*, a stolen East India Company frigate commanded by the same Robert Culliford who had run off with Kidd's brigantine at St. Martin years before. Culliford and his forty men were no match for the *Adventure*'s guns. They fled ashore in their boats and took cover in the woods.

Taking the *Mocha*, thought Kidd, would absolutely crown his voyage. He had honored his Admiralty commission by capturing a French merchantman, now he could honor the king's by bringing home a freebooter. But he reckoned without his men. The sight of a real pirate, unhampered by their captain's weak scruples, moved the *Adventure*'s crew to admiration. When

Kidd urged them to seize the *Mocha* they hooted that they
would rather fire two guns at him than one at the pirate. After
sharing out the *Quedah* cargo, ninety-seven of Kidd's 115 men
deserted to Culliford. Kidd was helpless. His former crew
plundered and burned the *November*, carried off from the *Adventure* and the *Quedah* cannon, small arms, sails, gear —
whatever took their fancy — and warned Kidd that if he made
trouble they would put a bullet in his head. For a time he bar-
ricaded himself in his cabin, bales of goods against the door, an
arsenal of muskets by his side ready-charged for instant use.
Deserters rifled his chest, which he had left with a settler
ashore, and took care to burn the *Adventure*'s log.

Being at Culliford's mercy, Kidd could only play out the
game in an atmosphere of strained jollity. He made Culliford
the gift of a gun or two. He chuckled over Culliford's theft of
his ship long ago in the Caribbean, swore that "before I would
do you any harm I would have my soul fry in hell-fire." He
went aboard the *Mocha* to relax at ease in the shade of a
spread sail and drink from a convivial tub of cooling, if unpirat-
ical, "bombo" — a mixture of lime, sugar and, alas, water. It
was a good act, and got its reward. Kidd stayed alive, his
brother-in-law (sick since the plague at Mahilla) stayed alive,
the *Quedah* stayed afloat, and he kept his share of booty. With
a sigh of relief he watched the *Mocha* sail out, now 130 men
strong and forty guns at her ports, in mid-June.

The *Adventure*'s first voyage was her last. She lay in the
shallows, half-full of water, gaping at the seams. After Kidd
had stripped her of everything useful, he burned the hull for its
iron. With men picked up off the beach to work the bulky
Quedah, it was possible to come clear of this sorry business yet.
Enough booty lay in the ship's hold to pay the backers and
make a bit for himself. Culliford and his footloose crew might
drift or make haven as they chose, but William Kidd — family
head, man of property, pewholder in Trinity Church — must
needs go home. He had to wait another five months for the

northeast monsoon to blow him around the Cape. On November 15, the *Quedah* put out from St. Mary's Harbor and lumbered south.

While Kidd plowed steadily homeward in unclouded weather, a storm was blowing up in London. On August 4 the East India Company had laid before the Board of Trade a sheaf of reports on Indian Ocean piracies. Kidd figured prominently among them. One report told how he had aroused suspicion in the English squadron west of the Cape, and then slipped away by night. Fort St. George had news of the *Adventure's* attack on the Mocha fleet; Carawar corroborated this, while the depositions of Kidd's two deserters there added the pillage of Parker's ship. Everything was given its worst turn. The Babs incident became unquestioned piracy; Parker's vessel was now English, and drubbing his men turned into hideous torture. Killing the native in revenge for the cooper's murder was exaggerated to sheer carnage. Kidd's known misdeeds may have been miniscule, but only as the fuse to a powder keg is miniscule. Every tapster in London now knew that the voyage was almost an official act of government, and Tories shouted that the leading Whigs were a "Corporation of Pirates."

Not to be outshone in righteous horror, the government hastened to condemn Kidd as an "obnoxious pirate." On November 23 Secretary of State Vernon instructed colonial governors from Massachusetts to Jamaica to seize him on sight. "Take particular care for apprehending the said *Kidd,* and his Accomplices, whenever he or they shall arrive in any of the said Plantations," read the order, "as likewise, That they secure his Ship, and all the Effects therein: It being their Excellencies Intention, that Right be done to those who have been injured and robbed by the said *Kidd;* and that he, and his Associates, be prosecuted with the utmost Rigour of the Law." In December King William proclaimed pardon to all Indian Ocean pirates who should surrender to designated authorities. Two villains, whose evil careers put them beyond God's mercy and man's, were excepted. One was the most notorious of the Red Sea men, "Long Ben" Avery — the other, Captain William Kidd.

Wild tales of Kidd's whereabouts flared up, skipped, vanished like Walpurgis sprites. The cloistered annalist, Narcissus Luttrell, snatched at them before they were gone.[10] Kidd was prisoner on a French ship bound for the grim justice of the Indian Mogul. Not so; he was snugged down in the Scotch settlement at Darien, where the treacherous Scots "received him with all his riches." No, he was at the West Indian port of St. Thomas, offering the Danish governor 45,000 pieces of eight for safe haven.

The last rumor brought Luttrell closer to the truth. Early in April, 1699, the *Quedah* made landfall at the Leewards island of Anguilla. The ship's boat hardly touched shore before it put out again with oars flying. It brought back shocking news that Kidd and all his men were now condemned pirates. Some wanted to scuttle the *Quedah* and scatter for their lives. Kidd would not hear of it; he would go free or to the gibbet; no middle way lay between those two, no hiding place in a strange land for the small pleasure of drawing breath. What good was life, if he lost all that made it worthwhile? He relied on powerful friends and the French passes to establish his innocence. The essential thing now was to avoid arrest until he was under Bellomont's protection. Within four hours he spread sail for the downwind run to the neutral Danish colony of St. Thomas.

A few days later the *Quedah* stood off the Danish port, requesting entry. If Kidd was "an honest man, and can prove nothing unlawful to have done," replied the governor, "he can come in freely." This permission sounded dangerously qualified to Kidd. He sent back a request for security against Eng-

---

[10] Luttrell's manuscript chronicle of contemporary events (1678–1714) remained unpublished and almost unknown until Macaulay called attention to it by quotation in his widely acclaimed *History of England* (1855). Since Luttrell depended primarily on newssheets for information, his entries about Kidd simply reflected the changing course of public rumor.

10. Captain Kidd receives visitors aboard the *Adventurer* in New York Harbour, before leaving on his cruise to the Indian Ocean. Painting by J. L. G. Ferris (Smithsonian Institution)

lish warships while he lay in harbor, which the governor's council debated, then rejected. Kidd had become a hunted man; no one dared give him sanctuary.

Samuel Bradley had come to the end of his voyage. Weak and emaciated from two years of sickness since the Comoros, he begged "with folded hands" to stay at St. Thomas. Kidd was dubious about facing Sarah without her brother, but finally relented. Four of his crew who rowed Bradley to shore never returned. The rats were finding their holes.[11]

In his fashion Kidd, too, was on the run. Every day in the bulky *Quedah* invited capture. She was quickly recognized and, once spied, her worn sails and matted bottom made her easy to overtake. If Kidd was to reach Boston before a royal frigate pounced on him, he needed a fast anonymous craft. Perhaps he could pick one up, and safely moor the *Quedah,* among the bays of Hispaniola.

In the still waters of the Mona Passage Kidd sent out a boat to hail a becalmed sloop. She was the *Antonio,* up from Curaçao on a trading voyage to Puerto Rico, her merchant-owner, Henry Bolton, aboard. After some negotiation Kidd bought the sloop for 3000 pieces of eight, and sold Bolton goods worth another 8200. But what to do with the *Quedah?* She carried 150 bales of cloth, eighty tons of sugar, some saltpeter, iron and, of course, her valuable guns and anchors. Kidd moored her up the Higüey River of Hispaniola, lashed bow and stern to the banks, and engaged Bolton to guard her for three months until he

11 Until recently it was believed that Kidd treated his brother-in-law cruelly, marooning him, sick as he was, on a wild, uninhabited rock near Antigua. Here, presumably, he left him to die. The story originated in affidavits submitted by two of Kidd's men in South Carolina (cf. General Edward McCrady, *History of South Carolina* I, pp. 262–63), and from a letter of Bellomont to Secretary Vernon on October 18, 1700 (*Docs. Rel. Col. Hist. N.Y.,* IV, p. 760). But the relationship between Kidd and Bradley had always been affectionate. Bradley's 1693 will, never altered, referred to Kidd as "my loving brother-in-law [who] hath been very careful of me," and named him a chief beneficiary. Following this lead, D. M. Hinrichs searched the Royal Danish Archives, Copenhagen, in 1953. He unearthed reports from the St. Thomas governor, and Bradley's deposition made there, both showing that Bradley was put ashore at his own desire, near the town. For full discussion, cf. Hinrichs, pp. 108–118.

could fetch her away to an Admiralty court. Three of his own men and eighteen from the *Antonio* went aboard the *Quedah* to protect the cargo from looters. Into the sloop Kidd stowed a little nest egg of gold in dust and bars, silver plate, gems, and bales of fine cloth. With a dozen of his men as crew, he pointed the *Antonio* north in mid-May.

The *Antonio* crept cautiously up the Atlantic coast, stopping only on the wild Jersey shore for repairs. On the supposition that Bellomont would be in New York, Kidd then skirted Long Island to drop anchor at Oyster Bay on June 10. From there he sent secret word of his arrival to his close friend and New York neighbor, James Emmott, who joined him at Oyster Bay in a day or two. Bellomont, it seemed, was in Boston, and Emmott agreed to go to him as Kidd's emissary, carrying the passes that would prove Kidd innocent of piracy. The *Antonio* put Emmott down on the Connecticut shore. By late evening of June 13, he was closeted with the governor at Peter Sergeant's handsome brick house in Boston.

Bellomont was as much on the razor's edge as Kidd. Guilty or not, he wanted the New York captain in his possession. Clearly, "menacing him had not been the way to invite him hither, but rather wheedling." Bellomont took custody of the passes, and framed a deceptively encouraging letter. The Council, he wrote, "are of the opinion that if your Case be as clear as you (or Mr. Emott for you) have said, that you may safely come hither and be equipped and fitted out to go fetch the other Ship, and I make no Manner of Doubt but to obtain the King's Pardon for you and those Men you have left, who I understand have been faithful to you and refused as well as you to dishonor the Commission you had from *England*." The Council approved, quite ignorant that tucked in Bellomont's pocket was Secretary Vernon's order to put Kidd in irons. "When I heard people say that the neighboring Governors had orders from Court to seize him," he recalled with some pride, "I laughed as if I believed no such thing." To give his letter added persuasion, he sent it by the hand of Duncan Campbell, a brisk young friend of Kidd, a fellow Scot, and Boston's postmaster. "I doubt not I shall be able to make my Innocency appear, or else I had no need to come to these parts of the world," wrote Kidd in return. He promised to come in with "about Ten of my own men" and clear himself of all suspicion.

Although his life depended on proving his hands absolutely clean, Kidd proceeded to dispose of booty in a way that could only arouse distrust. Admiralty law required him to bring in all goods for condemnation; instead, he treated the *Antonio's* cargo as his personal property. By Duncan Campbell he sent to Lady Bellomont an enameled box of gems, an obvious bribe, not too wittily made to the young wife of the aging governor. Small sloops appeared alongside the *Antonio,* loaded bales of cloth, and disappeared. When Sarah arrived in the care of one "Whisking" Clark, he left with a stock of goods in his hold. A couple of cannon went ashore on Block Island, a bag of gold bars into the cupboard of a Rhode Island freebooter friend, Captain Paine. Finally, with the lord proprietor's consent, Kidd buried a major cache of gold and jewels in the orchard of Gardiners Island. John Gardiner gave him a proper receipt. Kidd's treasure was now nicely scattered; anyone who wanted to find it would need his help. On June 26 the *Antonio* fired a salvo in salute to Gardiners Island, and pointed her bow for Boston.

Settled comfortably into lodgings with Duncan Campbell in Boston, Kidd did little to create an impression of forthright honesty. He had Campbell slip the governor's wife another bribe — £1000 worth of gold bars neatly sewed up in a green silk bag. The lady was giddy, but not enough for that, and sent it back. On June 3 the Council summoned Kidd to a session before the blue-tiled fireplace of Peter Sergeant's elegant parlor. The Council greeted him courteously and requested him to bring a written narrative of his voyage to its meeting next day. On the following day five of his men accompanied him, each bearing a written affidavit, but Kidd's own narrative was not ready. He pleaded the loss of his logbook at Madagascar. The Council gave him two days' respite, until their Friday morning session. He failed to show up. Sent for, he returned word that he had mistaken the time of meeting. His narrative would be ready that evening.

The delay had Bellomont writhing. Every hour of Kidd's freedom was a danger to him. Today Kidd took a cheering cup at the Blue Anchor and strolled the waterfront, tomorrow he might be off to the Indian Ocean again, leaving Bellomont a ruined man. Although sympathetic Council members inclined to excuse Kidd on his personal evidence, which included the French passes, Bellomont "fancied he looked as if he were on the wing, and resolved to run away." Afraid to wait a moment longer, the governor read to the Friday morning session his orders to seize Kidd. The instructions were too clear to ignore, and the Council so voted. Constables were alerted to lay hold of Kidd wherever he could be found.

He was neither at Duncan Campbell's nor the Blue Anchor. To prevent gossip of a backstairs deal, Bellomont had seen Kidd only at Council sessions. This irked Kidd; after all, Bellomont was the chief mover of the voyage; he had gotten Kidd into it, and should be man enough to stand by him in trouble. At two o'clock that afternoon Kidd knocked at Peter Sergeant's door. The waiting constables closed in; Kidd burst through the door, yanking at his sword; the constables plunged after him and pinned back his arms; Kidd was under arrest. Nine of his men were rounded up the same day.

Bellomont had Kidd, now to keep him. The jail proved unreliable when a pirate slipped out, taking a pert servant girl with him. Frightened, Bellomont sacked the jailer and paid the county sheriff forty shillings a week to set a strong guard. Still nervous in spite of this precaution, Bellomont ordered Kidd into the Stone Prison, in sixteen-pound irons.

As soon as Kidd was behind bars a frantic hunt for his booty began. Constables ransacked his lodgings so wholeheartedly that they scooped up Sarah's things, too, and twenty-five crowns belonging to her maid. The bright buttons on Kidd's waistcoat took Bellomont's eye. He hoped that they were diamonds, but they turned out mere "Bristol stones." Moreover, he brooded in a letter to London, "seven of the buttons were wanting when they were brought to me."

The *Antonio* was inventoried for its poor remains of shot, worn cutlasses, candles and tar. Duncan Campbell surrendered whatever personal gifts Kidd had made to him, as well as Lady Bellomont her enameled box with its few gems. Four prominent Bostonians dug up the cache at Gardiners Island. The constabulary rummaged through Captain Paine's house in Rhode Island; in New York they grilled Sarah's housekeeper, and made search for all sloops that had taken cargo off the *Antonio*. A warrant went out for "Whisking" Clark on the charge that he had whisked away a load of goods. Three weeks after Kidd's arrest, five Boston citizens of good repute drew up the official tally of collected loot. Its estimated worth: £14,000.

In September Bellomont received precise instructions from the London Treasury. He was to put all of Kidd's personal belongings, and the assembled booty, aboard a man-of-war, under care of an absolutely trusted person. He was to post ahead a detailed and exact list of the whole. He was to give a copy of this list to the said trustworthy person and, on the chance that said person might die en route, place a second copy in the hands of the ship's captain.

But where was the *Quedah*, that golden galleon? Could they lay hands on her? Kidd's overdue narrative, submitted the day after his arrest, added this postscript: "the said Ship was left at St. Katharina on the Southeast part of Hispaniola, about three Leagues to Leward of the Westerly end of Savano." In his first rush of excitement, Bellomont prepared to send a 300-ton salvage ship. The estimated £1700 cost staggered him, however, and he wondered if enough goods would be left to pay for the voyage. "What a knave and a fool Kidd must be," he wrote to Vernon, to leave the *Quedah* in far waters. On July 17 a Captain Evertse reported that he saw the *Quedah* burning to the keel on the Hispaniola coast. Still, thought Bellomont, some of the goods might be recovered. On August 2 a new crew aboard the *Antonio* posted south to see what could be done.

Kidd hoped that by withholding definite information on the *Quedah* he could pry himself out of jail. In December the jailer brought the governor a letter "to acquaint me," Bellomont wrote to the Board of Trade, "that if I would let him go to the place where he left the *Quidah Merchant* and to St. Thomas' and Curacao he would undertake to bring off 50 or three score thousand pounds that would otherwise be lost." A most unlikely proposition, as Kidd knew; Bolton's time had run out long ago, and in the lawless Indies nothing valuable stayed put.[12] Bellomont shrugged at the offer. He was busy with his paper work, at which he excelled: documents, depositions, inventories, appraisals, long reports to England. The more evidence he saw, the more he damned Kidd. A risky defense of him was unthinkable; if he could not be easily saved, let him be quickly condemned. A "monster," Bellomont described him to Somers, and told the Board of Trade that "there never was a greater liar or thief in the world than this Kidd." Bellomont was delighted to learn of Moore's death from the deposition of Joseph Palmer, a crewman who had deserted to Culliford. "Your Lordships will be pleased to observe he accuses Kidd of murdering his gunner . . ."

[12] Our only account of the *Quedah*'s treasure comes from the man who knew best, Henry Bolton. Whether he was telling the truth or not is another matter. He was arrested in Jamaica, and after December 24, 1700, was in Newgate prison, London. Bolton swore that during five weeks after Kidd's departure the men left to guard the *Quedah* sold her cargo to passing ships to the tune of £ 300–400 per man. He, and two or three honest ones that stood by him, were helpless against so many. Fearing Kidd's return, the looters then made their escape. Bolton left, as well, when a friend warned him that Hispaniola Spanish were on the way. Captain Evertse's story that the *Quedah* perished by fire has not convinced anyone. Richard Morris, in *Fair Trial* (1952), supposes the improbable: that the slow, clumsy *Quedah* roamed the Caribbean for many years as the pirate ship, *Widdah*.

Meanwhile Kidd suffered the rigors of the Stone Prison. As October frosts arrived the Council noted that the prisoners were in danger of "perishing by the cold," and permitted them their clothing; the Reverend Cotton Mather chilled them further with a New Year's sermon on the text, "Hee gets Riches and not by right; leaves them in the midst of Dayes and in his End shal be a Fool." Whatever their end, the prisoners had to be gotten to England. "Send hither in safe custody," King William instructed Bellomont, "all Pirates who are under your Government at the time of your receiving this direction." [13] In September, 1699, the man-of-war *Rochester* sailed for the colonies to bring the accused men home, but ran into a storm so fierce that she limped back to port for repairs. Nerves were raw in Parliamentary circles; a howl went up that the storm was all a Whig plot to prevent Kidd's trial, and the Lords Justices were driven to inquire as to the real extent of the *Rochester*'s damage. At last, on February 6, 1700, H.M.S. *Advice* arrived in the colonies to carry out the assignment. By the 16th Bellomont had thirty-one prisoners chained up in the ship's gun room. Kidd received special consideration — a steerage cabin, with a Negro servant to care for his wants. He had to be kept safe, but he also had to be kept alive.

Parliament shook with angry debate over what was now known as "the Kidd affair." On December 1, 1699, while Kidd shivered in the Stone Prison, Commons ordered before it all papers that related to his voyage. It expressed shock at what it

[13] Being committed on the high seas, piracy fell outside the jurisdiction of English shire courts. Admiralty courts were governed by civil law, however, which permitted conviction only by confession, or by the testimony of eye-witnesses. Inability to produce either of these before the court allowed so many accused pirates to escape sentence that a 1536 act of Henry VIII put their trials under common law, as though committed on land, and necessitated therefore that trial be held within an English county. Since at that date no colonies of England existed, the law did not provide for trials overseas. The inconvenience of the procedure led to ignoring the law in many cases, but the king could call any case home, as he did with Kidd. Almost at the hour that Kidd boarded the *Advice*, King William signed an act enabling special commissions to try pirates on colonial soil.

learned. The member from Oxford thought "these seemed to be horrid things" that deserved unsparing punishment. The member from Great Grimsby declared that Kidd's backers had encouraged him to plunder at will, and were eager for all that they could steal in this lawless manner. "What would become of this nation," demanded another voice, "if those in authority were not content to plunder and sweep away by grants all that could be got here, but likewise sent out their thieves to rifle whatever was to be met with elsewhere?"

In reply, the government's defenders pointed out that monarchs had awarded pirate goods to captors ever since Henry VIII. The solicitor-general added that every Lord Admiral for 300 years had received a share of goods seized from pirates; that a pirate is "*hostis humani generis*," and, as the enemy of all mankind, may be captured, executed and his booty claimed by anyone whatsoever; finally, that the king's grant to the backers gave only what he had clear right to, no more, which would not include the property of proved owners.

On December 6 the House heard motion "That the letters patent granted to the Earl of Bellamont and others of pirate goods are dishonorable to the king, against the law of nations, contrary to the laws and statutes of this realm, invasive of property, and destructive of trade and commerce." When Secretary Vernon revealed the real backers, for whom the dummy names stood, the member from Abingdon leaped up to demand if they would "be gagged by great names!" Debate on the motion began at noon and was still in full heat when candles were brought in at dusk. At nine o'clock the exhausted members defeated the motion, 189 to 133.

London awaited Kidd's approach as though he were a visiting prince — of evil. News that the *Advice* had blundered off course and into the Bristol Channel raised groans of treason. From the Downs, on April 8, Captain Wynne of the *Advice* sent posthaste word of their arrival to Secretary Vernon, who in turn hurried the message to Parliament. The royal yacht *Kath-*

erine spread sail to pick up Kidd in the Thames estuary and rush him to Greenwich. Admiralty orders kept him incommunicado; no one from shore could speak to him, no letter to him could be delivered. As he boarded the *Katherine* at noon of April 11, Kidd was able to dispatch to Russell (now Lord Orford) a briefer version of his Boston narrative and a letter protesting his innocence. He wanted his passes; he wanted Livingston examined before any trial was held; and, "when I am clear of this trouble," he wanted to bring in the *Quedah,* whose value he now jumped to £90,000.

The seething political pot in England began to boil. Tories were determined to beat the Whigs to their knees with any cudgel they could lay hold of, and Kidd was a handy one. They feared that if the *Advice* sailed in after the House dismissed its present sitting, Whigs would use the interim to hush up "the Kidd affair." On March 16, therefore, the House petitioned William that Kidd "not be tried, discharged, or pardoned, until the next session of Parliament." Secretary Vernon hoped that the matter could be settled sooner, for, as he wrote to Shrewsbury, "if this fellow is to lie in prison the whole summer, one cannot tell what lesson he may be taught by winter; whereas, if he were examined by members immediately upon his arrival, the naked truth would appear, and some people's jealousies would be found groundless . . ." Jealousies had grown venomous; on April 10 the House received a motion that the estimable Lord Somers be banished from the king's presence forever. It lost, but 106 members supported it. On April 11 Parliament rose.

Unlike Parliament, the Admiralty never dismissed. It ordered its marshal, John Cheeke, to take a file of soldiers and march Kidd to the Admiralty office as soon as the *Katherine* touched Greenwich. A messenger mounted the steps of the Admiralty at seven o'clock on the Sunday morning of April 14 to say that Kidd was ill in mind and body. Boston's biting cold, the cramped voyage, the somber prospects ahead, had unstrung him. He had asked for a knife, which was refused lest he do away with himself. Then he had fallen into a "fitt," and in his bewilderment handed Cheeke a gold piece to send home to Sarah. His papers were gone, Kidd lamented, and as a result he would surely be condemned. He hoped to be shot, rather than suffer the shame of hanging. Cheeke also had whispers of dark doings — a muffled figure had rowed alongside the *Katherine* in a wherry, asking for Kidd.

The prisoner gathered strength by afternoon, and Cheeke was able to present him at the Admiralty office. The Board interviewed him twice during the day. The result was read out to him; he and the Board signed it, and sealed it fast.

Every act of the Admiralty at this point was calculated to be thorough and aboveboard. Both principal Secretaries of State opened the "two Deall Boxes" of evidence shipped by Bellomont, so that they could vouch for each other. All letters bearing on Kidd's case were slit in public and read before the assembled Board. Orford saw to it that the Board took possession of Kidd's protest addressed to him from the Downs. On April 26 the "trusted person" of the *Advice*, Lieutenant Hunt, handed over the keys to Kidd's iron chest. The Board found all his papers neatly tied up with white tape. After a jeweler weighed the gold and put the gems under his glass, the Board clamped shut the double locks again. Kidd would not need the chest; he was already in Newgate prison.

Newgate adjoined the court chambers of Old Bailey, both so smelly that visitors brought flowers to bury their noses in. Here Kidd lay for more than a year, in strict confinement. He was ill much of the time. In mid-May the Newgate keeper notified the Admiralty Board that "Capt. Kidd was troubled with a great Paine in his Head, and shaken in his Limbs, and was in great want of his Cloathes." The anxious Board ordered that he have them. On December 30 he was little better. "I have had a great fit of sickness, and am in continuall danger of a relapse," he told the Board in a shaky hand. He asked for the same freedom to exercise in the yard that other prisoners enjoyed. After nervous debate the Board allowed it, so long as a guard stayed by his side.

When Kidd entered Newgate, the Admiralty attorney argued that he should be kept both "safe" and "close." The Board scrupled a bit at this, since such extreme deprivation of rights was usually enforced only in cases of treason, when the whole realm was threatened, and then only on order from the King in Council. Well, said the attorney, it was prudent all the same, and "he could not see any harm in it." For a full year, therefore, Kidd was shut off from communication with anyone concerned in his trial. His only visitors were a Thames Street fishmonger and a butcher's wife from Wapping, his aunt and uncle, plain folk indeed, who could see him if a keeper stood by. He was allowed writing materials for one purpose — to address the Admiralty Board. Not even a letter to Sarah. On March 20, 1701, he wrote of his inevitable trial, "I am wholly unprepared, having never been permitted the least use of pen, Ink and paper to help my Memory, nor the advice of friends to assist me, in what so nearly concerns my life." Next day, Commons ruled that "according to law" he was entitled to these privileges. The Admiralty still dallied; not until April 16 did it inform the Newgate keeper that "Capt. Kidd is now to be look't after in no other manner than as other Criminalls are in his circumstances." By then, Kidd was no longer dangerous.

On March 6, 1701, the new House of Commons had called on the Admiralty to deliver up all its papers relating to the Kidd affair. They arrived in such confusion, mixed helter-skelter with reports on other pirates, that a large committee had to be appointed to sort them out. On March 22, the House listened to relevant extracts from the Council minutes of New York and Massachusetts. One of the *Quedah* merchants, Cogi Baba, personally presented his version of the ship's seizure, and a claim for indemnity. The House instructed the sorting committee to report on March 27, and ordered Kidd to be brought before it on the same day.

Kidd's appearance before the House was a disappointment to both. Members thought him stubborn, truculent, perhaps slightly drunk. His purpose and theirs were quite opposite: he cared only to exonerate himself, they cared only to implicate his backers. It was commonly speculated that if he had turned savagely against the Whig statesmen, damned them as dishonest rogues, and painted himself as their hapless victim, he might have won a pardon from grateful Tories. Instead, he insisted on his innocence, and that of all concerned in his voyage. "I had thought him only a knave," commented one member, shaking his head; "now I know him to be a fool as well." [14]

Next day the House took up the matter again and gnawed it like an old bone. The members examined Sir Edmund Harrison, listened to the clerk drone out the Articles of Agreement, both commissions, Bellomont's sailing orders, and the king's grant. It must have been a weary session. Motion made to declare the grant "illegal and void" lost by a close vote, 185–198. They were done with Kidd, bored with him, in fact; let him, they declared, "be proceeded against according to law." [15] The House had its eye on bigger game. By April 14 it forced through motions to impeach Somers, Orford, Halifax and Portland.[16]

As Kidd saw it, his whole defense rested on the French passes. With them he had a chance, without them he had none.

[14] Bishop Gilbert Burnet admired Kidd's courage: ". . . all endeavors were used to persuade him to accuse the lords; he was assured, that if he did it, he should be preserved; and if he did not, he should certainly die for his piracy: yet this could not prevail on him to charge them . . ." As Kidd's case became more desperate, he weakened in his resolve to stand or fall alone. In an April letter to Speaker of the House Robert Harley, he said that his backers "made me the Tool of their Ambition and Avarice," and now served their selfish political ends by abandoning him. But even this letter repeated his claim that he had done nothing wrong. If Kidd was in no way guilty, neither, of course, were the other participants in the voyage.

[15] On March 31 the House received word that Kidd wished to appear before it again. He was sent for, heard and remanded to Newgate; the record says no more. On April 1, the king informed the House that he had ordered Kidd's trial to proceed in the usual manner.

[16] In 1700 the English sovereign appointed and dismissed ministers in fact as well as in form. Parliamentary control of the executive was exerted through

He requested of the House all papers that he needed for his trial. The House returned them to the Admiralty, and on April 16 ordered the Admiralty to deliver them to Kidd. When the Admiralty clerk brought them to Newgate, the passes were missing. Nor could Kidd find Bellomont's letter to him at Long Island, which acknowledged their existence and foresaw their effectiveness in obtaining his release. Both had vanished. In a frenzy Kidd begged the Admiralty for them. The Board was surprised — it really did not know what to do about it — perhaps he might apply to the Admiralty judge. On May 3 it directed Captain Wynn of the *Advice* to see if he could dig them up somewhere. Who knows, the Board speculated, Bellomont might still have them.

The trial was set for May 8. Two weeks before that date Kidd was informed of it, and the court appropriated £50 for him to engage counsel. The same Admiralty clerk who failed to deliver the passes now failed to deliver the £50. He brought the money to Newgate at the last moment, on the night of May 7. Since Kidd's two legal advisors, Dr. Oldish and Mr. Lemmon, would not go to work until they had their fee in hand, Kidd held only one hurried conference with them, on the morning that court convened. He had just enough time to urge them to demand his French passes.[17]

---

votes of censure, or by impeachment. Commons brought the charges, Lords judged their validity. This ancient right of Parliament to impeach was kept polished by frequent use, and in some periods amounted almost to a pastime. Of the four accused in this instance, only Somers and Orford were charged with complicity in the Kidd affair. All were acquitted; Commons had no expectation of a favorable verdict from the House of Lords, and did not even appear to press the charges.

[17] Court procedures of the day put the accused at an enormous disadvantage. He was not informed, prior to trial, what specific charges would be brought against him. Worse, counsel could aid him in the courtroom on matters of law, but not of fact. Strangely, to us, the prosecution did not seem equally dispensable. In theory, the court itself defended the accused as to the facts of the case, and assured him justice, but the disadvantage remained. However ignorant and fumbling the prisoner might be, he had to carry on all cross-examination himself.

A special court of commission sat to try the many accused pirates gathered into London jails. With one exception, its justices were able men. As Lord Chief Baron of the Exchequer, the presiding judge, Sir Edward Ward, headed England's courts of common law; Sir Henry Hatsell ranked as a baron also; Justices Turton and Gould were judges of the King's Bench. John Powell, a man of large and hearty spirit, had served twenty-two years on the bench without reproach, a record in that vindictive age.[18] The one clearly incompetent member was Sir Salathiel Lovell, Recorder of London, over ninety, and so forgetful that wags called him the "Obliviscor" of the city.

The solicitor-general, Sir John Hawles, headed the prosecution. Dr. George Oxenden, authority on Admiralty law and former Regius Professor at Cambridge, was present to supply learned advice and serve as clerk. William Cowper, later lord chancellor and the first Earl Cowper, was chief prosecutor, assisted by Dr. Newton, Advocate of the Admiralty, and Messrs. Knapp and Coniers, Crown counsels. A formidable array of legal talent, all told; not great men, but the best that England could put into the courtroom.

On the morning of May 8 a seventeen-man grand jury assembled at Old Bailey under the rheumy eye of Sir Salathiel Lovell. Dr. Oxenden explained to them the nature of the indictment. Possibly for the first time Kidd knew that the charge against him was murder — the killing of gunner Moore — as well as piracy. The grand jury found for the bill of indictment. Kidd was called to the bar to plead.

"William Kidd, hold up thy hand."

Kidd objected, to the irritation of the court. "I beg your lordships I may have counsel admitted, and that my trial may be put off; I am not really prepared for it."

[18] A decade later Swift told Stella that Powell, "an old fellow with grey hairs, was the merriest old gentleman I ever saw, spoke pleasing things, and chuckled till he cried again." Powell once presided at a witchcraft trial in which the defendant was accused of flying through the air. He smilingly observed that no statute forbade it.

"Nor never will be, if you can help it," snapped Sir Salathiel. The court advised Kidd that counsel could not be admitted until after he had pleaded. It pointed out that if he refused to plead, his case would suffer, since he could then make no defense. Roared the exasperated clerk of arraigns for the fifth time: "William Kidd, art thou guilty or not guilty?"

Kidd gave up. "Not guilty."

"How wilt thou be tried?"

"By God and my country."

"God send thee good deliverance." [19]

Five justices took their seats; the clerk intoned the charge. Kidd, it said, "being moved and seduced by the instigation of the devil," had struck one William Moore "with a certain wooden bucket, bound with iron hoops, of the value of eight pence, which he the said William Kidd then and there had and held in his right hand, did violently, feloniously, voluntarily, and of his malice aforethought, beat and strike the aforesaid William Moore in and upon the right part of the head of him the said William Moore, a little above the right ear of the said William Moore, then and there upon the high sea, in the ship aforesaid, and within the jurisdiction of the Admiralty of England aforesaid, giving the said William Moore, then and there with the bucket aforesaid, in and upon the aforesaid right part of the head of him, the said William Moore, a little above the right ear of the said William Moore, one mortal bruise; of which mortal bruise the aforesaid William Moore, from the said thirtieth day of October in the ninth year aforesaid, until the one and thirtieth day of the said month of October, in the year aforesaid, upon the high seas aforesaid, in the ship aforesaid, and within the jurisdiction of the Admiralty aforesaid, did languish, and languishing did live; upon which one and thirtieth day of October, in the ninth year aforesaid, the aforesaid William Moore, upon the high sea aforesaid, near the aforesaid

[19] For the most reliable verbatim report of Kidd's trial, see T. B. Howell, *State Trials*, XIV, 123–234. Quotations given in the present account are excerpted from it, and not always in consecutive order.

coast of Malabar, in the East Indies aforesaid, in the ship aforesaid, called the *Adventure Galley,* and within the jurisdiction of the Admiralty of England aforesaid, did die . . ."

Although on trial for murder, Kidd was obsessed with the French passes. If he could get them they would prove him innocent of piracy, at least, while their absence at the moment might delay the trial. Dr. Oldish requested that Edward Davis, one of Kidd's Madagascar passengers now prisoner in Newgate, be called as witness. "There are several other letters and papers that we cannot get," explained Mr. Lemmon, "and therefore we desire the trial may be put off till we can procure them." Davis had seen the passes; he would prove their existence.

The court had no mind to postpone a murder trial for evidence dealing with piracy. "They have had a fortnight's notice to prepare for the trial," grumbled the solicitor-general.

"We petitioned for the money," replied Dr. Oldish, "and the Court ordered £50; but the person that received the money went away, and we had none till last night."

"I ordered that the money might be paid into his own hands," exclaimed Dr. Oxenden.

"I paid the £50 into his own hand on Tuesday morning," the Admiralty registrar put in hastily.

"I had no money nor friends to prepare for my trial till last night," Kidd told the court.

"My lord," said the solicitor-general to Chief Baron Ward, "this we will do; let Davis be brought into Court; and if that be a just excuse, we are content. In the meantime, let him be tried for the murder, wherein there is no pretence of want of witnesses or papers."

The court agreed, and Kidd went on trial for the murder of Moore. "My lord," began Mr. Coniers, when the charge had been read, "it will appear to be a most barbarous fact, to murder a man in this manner; for the man gave him no manner of provocation." To prove his case Coniers summoned Joseph Palmer, Kidd's deserter to Culliford, now groomed as king's

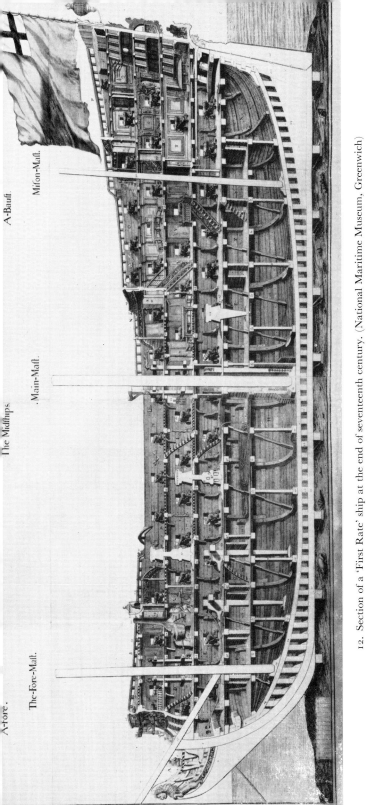

A-Fore.

The Midships.

A-Baust.

The-Fore-Mast.

Main-Mast.

Mison-Mast.

12. Section of a 'First Rate' ship at the end of seventeenth century. (National Maritime Museum, Greenwich)

13. Shipping on the Bristol Avon seen at about the period of Woodes Rogers' exploits; Painting by Van Beecq. (National Maritime Museum, Greenwich)

witness. Palmer's evidence was shrewdly calculated to put Kidd in the worst light. It made Moore out a peaceable fellow, described Kidd pacing the deck before he struck the blow (thus precluding an uncontrollable rush of anger), and told how Palmer himself laid his fingers on Moore's broken skull. Cross-examining, Kidd tried to force an admission that mutiny was brewing. "There was no mutiny," Palmer maintained; "all was quiet."

Coniers now called the *Adventure*'s surgeon, Robert Bradinham, another deserter to Culliford who had turned witness for the Crown.[20] He did not see Kidd strike the blow, but could testify to its mortal effect. The skull was definitely shattered. No, he did not know of any previous quarrel between Kidd and Moore.

Mr. Cowper called Palmer back. Did Kidd throw the bucket or keep it in his hand? He held it by the strap, said Palmer, in his hand.

Kidd summoned what spotty defense he could. Hugh Parrot was able to say that "my commander was in a passion." Richard Barlicorn had heard Bradinham attribute Moore's death to his earlier sickness. Called back to the stand, Bradinham flatly denied it. "My lord, I never said so . . . He was not sick at all before." Abel Owen told the court that there was a mutiny, but on cross-examination admitted that he meant weeks before Moore's death, at the time when Kidd refused to seize the *Loyal Captain.*

---

[20] Palmer, a young Rhode Islander, was one of those sent back to Kidd at the Nore — no commendation if the *Duchess*'s captain was yielding his worst seamen. At first Bellomont took a harsh view of both Palmer and Bradinham. He set Palmer down as a liar and, having examined nine pirates in Boston, decided that "Robert Bradinham, Kidd's surgeon, is the obstinatest and most hardned of 'em all." Bellomont softened when it became plain that Palmer would turn Crown's evidence. Palmer became "an honest young man in his own nature," whose testimony "is pretty home against Kidd," and Bellomont trusted that this service would earn him speedy pardon. Indignant defenders of Kidd disparage the prosecution's two witnesses on the grounds that they would tell any falsehood to save their lives. If so, the same was doubly true of Kidd, for they were relatively sure of pardon, whereas he was in grave danger of hanging.

Plainly, calling further witnesses on Kidd's part would not help. "Have you any more to say for yourself?" asked Justice Ward.

"I have no more to say," replied Kidd, "but I had all the provocation in the world given me, and I had no design to kill him . . . It was not designedly done, but in my passion, for which I am heartily sorry."

Ward's charge to the jury summarized the evidence admirably, without giving Kidd an ounce of credit beyond what the testimony dictated. He did not see how so few words, and so slight, could justify killing. No proof had been offered that mutiny threatened. "I cannot see what distinction can be made, but that the prisoner is guilty of murder."

After an hour's retirement, the jury agreed. "Guilty," said the foreman.

The clerk of arraigns turned to the Newgate constable. "Look to him, keeper," he said.

Next morning Kidd and his nine men shuffled into Old Bailey for three separate trials on five counts of piracy. The first charged them with "piracy and robbery, on a ship called the *Quedagh Merchant.*" In his opening speech, Dr. Newton made a carefully biased review of the voyage. He mentioned the commission for seizing pirates, but not that for privateering on any vessel under French authority. He treated the Babs incident as a heinous offense, and berated Kidd for not capturing Culliford. His invective had a grand sweep to it: Kidd was "an arch-pirate . . . equally cruel, dreaded and hated both on the land and at sea . . . no one in this age has done more mischief, in this worst kind of mischief, or has occasioned greater confusion and disorder, attended with all the circumstances of cruelty and falsehood . . ."

The prosecution set out to prove not only that Kidd took the *Quedah* without cause, but that he intended piracy from the beginning. "If you can prove that he was a pirate all along," Justice Powell nodded, "this will be a great evidence against him." Bradinham took the stand to recount the whole voyage at length. "Now you are come to the *Quedagh*, for which they are indicted," Justice Powell reminded him, "go not beyond it" — which Bradinham promptly did. At Madagascar, he continued, Culliford's men "heard that he (Kidd) was come to take them, and hang them. He told them it was no such thing; and afterwards went aboard to them and swore to be true to them. I know all this," said Bradinham to Justice Ward, "because I was aboard then and heard the words." Kidd had shared out the *Quedah* goods at Madagascar. The surgeon, gifted with an uncanny memory, recalled exactly the shares and half-shares, money and goods, received by each of the prisoners.

"Did you not see any French passes aboard the *Quedagh Merchant?*" demand Kidd.

"You told me you had French passes," Bradinham replied, "but I never did see them."

Joseph Palmer corroborated Bradinham's testimony in its main essentials. He had been away for water in the *November* when the *Quedah* was taken, but could vouch for shares of plunder received by the prisoners. He, too, was silent on the *Quedah* pass.

"I ask you whether I had no French passes," demanded Kidd in cross-examination.

"Indeed, Captain Kidd, I cannot tell. I did hear you say that you had French passes, but I never saw them."

"I had a commission to take the French, and pirates," Kidd declared, "and in order to that, I came up with two ships that had French passes both of them. I called you all a-deck to consult. Did not a great many of the men go aboard? Did not you go? You know, I would have given these ships to them again but you would not; you all voted against it. Did not you?"

"This Armenian offered you 20,000 rupees for the ship, and you refused," Palmer retorted.

"Did not I ask where will you carry this ship?" cried Kidd. "And you said that you would make a prize of her, that you would carry her to Madagascar?"

All that was a hoax, in Palmer's opinion. "The Armenians

came crying and wringing their hands; upon which, you said, 'I must say my men will not give them the ship.' And so some of the men went on the forecastle, and pretended they would not give them the ship; but there was not a quarter part of the men concerned in it."

In cross-examining Kidd was simply inept — petty, illogical or irrelevant, by turns, and never seemed to strengthen his case. Justice Ward stuck with the solid facts. Kidd had produced no evidence that the *Quedah* was a legal prize. Even if he proved it, he was guilty of sharing goods prior to condemnation, just as a pirate would. And instead of seizing Culliford, as his commission bade, he consorted with him. "These things press very hard upon you," the chief baron warned Kidd. "We ought to let you know what is observed that you may make your defense as well as you can."

But Kidd could do no better. He called Edward Davis, his passenger from Madagascar, who could only state that Kidd showed him passes — he was not sure what kind. A garrulous fellow, suitably named Mr. Say, testified that Bradinham, while in Marshalsea prison, seemed certain that Kidd would successfully answer his accusers. Captains from Kidd's West Indian days certified to his character and good standing at that time. The court did not see what this had to do with seizing a ship ten years later.

"You must bear this in your minds," Justice Ward summed up to the jury, "that to make it piracy it must be the taking piratically and feloniously upon the high sea, within the jurisdiction of the Admiralty of England, the goods of a friend, that is, such as are in amity with the King." At the Babs Kidd had attacked ships at amity with the King, Ward went on, and at the Maldives had brutally mistreated natives of a friendly power. Seizing the *Quedah* was equally lawless, Ward reminded the jury; both ship and goods belonged to persons whose countries were at peace with England. Kidd had to show that they were subjects of France, or had a French pass, otherwise the act could only be considered piracy. "As to the French passes, there is nothing of that appears by any proof; and, for aught I can see, none saw them but himself, if there were ever any."

The jury was out half an hour. When it returned, the clerk ordered Kidd to hold up his hand. "How say you," the clerk asked of the foreman, "is he guilty of the piracy whereof he stands indicted or not guilty?"

"Guilty," answered the foreman.

The prosecution was nothing if not thorough. With Kidd condemned twice over, the third trial opened. A new jury was cried and counted. The charge accused the defendants of plundering Parker's ship and seizing the *Rouparelle*. For the benefit of the fresh jury, Bradinham labored once more through the narrative of the voyage. Kidd had "drubbed with a naked cutlass" crewmen of Parker's ship, and taken out of it coffee, pepper, myrrh, clothing and some Arabian gold; he had plundered the *Rouparelle* and sunk her at Madagascar. Both ships were Moorish.

"This man contradicts himself in a hundred places," groaned Kidd.

Bradinham named some of the crew who took shares at Madagascar. "How can he attest these wicked lies?" spoke up one of them. "I had nothing."

"The captain divided out the shares," Bradinham retorted.

"He tells a thousand lies," said Kidd. By now, he was tossing his hands in despair.

"Will you ask him any more questions?" inquired the solicitor-general.

"No, no, so long as he swears it, our words or oaths cannot be taken."

"Will you ask him any more questions?" repeated the clerk of arraigns.

"No, no; it signifies nothing."

And it did not. Unable to dent Palmer's testimony, Kidd gave up trying. "Mr. Bradinham," he broke in as the trial neared its end, "are not you promised your life to take away mine?"

Summing up, Justice Turton concluded that if the jury believed the Crown witnesses, "you will think fit to find them guilty." The jury thought fit; after a brief half-hour of deliberation it found for the prosecution.

The final trial charged that the defendants "did piratically and feloniously set upon board, break and enter" two unnamed ships, one Moorish and one Portuguese. In defense, Kidd was reduced to abusing the Crown witnesses. "It is hard that a couple of rascals should take away the King's subjects' lives," he said bitterly. "They are a couple of rogues and rascals." The jury brought in a quick verdict of guilty.

"William Kidd, hold up thy hand," ordered the clerk. "What canst thou say for thyself? Thou hast been indicted for several piracies, and robberies, and murder, and hereupon hast been convicted. What hast thou to say for thyself why thou shouldst not die according to the law?"

"I have nothing to say, but that I have been sworn against by perjured and wicked people."

"You have been tried by the laws of the land," the clerk went on. "Nothing now remains but that sentence be passed according to the law. And the sentence of the law is this:

'You shall be taken from the place where you are, and be carried to the place from whence you came, and from thence to the place of execution, and there be severally hanged by your necks until you be dead. And the Lord have mercy on your souls.' " [21]

"My lord," said Kidd, "it is a very hard sentence. For my

---

[21] Three servants were acquitted, the other six received sentence along with Kidd. Only one, for reasons that remain obscure to us, got as far as the gallows. On the day that Kidd was sentenced Culliford was convicted as well, but reprieved. He had surrendered properly under the king's pardon, and had a receipt to show for it. Queen Anne freed him April 9, 1702.

part, I am the innocentest person of them all, only I have been sworn against by perjured persons."

The condemned shambled back to their cells, to the comforts of God and the fierce exhortations of the Newgate chaplain, who preached next Sunday on the cheerless text: "And they shall go away into everlasting punishment." Kidd made one last attempt to escape that fate. On May 12 he got off a letter to Robert Harley, speaker of the House of Commons, urging that he be sent, under guard, to bring in the *Quedah.* He now valued her at £100,000, and thought it a pity if so great a treasure were lost to the government. Of course, Harley paid no heed.

On May 17 the Admiralty issued a Latin precept setting the execution for May 23, at Wapping. Two days later a warrant instructed Marshal Cheeke to hang Kidd's tarred body at Tilbury Point, "and at such place on ye said Point where he may be seen quite plaine by persons passing into and out of ye River of Thames." So long as his bones lasted, Kidd would serve "as a greater Terrour to all Persons from Committing ye like Crimes for the time to come."

A little before three o'clock in the afternoon of May 23 the keeper's key grated in the door of Kidd's cell for the last time. Outside Newgate the grim procession formed up. At its head, in an open carriage, the deputy marshal carried over his shoulder the short silver oar of the Admiralty. The bewigged marshal followed, then the black-draped cart of the condemned, surrounded by constables. They clattered slowly through Cheapside, past the Royal Exchange and Aldgate Pump. The square keep of the Tower rose on their right hand, above the broad reach of the Thames. Kidd could see the moored barges now, the little boats plying up and down with their passengers, London Bridge steep with buildings along its great piers, the late sun dimly glinting on Southwark roofs. They lurched over the potholes of Catherine Street. A raucous crowd trailed them, children trotting alongside and stretching up their hands for coins. For a while the shabby tenements of Wapping shut out the river.

Wapping was originally marshland, and remained a damp, pestiferous hole. Uninhabitable before Elizabeth's reign, it had then been banked against the Thames tides; frogs and salamanders departed, rivermen took their place in the foggy bottom, rows of miserable hovels were thrown up along the roadside, and cheap taverns moved in to take the workers' pay.

Even the gibbets at Wapping were makeshift. Other criminals went to their Maker with some respectability on Tyburn hill, but the Admiralty, due to an old quarrel with common-law courts over jurisdiction in pirate trials, used the dank riverside. It footed its scaffolds at low tide — *"infra fluxum ac refluxum,"* as the precept carefully specified. After an execution, the hangman cut down the body from its "wet tree" and chained it to a post until tidewater had ebbed and flowed over it three times. The Admiralty wanted no doubts as to whom the dead belonged.

In the muddy flats beyond the last tenement the procession halted and the prisoners climbed down. Kidd was unsteady; he was drunk. The chaplain prayed hard for him without getting much of his attention. It was not too late to repent, the chaplain urged, and Kidd was ready to repent his sins in general, but not any piracies in particular. "He expressed abundance of sorrow for leaving his wife and children, without having the opportunity to take leave of them," the chaplain recalled, "so that the thoughts of his wife's sorrow at the sad tidings of his shameful death was more occasion of grief to him than that of his own sad misfortunes." The constables pushed Kidd onto the rickety platform, and the noose tightened around his neck. When he was "turned off," the rope broke and he fell to the ground, splitting the scaffold. He had to be put up a ladder. The chaplain mounted the rungs in a last exhortation to repent his evil deeds. Stunned, Kidd muttered that he was sorry, sorry for all, sorry for everything, and the hangman pulled away the ladder. This time the rope held.

Did Kidd have a fair trial? The answer to that question depends upon the standard of fairness applied. According to court procedures of the day, he did. Twentieth-century jurisprudence, however, considers those procedures grossly unfair to the accused. In conducting his own blundering defense, the defendant was pitted against barristers of skill and experience. Further, he could not testify in his own behalf, therefore none of Kidd's men, being under the same indictment, could take the stand for him. Palmer and Bradinham spun out their narratives at great length and in convincing detail, while Kidd could reply only with feeble cross-examination. As long as the opposing witnesses stuck to a consistent story, he was doomed.

Within this faulty framework of court custom, the justices showed clear bias in their conduct of the hearings. They treated the Crown witnesses gently, but were short and sharp with the prisoners in the dock. Much was made of the Babs incident and the friendship with Culliford (neither of which was included in any indictment), inference of Kidd's evil intent being drawn from them, whereas inference of good character from Kidd's past was thrown out as irrelevant. During the *Quedah* hearing Justice Ward referred to Kidd as a pirate before the jury had rendered verdict, a slip that today would result in mistrial. Summing up evidence by the justices was nothing less than a signpost to the gallows. In theory, the court safeguarded the defendant's cause; in fact, this one lined up with the prosecution against him.

These abuses were small compared to those inflicted on him before the trial began. The first was to shut him up "close" in Newgate, unable to communicate with anyone who might assist him. Most outrageous, of course, was the theft of the passes, and of Bellomont's letter confirming them. They had been seen by various witnesses on the voyage; in its minutes for

June 19, 1699 the Massachusetts Council had recorded them; the Admiralty examined and endorsed them on September 26, 1699; the Board of Trade had copies; they were read out to the whole House of Commons a month before the trial and went, word for word, into its journal. Kidd repeatedly appealed for them to men who should have leaped to right an obvious wrong. Incredibly, no one in all London lifted a hand to find them. In their absence the court could treat the passes as if they did not even exist.[22] The third act of this tragedy of deception was the delay in delivering the money for Kidd to hire counsel. This effectively prevented him from receiving adequate legal advice, or taking any embarrassing steps toward recovering the passes before court convened.

Yet, supposing all injustices done to Kidd erased, would it have made a difference? Was he, in fact, guilty of piracy? Opinion breaks almost even on the issue. His defenders have called him "no pirate at all," the evidence presented against him "flimsey, doubtfully substantiated" and "precarious"; one concluding bluntly, "the essential fact is simple: Captain Kidd was innocent." At the other extreme, a few have argued that the court decision was correct in every one of the four trials, even those to which the missing passes applied.

Apologists for the court maintain that the status of a ship was determined solely by the nationality of her owner, or his place of domicile. Since both the *Quedah* and the *Rouparelle* were Moorish-owned, they were not liable to capture. Scholarly opinion, however, supports Kidd. "It is a known and established rule with regard to a vessel," states Richard Wildman, "that if she is navigating under the pass of a foreign country, she is considered as having the national character of that nation, under whose pass she sails; she makes a part of its naviga-

[22] The passes not only existed then, but still do. They can be seen in the Public Records Office, London, where Ralph D. Paine discovered them in 1911.

tion, and is in every respect liable to be considered as a vessel of that country." [23] Further, everyone connected with Kidd's case recognized their validity. Certainly Bellomont did, as well as those who stole them, but, most conclusively, so did the learned justices on the bench. "If there was a French pass in the ship," Chief Baron Ward told Kidd, "you ought to have condemned her as a prize."

The passes, however, covered only two of the five piracies with which Kidd was charged. He offered no sound excuse for the other three. Corroborative evidence from his own men established beyond reasonable doubt the treatment given Parker and his ship. Plunder of the others rests upon the sole testimony of Crown witnesses, scorned by some critics as unreliable, yet neither Kidd nor his men straightforwardly denied them. When Kidd accused Bradinham of lying, and Justice Turton demanded an instance of it, he could only scrape up a pair of trivial points unrelated to the ships in question. We are left with the conclusion that if Kidd were judged not guilty of taking the *Quedah* and *Rouparelle* illegally, he would have been condemned for the other three.

Finally, Kidd transgressed every regulation governing lawful privateers who took prizes. His Admiralty commission ordered him to follow the royal Instructions issued in 1693 (of which he was given a copy), and to comply with Admiralty practice and the recognized Law of Nations. These made it abundantly clear, and the same was restated in Kidd's Articles of Agreement, that a captured ship became a legal prize only after an Admiralty court had examined it. T. H. Horne, *A Compendium of Prize Law*, puts it in italics: no captured goods may be disposed of in any way until "*after final adjudication* of the same,

[23] Richard Wildman, "International Rights in War Time," *Institutes of International Law*, Vol. II (Philadelphia: T. and J. W. Johnson, 1850), p. 39. Cf. also Joseph Story: "Ships are deemed to belong to the country under whose flag and pass they navigate, and this circumstance is conclusive upon their character," *Notes on the Principles and Practice of Prize Courts* (London: William Benning and Co., 1854), p. 61.

as lawful prize, in any duly authorized court of admiralty in his
Majesty's dominions; *and not before.*" [24]   Further safeguards
specified that the papers of a captured ship be submitted, and
her principal officers be presented before the Admiralty judge.
These regulations were extremely difficult to obey, and were
honored more in the breach than the observance, but an un-
friendly court could always enforce them against a hapless defendant. Kidd obeyed none of them. He shared out cargo; he
brought in neither ships nor officers and, according to Cogi
Baba, threw the *Quedah*'s papers overboard. So when Kidd
talked of his passes, the court had a pat reply: if his prizes were
legal, why hadn't he brought them in?

It seems unlikely that anything could have saved him. Piracy charges failing, the prosecution still had him in its grip for
the killing of Moore. Today that verdict would be manslaugh-
ter, but seventeenth-century judges were not in the habit of
drawing so fine a line. Hang the villain, or let him go; and
many an Englishman swung for less.

Appalled by the injuries done to Kidd, some enthusiasts have
raised him to virtual martyrdom — the simple-hearted provincial duped, then crushed, by despicable politicians. The tragedy of his end goes deeper, as it always must, to faults of character. Ambition drove him into the trap, and he was never
shrewd enough to get out. He stumbled from one miscalcula-
tion to the next — thinking that his royal commissions gave him
superior status, that he could control his shiftless crew, that
Moorish ships might be taken with impunity, that small piracies would go unnoticed, that the French passes covered all
offenses, that a show of friendship with Culliford would never
be questioned, that Bellomont's subtle reassurances were trustworthy, that the great men in London would protect him,
that — . All wrong, all delusions. Entangled in these blunders,
his very respectability betrayed him to his death. He refused to
cut and run; he lacked the infinite cunning of the true criminal,

[24] P. 86. London, 1803.

who puts survival above all else. Was he not an honored citizen of New York? Did he not head a family, own property, hold a pew in Trinity Church? Without these, life was little. Better to die maintaining his innocence, than live with the stain of guilt. Shameful — that was the worst of Wapping. He had hoped to be shot, like a gentleman.

Ironically, this "milk-and-water amateur," whose modest desire was to serve the king as commander of a royal frigate, has been remembered as history's most atrocious pirate. Broadsides and ballads recounting his evil deeds were hawked in London streets before the tides had washed his body thrice. Mothers sent wakeful children scurrying to bed, if not to sleep, by threats that Kidd would get them. When spiritualists summoned up his ghost, candles burned blue and the air smelled of sulfur. If tales of his buried treasure are true, he sowed the coves and islands of America with the wealth of India. So many midnight diggers pitted a New York farm in 1762 that the owner begged them to dig by day — and fill in the holes. A housewife's "mesmeric revelation" in 1846, placing the sunken *Quedah* on the Hudson bottom, jewels heaped in her "like ducks' eggs in a pond," started a gold rush up the river. The more occult have searched with Bible and key, sieve and shears, hazel wand, incantations, while business corporations, lacking the psychic gift, resorted to dredges and dynamite. By one means or another, they have scoured the Atlantic coast from Nova Scotia to Key West, and the treasure was usually called Kidd's.

Early American folklore tells us that Kidd kept a watchful eye on these weird doings. Many a boatman saw his ship glide by in the mist, silent, needing no wind. Many a digger by moonlight, whose shovel thudded on a buried chest, ran screaming as Kidd loomed over him with raised cutlass. One melancholy yarn treated him more kindly. For some years after

Kidd's death, a seafarer, his clothes reeking of saltwater, knocked at lonely farmsteads around New York, asking his way. He would stay the night, pay for the hospitality with Moorish gold, and depart, his clothes as wet as ever. It was Kidd, of course, trying to get home.

CAPTAIN WOODES ROGERS

"Fight on, my men, Sir Andrew says,
A little I'm hurt, but yet not slain;
I'll but lie down and bleed awhile,
And then I'll rise and fight again."
Old English Ballad

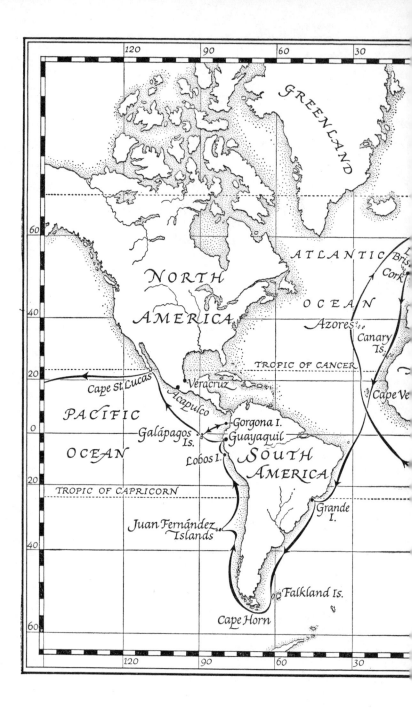

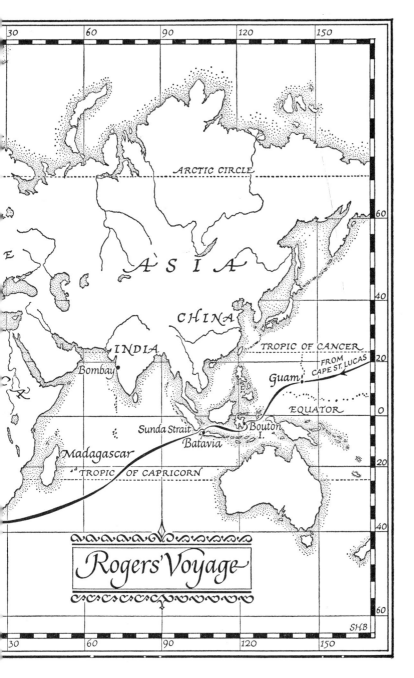

30 60 90 120 150

ARCTIC CIRCLE

60

A S I A

40

CHINA

TROPIC OF CANCER   20

INDIA   FROM
                    CAPE ST. LUCAS
Bombay   Guam

EQUATOR   0

Sunda Strait   Bouton
Batavia   I.

Madagascar   20
TROPIC OF CAPRICORN

40

Rogers' Voyage

60

SHB

30 60 90 120 150

WOODES ROGERS was a tall young man with a heavy torso balanced on legs too short for it, a round face, a thick, slightly curved nose, genial mouth, dark eyes, and high-set brows that gave him a perpetual look of mild surprise. In 1708 he had more cause than usual for astonishment. Though he was but twenty-nine years old, and had never gotten beyond apprentice mariner, he was about to command a voyage that made thoughtful men shudder — around the wintry Horn.

From his house in fashionable Queen Square, Bristol, Rogers could cross the old parade grounds and the cobbled quay to inspect his ships fitting out in the Froom. They were sound enough, and admirably equipped; the owners had seen to that. Rogers' *Duke* rated at 320 tons burden, thirty guns; her consort *Duchess* at 260 tons, twenty-six guns. Both were double-sheathed in the hull against worms, both spread new canvas on new rigging; flour, salt meat, beans and biscuit jammed their holds; powder kegs were lashed in the gun rooms, and ball filled the racks. Both ships carried privateering commissions; both aimed to pursue, attack and seize enemy ships in the South Sea.[1]

The enemy was France, allied to Spain. Marlborough's victories had shaken the French without destroying them, and in 1708 Louis XIV still hung grimly on, his waning strength fed by expanded commerce with the Spanish colonies. French merchantmen flocked to Pacific ports, French men-of-war convoyed

[1] Since the isthmus of Darien lay east and west, Balboa, who crossed it in 1513, viewed the Pacific southward, and called it the "South Sea" in distinction from Caribbean waters north of the isthmus. The name stuck, and the term "pacific," first applied by Magellan (1520), did not supplant it for more than two centuries.

the Spanish treasure fleets home from the Caribbean. "By this means," Rogers observed, "they are now absolute Masters of all that valuable Trade, which has enabled their Monarch hitherto to carry on the War against most of the Potentates of *Europe,* which otherwise could not be done."

To cut the enemy's overseas lifeline, Queen Anne encouraged the privateers. They were patriotic enough, but they wanted their money back. In 1707 the queen surrendered all government shares in their booty. This sweet union of patriotism and profit induced a group of Bristol investors to strike Spain where her armor was thinnest — in the South Sea. The list read like a register of town fathers: three mayors, the borough clerk, two sheriffs, the revered past Master of the powerful Merchant Venturers, a prominent Quaker who did not scruple at a little honest pillage, and the town's leading physician, who guarded his large investment by going on the voyage himself.

Bristol men had been privateering for three centuries, and knew every trick of the hazardous trade. "There never was any voyage of this nature so happily adjusted," thought an early historian, "so well provided for in all respects, or in which the accidents, that usually happen in privateers, were so effectually guarded against." The "accidents" were scurvy, inevitable as the fall of night, and mutiny, almost as sure.

Scurvy plagued any voyage that strayed more than a month from shore. Gums softened, teeth fell out, black blotches grew under the skin, the heart weakened, absolute lethargy set in. Men moved in a dream, if they moved at all. At the shout to set sail they reached for the rope with the weaving concentration of a drunkard aiming for the bottle. Sooner or later they dropped exhausted and were slung down the hatch to their hammocks, where they lay, eyes glazed and fingers fishing aimlessly at their swollen bodies, until they died.[2] To prevent this

[2] Scurvy's frightful toll for three hundred years provides one of the most pitiable examples of stubborn ignorance to be found in all medical history. Although John Woodall's 1636 survey of naval medicine, *The Surgeon's Mate,*

horror, or ease it at least, the Bristol owners put six medical
men aboard the ships. Leyden-trained James Wasse, "a very
honest useful man" skilled in both medicine and surgery, took
charge in the *Duchess*, with two orderlies to help him; apothecary Samuel Hopkins and surgeon John Ballet were assigned to
the *Duke*. Dr. Thomas Dover, the bristly physician who had
put money into the voyage, presided over the entire medical
staff.[3]

The owners met the threat of mutiny by doubling the usual
complement of officers. As commander of the *Duke* Rogers was
backed by a second captain, a master, three lieutenants and a
trio of mates. Captain Stephen Courtney of the *Duchess* had
Edward Cooke as second captain, three lieutenants (of whom
one was Woodes Rogers' younger brother, John), a master, and
no less than five mates. Each ship carried an owners' agent:
Carleton Vanbrugh on the *Duke*, William Bath aboard the
Duchess. Not all the officers were seasoned mariners, to be
sure. In keeping with England's tradition that every one of her
sons had saltwater in his veins, Rogers' second in command, Dr.
Dover, hardly knew a bight from a binnacle; two of his mid-

---

recommended daily orange juice as an antidote, 159 years passed before the
British navy made it official. Meanwhile an estimated 800,000 British seamen
died, most of them needlessly. We now know that the remedy is ascorbic acid
(vitamin C). An ounce of citrus juice daily will supply it, and leafy vegetables
are also useful, as well as some more easily preserved, such as potatoes and
onions. The beef-and-bread diet of early ships grievously lacked this necessary
ingredient. By a controlled experiment Dr. James Lind established the fact in
1747, and published it to the world in 1753, yet in 1779 the Channel fleet came
in from a ten-weeks cruise and put 2400 scurvy-ridden seamen into shore hos-
pitals. When the Admiralty finally prescribed citrus juice on all naval vessels
in 1795, scurvy vanished overnight.

[3] Medical opinion in the early eighteenth century was a frightening jumble
of superstition, guesswork and common sense. In the hierarchy of its practice
the university-educated physician occupied a place of lordly grandeur. Usually
he began practice without ever having seen a patient, and rarely condescended
to do so thereafter unless the patient was rich. This inferior role was left to
the apothecary, who waited on the physician at a coffeehouse and paid him
for his diagnosis. Surgeons were, literally, sawbones, not much more knowl-
edgeable than the barbers from whom their profession emerged, and were
forbidden (ashore) to operate without a physician present. Often ships carried
only a surgeon for the essential functions of amputation, bone setting and
wound dressing.

shipmen were young lawyers hungry for adventure before settling to their dusty briefs; and the steward had dealt in oil before sea fever struck him. They would beat into shape. If all
the officers hung together and kept their pistols handy, they
could snuff out any petty insurrection in the crew.

They might not hang together, of course. Many a voyage
had been ruined by violent disagreement among the officers.
To avoid this, the *Duke* and *Duchess* sailed under a written
Constitution which stipulated an officers' committee on each
ship and a joint council for both. On the strength of his large
investment in the venture, Dr. Dover had pushed his way to
chairmanship of the council, with a double vote in case of deadlock. But the man who had to be consulted in any decision of
major importance was their "Pilot for the South Sea," Captain
William Dampier.[4]

Lean, long-jawed, moody Captain Dampier had already circled the globe twice. In 1680 he joined the wild scramble of
buccaneers that debouched into the Pacific across Darien, and
had come home after a twelve-year odyssey around the world
with two assets: a tattooed native prince whom he hoped to
exhibit for a fee, and the intensive notes of his wanderings, kept
dry from tropic rains and river fords in wax-sealed bamboo
cases. He sold the prince to fend off starvation, and converted
the notes into two classic volumes of travel to strange shores:
A New Voyage Round the World (1697), and *Voyages and
Discoveries* (1699). In 1699 he explored along the west coast
of Australia; in 1703 he once more privateered around the
world. No Englishman could match his knowledge of lands,
currents and winds in eastern waters. But he had twice quarreled with his officers, and had been courtmartialed out of any
naval command. The present cruise needed a commander who

---

4 Edward Cooke, second captain of the *Duchess*, credits Dampier with originat-
ing interest in the enterprise. He pushed the idea, says Cooke, " 'till he had
prevailed with some able Persons at Bristol to venture upon an Undertaking,
which might turn to a Prodigious Advantage." Rogers' narrative of the voyage,
however, is dedicated to the Bristol merchants who "did me the Honour to
approve my Proposals for the following Voyage."

could be both mild in controversy and bold in attack. Dampier was neither. For those requisites, Woodes Rogers was exactly the man.

He came of a solid East Dorset family. Old John Rogers had been sheriff there in the time of Queen Bess, had sat in her Parliament and been knighted by her, and had rested since in his marble tomb in the Blandford church, where the stained light glowed through his arms etched in the leaded panes. Though born in Poole, Woodes Rogers was Bristol-trained — a point to his credit. For a seven-year apprenticeship he had studied the complex art of seamanship with a respected captain of the port. In 1705 he married a Queen Square neighbor girl, Admiral Whetstone's daughter Sarah, who had presented him with offspring at becoming intervals: little Sarah, 1706, William in 1707 and Mary 1708 (who died in childhood), all properly baptized in the medieval church of St. Nicholas. By marriage he was now a free man of Bristol, privileged to vote for Parliament and to trade at will.[5] His sea captain father's death had left him the Queen Square house, and his small legacy went into a pottery across the Froom, at the foot of Brandon Hill.

However, the owners had chosen him for reasons less visible. Beneath his staid manner ran a deep current of idealism, like a distant river, underground. *Je ferai mon devoir*, read the family motto in the Blandford church. He would do his duty, regardless of personal distress. If Louis of France was dragging out the war on Spanish goods, then leave wife and child, beat round the Horn, risk strange seas, but strike at the root. He would serve the owners' interest with the same selfless fidelity. A man to endure all weather, they agreed. So they bypassed Dampier, Courtney, Cooke and a score of competent Bristol captains, to put this untried young man in command.

---

[5] Prior to male suffrage in 1832, about one Bristol citizen in ten achieved this enviable status. It was gained by being born in the town son of a free man, by marrying a free man's daughter, by seven years of apprenticeship to a free man, or by paying a sum commensurate with one's station.

A commander, Woodes knew, can be little better than his ships and men. As they eased down the Bristol Channel in the late afternoon of August 1, 1708, he was chagrined to see that other vessels, likewise bound west for Cork, showed the *Duke* and *Duchess* their heels. "Our Masts and Rigging being all unfit for the Sea, our Ships out of trim," he lamented, they tagged dolefully behind the rest of the fleet. They were poorly manned as well: too few hands, too many green landsmen and waterside vagrants, "not 20 Sailors in the Ship." An ill-omened beginning. The ships blindly groped into Cork through fog that blotted out their mastheads, and for a week lay buffeted by whipping winds and drenched by rains.

However, ten sunny days followed. They hastened to shift gear, stow last-minute provisions, tallow bottoms and recruit men. Forty of their Bristol crew vanished into Cork taverns or were dismissed, and 150 new hands hired. Crewmen married Irish biddies with the careless abandon of soldiers doomed to the cannon's mouth. At parting, Rogers observed, the couples "drank their can of Flip till the last minute, concluding with a Health to our good Voyage, and their happy Meeting, and then parted unconcerned." Only a gloomy Dane, who had won an Irish girl as deficient in Danish as he in English, took his vows seriously. The two parted with tears, and the Dane moped about the ship for days, desolate at losing his love as soon as he found her.

On the morning of September 1 the man-of-war *Hastings* shepherded a twenty-ship convoy south from the spit end of Cork. Rogers noted with satisfaction that his ships now sailed as well as any, "crouded and pester'd" as they were with new hands. He had 181 men on the *Duke* and 153 on the *Duchess*, a third foreigners, "Tinkers, Taylors, Haymakers, Pedlers, Fidlers, etc. one Negro, and about ten Boys." They would have to do. He could teach them the use of firearms and "bring them to discipline" as soon as they got their sea legs. Some might be squeamish about so long a voyage, of course; Rogers thought it best to tell them while still in convoy, so that "we might have exchang'd our Malcontents whilst in Company with one of Her Majesty's Ships." Four days at sea he called all hands aft and announced that they would be cruising to the South Sea. For how long? Two or three years, perhaps. One fellow complained that he was to be tithing man in his parish that year, and if he failed to show up for it, his wife would have to pay the forty-shilling tax. The rest simply stared until he quieted, and "all Hands drank to a good Voyage."

Under the bright clear night sky of September 6 the *Duke* and *Duchess* saluted the *Hastings* and bore away south on a brisk wind, in company with the Madeira-bound *Crown Galley*. The voyage had begun. How many would come back whole and sound? How many would go over the side in a canvas shroud? Let God decide.

Possibly the steward should have stuck to peddling oil. He allowed the ships to leave Ireland short on liquor, a mistake that could only be made, it would seem, by a violent effort. For seamen, liquor was one of the grand processions of nature, like the trade winds or the Gulf Stream. Seamen without a nip of spirits were no better than plumbers without kits — they could not be expected to work seriously at their trade. "Now we begin to consider the Length of our Voyage," Rogers reasoned, "and the many different climates we must pass, and the excessive Cold which we cannot avoid, going about Cape Horne; at the same time we had but a slender Stock of Liquor, and our Men but meanly clad, yet good Liquor to Sailors is preferable to Clothing." Exactly, as any masthand would testify: if you were warm enough inside, it didn't matter how much you puckered outside with the cold; and, strangely enough, the obverse was equally true: when the sky was brassy, and the sun melted tar out of the deck seams, nothing cooled like a can of spirits. Rogers called a general council to ponder the low state of this strengthening element in their diet. The council's duty was clear: lay course for Madeira, where the white wine was tangy as a summer breeze, next to the Cape Verdes for more of the same, then strike down the Atlantic to Grande Island in Brazil.[6] All officers present signed the order, Rogers in a clear bold hand, with a slight romantic flourish.

Next day at dawn they glimpsed a white square of topsail dead ahead and clapped on all canvas in pursuit. By midafternoon the *Duke* was close enough to put a shot over the stranger. She hove to, and broke out the colors of neutral Sweden. Rogers took a dozen men aboard to make search. Although a drunken seaman on the Swede whispered that she had contraband lining her keel, he could turn up nothing questionable. To prove her a legal prize would necessitate emptying her hold in port — a time-consuming distraction — and if the Swede was innocent, Rogers could draw an embarrassing fine. He let her go.

The *Duke*'s crew raised a howl of protest as the Swede made sail. Whipped on by a coxswain named Cash, an angry knot of men clustered at the forecastle. Rogers could see their hunched backs leaning toward the voluble Cash, and the looks of disgust that they threw over their shoulders toward the quarterdeck. He quietly called the officers aft, handed out pistols, and they advanced down the waist of the ship in solid force. The mutineers broke up, sullen but helpless. Rogers put ten of them in irons, and saw to it that one abusive fellow was drubbed with a rope's end. Then he summoned the rest of the crew to the mainmast where he carefully explained why it was inadvisable to seize the Swedish ship.

The grumblers were willing to forget the Swede, but keeping their cherished coxswain in irons was another matter. In a few days half the crew lined up at the steerage to demand his release. Rogers had to win this early battle of discipline or risk chaos for the whole voyage. He called the spokesman to the quarterdeck, tied him to the rail, and had him lashed until his bare back rose in welts. The men had seen enough; they

[6] All these islands were possessions of England's ally, Portugal.

trooped away in silence to their posts. Cash, obviously, was going to be more trouble than the voyage could bear. Rogers sent him aboard the *Crown Galley,* to be put ashore at Madeira, and after a few days took the rest of the culprits out of irons on their promise of good behavior. He had chased down his first prize and smothered his first mutiny, both hopeful signs. "Fine pleasant Weather, and moderate Gales," concluded his journal entry for the day.

Pursuit of the Swede had carried them past Madeira. The council elected for the Canaries instead, those Fortunate Isles of the ancients, where nymphs guarded the golden apples, and Hesiod's dead heroes made their eternal home. As morning broke on September 17 the voyagers spied Tenerife's green, cloud-sheltered peak and below it, toward Fuerteventura, a sail. She was a small Spanish barque blessed with two butts of wine, a hogshead of brandy, and four friars among her forty-five passengers. All were relieved to be captured by Christians rather than heartless Turks, and the chief friar, "a good honest old Fellow," ready to toast anyone for the sake of a drink, downed his wine with gusto when Rogers gravely proposed the health of Archduke Charles of Austria.

Jollity, however, put no money in the bank. The vessel was Spanish, the passengers were Spanish, and some profit should be made from them. At the port of Tenerife, Rogers prepared to send in a boat oared by prisoners, and carrying a friar as his emissary to the local government. He had no intention of handing the Spanish a hostage, but the *Duke's* brash agent, Vanbrugh, insisted on going along. Vanbrugh was sure that he alone could represent all those august Bristol owners totting up their accounts at home, he alone could strike a favorable bargain where other men bungled. Rogers reasoned, Vanbrugh became vehement; finally, he went. Ashore the Spanish authorities welcomed the agent to their bosoms, and locked him up.

Next morning the boat brought out from the town three nervous English dealers in Canary wine. A letter from the English vice-consul begged Rogers to remember that by agreement between the English and Spanish sovereigns these islands were outside the continental war, and should not be molested. Hostile acts on Rogers' part would injure the wine trade with England, and surely invite reprisals against her citizens in the islands. The proper thing was to free the barque at once. Vanbrugh was being held by Spanish authorities until this was done.

Rogers framed a courteous but firm answer to this plea. The privateers had no instructions to spare the Canaries, he said; furthermore, the barque had been taken in the open sea. As for Vanbrugh, Rogers would release the passengers in return for him, but barque and cargo had to be ransomed. "It was Mr. Vanbrugh's misfortune to go ashore; and if he is detain'd, we can't help it." The ships awaited prompt reply.

At sunset the boat brought them what Rogers brushed aside as "dilatory Answers to our last." The Spanish were up to their beloved game of haggling. They would ransom the barque, yes, but insisted that he surrender the cargo. He fired back a sharp ultimatum: produce supplies worth 450 Spanish dollars by eight o'clock tomorrow or he would bombard the town. This sobered the hagglers. As the ships stood for shore next morning with guns run out, a longboat hastened to meet them, loaded with wine, hogs, grapes — and Vanbrugh. Placated, Rogers returned the friars' books and beads, and bestowed a plump head of cheese on the jolly old winebibber. By afternoon the ships struck south across Tenerife's broad shadow toward the Cape Verdes.

Vanbrugh was furious at Rogers' willingness to abandon him in the Canaries. Both inhumane and contrary to the best interests of the voyage, he cried, buttonholing anyone who would listen. He got little sympathy. A council dining aboard the *Duke* approved all actions taken at Tenerife. After the brandy went round, they hammered the point home in a second motion: "Whereas there has been some Difference between Capt.

Woodes Rogers and Mr. Carleton Vanbrugh the Ship's Agent; it being refer'd to the Council, we adjudg'd the said Mr. Vanbrugh to be much in the wrong." As well try to cap a volcano; Vanbrugh merely subsided until the next eruption.

To the crew, who worried not a whit about Vanbrugh, the young voyage was still something of a lark. On September 25 Rogers took a sighting on the sun, called the boatswain to the steerage, and informed him in sepulchral tones that the ships stood under the Tropic of Cancer. Old hands lined up sixty culprits charged with previous failure to cross the line. A toothless ogre of a judge heard the evidence with a great show of horror at such intolerable evil, and sentenced the lot of them to death by drowning. Driven to the main yard, they crept to a rope attached to its end, straddled the cross-board, and were plummeted into the water in a spout of foam. After each was hauled up dripping and blowing for the third time, the judge pronounced glum pardon over him and let him live. Rogers watched the fun with his faint smile. The ducking, he noted, "prov'd of great use to our fresh-water Sailors, to recover the Colour of their Skins which were grown very black and nasty."

Really good-hearted fellows under their dirt, thought Rogers. Unpredictable though, flighty as children. Sooner or later — no avoiding it — he would have to put muskets into their hands. Two hundred men with muskets! it made his skin crawl. He could predict one thing of these bogtrotters: if they did not like their share of plunder they would take their muskets off the enemy and train them on their own officers. Shares set by the articles allotted twenty-four to a captain, sixteen to a first lieutenant, ten to a surgeon, descending then through all grades to two and a half for a seasoned hand and one and a half for a green landman. The owners would gobble up a huge two-thirds of all clear booty, leaving but a third for the men who would win it with their blood.

"We found," Rogers jotted in his journal, "it would be next to a miracle to keep the Men in both Ships under Command, and willing to fight resolutely on occasion, if we held 'em to the Letter of Agreement with the Owners, which was not duly consider'd of at home." If a sacrifice was to be made, Rogers would be first to make it. *Je ferai mon devoir.* By custom a captain took cabin plunder, a profitable right, since jewels and coin often lay for safekeeping in the cabin of a captured ship. At the Cape Verdes on October 8 Rogers told the council that "for the Good of the Voyage" he would surrender his cabin plunder as a move to forestall "continual Scenes of Mischief and Disorder." [7] That night the ships sailed out of St. Vincent harbor, past the ghostly sugarloaf of Monk's Rock, to point south for the long haul to Brazil.

Rogers was almost at once in the case of poor Job — "the thing which I greatly feared has come upon me" — for the very mischief and disorder which he dreaded rose in the person of Page, the abusive mate of the *Duchess.* Amiable Captain Courtney simply could not put up with the fellow any longer. In the middle of the Atlantic, Rogers and Courtney decided that a change of ships might help; Page could come aboard the *Duke,* and John Ballet, who doubled as surgeon and third mate, could take his place on the *Duchess.* Page would have none of it; he refused. When Second Captain Cooke ordered him to pack up, he refused. The boat came alongside; he refused to get into it. Cooke hit him a clout, and the two of them brawled across the deck until other officers leaped in and forced Page over the side, Cooke after him in a panting fury.

A mutinous officer could not be tolerated; worse than an unruly seaman, he corrupted the whole command. Into bilboes on the *Duke*'s forecastle went Page, under guard of an armed corporal and in full sight of the surprised crew. He did not stay long. Soon he begged the corporal to be a good fellow, let him relieve himself in the head. Why not? the corporal loosened his

[7] Gentlemanly Stephen Courtney of the *Duchess* joined him at once in giving up cabin plunder. Rogers estimated his own personal loss at ten times the value of his shares.

shackles. In an instant Page kicked off his shoes and was over the side. By the time the boat crew scrambled down the ladder, he was swimming strongly for the *Duchess*. He dove underwater to escape his pursuers, bobbing up unexpectedly and wrenching at their oar blades, until the boat crew hauled him inboard, swearing and spewing saltwater. Back on the *Duke*, Rogers had him whipped with a rope's end and put in irons.

Mischief and disorder, groaned Rogers, enough to drive a man to prayer. He established daily services, according to the Prayer Book, on both ships. It helped, no doubt, to bring them safe to the steep cove of Grande Island on November 20, but did not save further nuisance during their stay. After six weeks in the crowded ships the men were wild to be ashore. When Rogers forbade it, fearing both desertions and malaria, one *Duchess* seaman let it be known that he intended to put solid ground under his feet no matter what the commander said. The *Duchess* lieutenant threw him into the brig. Seven others demanded his release or the pleasure of joining him, so the brig now had eight. At dusk two more slipped down the anchor cable and swam to the island, but weird night sounds drove them back into the water up to their knees, where they screeched for a boat, "begging for God's sake to be brought aboard, or they should be devour'd." Probably no more than the harmless hooting of monkeys, recorded Rogers. Into the brig they went, and that made ten.

Mischief and disorder; if there was not enough of it, Vanbrugh could be counted on for more. One dawn the *Duke*'s watch hailed a canoe gliding furtively across the cove. It made no answer, only dug its paddles deeper, and Rogers sent the pinnace in pursuit. Before Vanbrugh could be stopped he leaped aboard, rummaged the locker for muskets, and in the chase toppled one of the fugitive paddlers with a chance shot. When the pinnace caught the canoe on the beach, it turned out quite innocent: a friar bound for his cache of coins on the island, and stomping mad because he had lost 200 pieces of eight overboard in the confusion. Worse, the wounded boatman died in two hours. Rogers did his best to smooth matters, but the friar shouted that he would make the royal courts of Portugal and England ring with his grievances.

Even Rogers' patience ran out. He was so utterly weary of Vanbrugh's foolishness that a few days later the council thought it "necessary for the Good of our intended Voyage to remove Mr. Carleton Vanbrugh from being Agent of the Duke Frigate to be Agent of the Dutchess, and to receive Mr. William Bath Agent of the Dutchess in his Place." The exchange was quite fair; Rogers gave up a brainless hotspur and got, in Bath, a drunken sot.

Since the green slopes of Grande supplied only wood and water, provisions had to come in from the village of Angra, nine miles across the sluggish water of the mainland bay. Angra was little more than a string of mud-and-thatch huts at the waterside, overshadowed by two churches and a monastery. The tiny garrison greeted the ships' pinnaces with a splatter of musketry, thinking them enemy French, but was soon reassured, and the Portuguese governor welcomed them with profuse apologies. He hastened to tell Cooke that next day Angra was to celebrate the Conception of the Virgin. Would the ships' officers favor him with their presence? Cooke reminded him stiffly that they were Protestant to a man. No matter — the governor waved it aside — was there not one Christ for all? Was there not one God? Well, yes, since the governor put it that way. Cooke would relay the invitation to Captain Rogers.

The officers accepted, and fetched along a ragged little orchestra — two trumpets, a hautbois, and some fiddlers that would have delighted Nero. These clambered to the church gallery for the service, where they struck up "all manner of noisy, paltry Tunes" while the officers below struggled to keep their faces straight. Besides their instruments the musicians had brought their bottles, and were excellently attuned by the time the procession lined up after the benediction. They led it, tootling between nips and coughing outrageously at the smoking censers; next, four citizens of known uprightness bore on their shoulders the Virgin's image; forty priests followed, each clasping his missal; while Angra's petty officialdom and their English guests carried long burning tapers in the rear. After the village had been crisscrossed with prayers and holy water, the friars entertained the Englishmen with sweetmeats at the monastery.

In return, the privateers dined Angra's chief gentlemen aboard the *Duke*, with ecumenical toasts to the Pope, the Archbishop of Canterbury and, for the sake of Dissenters, William Penn. "At parting," runs Rogers' thrifty note, "we saluted 'em with a Huzza from each Ship, because we were not overstocked with Pouder." The ships were ready to sail: bottoms scraped, mainmasts re-rigged; limes, fowl and corn loaded in; as well as what Rogers called "necessaries for our next long Voyage," namely, liquor. On December 3 they dropped the notched peak of Grande behind them and made south under a brisk gale.

Inside the Falklands three weeks later the sea darkened with forebodings of Antarctica: murky water, fog, flaws slapping the canvas from every direction. Albatross coasted in their wake, and cold-water porpoises shook white bellies in the bleak intermittent sunlight. The officers gave up their extra clothing to be altered for the men, and the tailors, who had spent weeks cutting rough garments from blanket cloth, stitched faster than ever. On New Year's Day, in a brief respite of following winds and calmer seas, the musicians marched up and down the *Duke* saluting each officer with a blary tune. The men dipped their pint from a tub of hot punch to drink health "to a happy new Year, a good Voyage, and a safe Return." From the bulwark they sent three huzzas echoing across the gray water toward the *Duchess*, and heard three, faint but cheery, in response.

It was their last moment of comfort for two weeks. By noon

14. A late seventeenth-century painting by Van de Velde shows an English ship *Kingfisher* engaging 'Barbary' pirates. (National Maritime Museum, Greenwich)

15. Captain Woodes Rogers and his children, a portrait painted in 1728 by Hogarth; the only known portrait of the privateer. (National Maritime Museum, Greenwich)

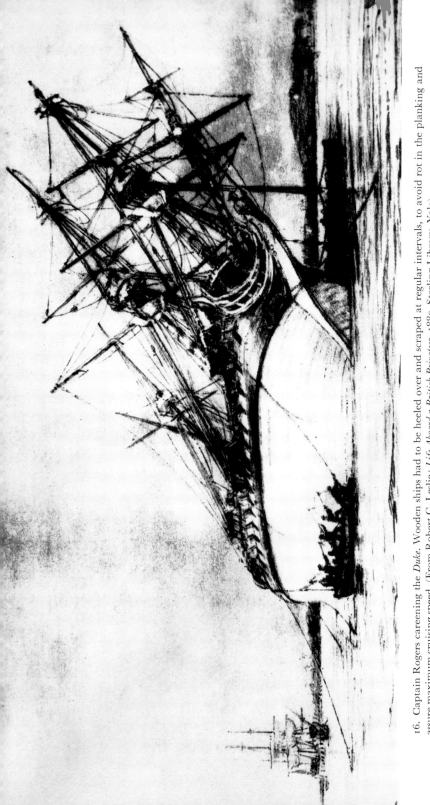

16. Captain Rogers careening the *Duke*. Wooden ships had to be heeled over and scraped at regular intervals, to avoid rot in the planking and assure maximum cruising speed. (From Robert C. Leslie: *Life Aboard a British Privateer*, 1889. Sterling Library, Yale)

on January 6 the seas of the Horn pitched about them like watery alps. Great sheets of spray stung men aloft and whitened their fingers as they clung to the yards. All that afternoon the ships drove before the gale, wallowing in immense valleys and rising on vast slopes, with no more canvas set than would keep the tiller steady.[8]

"A little before six we saw the Dutchess lowering her Main-Yard," Rogers recorded. "The Tack flew up and the Lift unreev'd, so that the Sail to Leeward was in the water and all a-back, their Ship took in a great deal of Water to Leeward; immediately they loos'd their Sprit-sail, and wore her before the Wind: I wore after her, and came as near as I could to 'em, expecting when they had gotten their Main-Sail stow'd they would take another Reef in, and bring to again under a two-reef'd Main-Sail, and reef'd and ballanc'd Mizen, if the Ship would not keep to without it; but to my surprise they kept scudding to the Southward. I dreaded running amongst Ice, because it was excessively cold; so I fir'd a Gun as a Signal for them to bring to, and brought to our selves again under the same reef'd Main-Sail. They kept on, and our Men on the lookout told me they had an Ensign in the Maintop-Mast Shrouds as a Signal of Distress, which made me doubt they had sprung their Main-Mast; so I wore again, our Ship working exceeding well in this great Sea. Just before night I was up with them again, and set our Fore-Sail twice reef'd to keep 'em Company, which I did all night. About three this morning it grew more moderate; we soon after made a Signal to speak with them, and at five they brought to: when I came within haile, I enquir'd how they all did aboard; they answer'd, they had ship'd a great

[8] Unsure of any passage southward Drake, Cavendish and other early captains followed Magellan's route through the 330-mile straits between the great island of Tierra del Fuega and the South American mainland. It was disadvantaged by being narrow, tidal, shelterless, and swept by sudden flaws from the steep mountains along its course. In 1615 a Dutchman, James Le Maire, ventured through the wide passage which bears his name, between the coast of Tierra del Fuega and Staten Island. Even this gave too little sea room for Rogers, who kept still further south through open water halfway to Antarctica.

deal of Water in lying by, and were forc'd to put before the Wind, and the Sea had broke in the Cabin-Windows, and over their Stern, filling their Steerage and Waste, and had like to have spoil'd several Men; but God be thank'd all was otherwise indifferent well with 'em, only they were intolerably cold, and everything wet." Clothes hung to dry all over the *Duchess*'s rigging had frozen to boardlike stiffness. But she was orderly, and had put six heavy guns into her hold for more ballast. The sea that pooped her had all but drowned some of the officers like rats in a hole. They were sitting down to a hasty bite of hot supper as the stern windows crashed in. The forward bulkhead fortunately burst, and everything movable washed helter-skelter down the deck in a tumble of debris, including a sword which the wave's shock had driven through a rolled-up rug.

South and south the ships drove through rain, sleet, head-on gales, towering seas, in the unblinking day of the Antarctic summer. Scurvy put seven men where they would never reef sail again, and more were sick. At latitude 61.53 degrees they bore west at last; by January 15 they were beyond the Horn and had risen to latitude 56. Rogers jotted down a laconic entry: "We now account our selves in the South-Sea."

Exhausted by the miseries of the Horn, the crew hated any sea that one could name, the whole liquid, impenetrable world of ceaseless motion and empty horizons on which they tossed, and longed only for stable earth underfoot and a bit of green food in their stomachs. Dampier held the ships close in along the continent until he hit on a familiar landmark, then set course due west 400 miles for the islands known as Juan Fernández. On January 31 the nearest of them, *Más a Tierra*, showed its ragged outline on their port bow.

Getting in against the faint contrary breeze was deadly slow. Twelve miles out and no nearer, hardly a ripple at the bow. Dover argued for trying with the pinnace. In the early afternoon it was hoisted out, but he did little better on the flat sea, and at nightfall was still three miles from his destination. As darkness settled, a large fire blazed up landward. Dover made about at once and returned to the ships. One could only guess that French or Spanish were bivouacked in the bay.

The ships jogged off and on southward through the night, and next morning were able to run back up the island to make the bay. Not an enemy ship in sight, but Rogers thought that they might have slipped out in alarm and left a holding garrison behind. At noon the yawl put in carrying Dover, the *Duke*'s mate Robert Frye, and six armed men, while the ships, beaten by gusts off the island, stood out to sea.

The yawl did not return. Alarmed, Rogers sent the pinnace after it, loaded with musketeers. The pinnace did not return. Now frantic with worry, Rogers ran up signal flags, while the *Duchess*, in a vain gesture, put out a French ensign. The pinnace launched from shore at last and, along with a welcome load of crayfish, brought the lone cause of their distress — a barefoot, heavily bearded man, dressed in goatskins. His eye had a remote, inward look; his speech was choked and broken, as though something clogged his throat. Who was he? Alexander Selkirk, a Scot, Dover explained. How long had he been on the island? Four years and four months; the man had kept exact count by marking sticks of wood. How in heaven's name had he gotten there? Seems that he had been master of the *Cinque Ports* —. No need to go further; Dampier knew him well.

Dampier fished back into his memory. Late summer of 1704, it must have been, Bay of Panama — Dampier captain of the privateer *St. George*, Stradling commanding her consort the *Cinque Ports*, this Alexander Selkirk her master. Dampier and Stradling had a difference of opinion — wretched fellow, Stradling — the *Cinque Ports* had deserted — deserted was the only word for it — gone south to coast along Peru. In September the *Cinque Ports* caulked up at Juan Fernández. Selkirk quarreled with Stradling there, claimed the repairs were haphazard and the ship still leaky as a barge, and if Stradling insisted on

putting out in her, he could go to the bottom alone.[9] Just leave
Selkirk safe ashore. Very well, blast you, growled Stradling.
He dumped Selkirk and his sea chest on the beach. Selkirk
hoped that other malcontents would move to join him, but none
did. When the ship's boat launched from shore, leaving him
quite solitary, he waded into the surf and shouted after it that
he had changed his mind. I haven't changed mine, Stradling
shouted back; stay where you are, and may you starve.

At first, overwhelming loneliness had troubled Selkirk far
more than bodily discomfort. For weeks he ate only when
hunger drove him, and slept only when he could no longer
watch. He pored over his Bible, prayed for rescue, repented all
sins remembered or forgotten, and was in general more devout
than he had ever been or, he shrewdly guessed, would ever be
again. Gradually he got used to his solitude, and almost liked
it. Two trim huts, grass-covered without and lined with skins
within, served him as living quarters and cookhouse. When his
clothes fell to rags he made more of goatskin, using a nail for
needle and raveled stockings for thread. His knife wore to the
handle; he ground new blades from discarded barrel hoops. As
the soles of his bare feet toughened and his scant store of ammunition gave out, he simply ran down his quarry on foot.
More than four years on Juan Fernández left him lean, agile
and robust.

Rogers hurried his men ashore in hope that a sojourn on the
island would treat them as well. Fifty of them were knocked
out by some degree of scurvy. Those who could walk tottered
on trembling legs to the waiting boats; those who could not,
stared feebly as they were hoisted up through the hatch and
lowered over the side in a canvas sling. Selkirk played host,
and Juan Fernández proved as good as a dinner table spread on
the tropic sea. A few goats left by the Spaniards had multiplied
to great flocks; buccaneer ship parties had planted turnips and

[9] A sound estimate, for Stradling soon ran the *Cinque Ports* aground in the
Mapella Islands in a sinking condition. Captured by the Spanish, the survivors
were thrown into Lima dungeons, and Stradling spent six years behind bars
in Peru and France before he escaped.

parsley for their next stopover, and these throve; wild cabbage dotted the forest, shellfish swarmed the shore. The men smacked their lips over young seal — as good as English lamb, they declared — and picked their teeth with the whiskers of sea lion. Snug in tents strewn with leaves fragrant as balm, fed on strengthening goat-meat soup mixed with greens, the sick recovered at marvelous speed.[10]

Balm indeed, this lotus land, but the privateers had come for more negotiable goods. After two weeks in the grassy valleys of Juan Fernández they loaded the last wood, dipped up the last barrel of water from the bright streams, and on February 13 made sail on a fair breeze for the coast of Peru.

Snow-capped mountains daubing the eastern horizon announced that the privateers had come for the first time into waters of the chase. They heeled and tallowed on the placid sea, and rigged the pinnaces with pursuit guns. The council appointed reliable hands to search all boarders returning from a prize. Gambling was outlawed "to prevent men losing all they had," swearing was forbidden as well, the officers being armed with "ferulas" to rap any foul-mouthed fellow, "by which we found the men much broken of that vice."

Two weeks of tedious patrol without a catch made these precautions look like a sorry joke. Rogers worried about crew morale: "Our Men begin to repine, that tho come so far, we have met with no Prize in these Seas." On March 15 a scrap of

---

[10] Including the recuperative visit to Juan Fernández, Rogers lost but eleven men by sickness or mishap up to that point, a remarkable record. Crossing the Atlantic, one seaman fell from the main yard without a sound and disappeared overboard; another on the *Duchess* broke his skull falling from the mizzen top; seven died of illness doubling the Horn, and two more at Juan Fernández. Of scurvy Rogers casually remarked that "the Methods to prevent the ill Effects of it are so well known, that they may easily be provided against," without offering the least indication what those methods were. We note, however, that he took on limes at Grande, and may have put lime juice into the punch which he heartily commended to all. Dover handed down his own Olympian verdict: give the men alum, mixed with wine. "This I have experienced for thirty-five years," he said later, "and do not remember that it ever failed"; a strange testimony, since alum is useless for the purpose.

a vessel, a sixteen-tonner, sailed innocently under their guns. She wasn't much, but she was a beginning and Rogers renamed her that. She would come in handy as courier, or for river work. He took her along to the inshore Lobos Islands where next night, by the light of a full moon, they anchored.

The gaunt clay islands were named for their combative breed of seal — *lobos marinos,* sea wolves — noisy, stinking brutes, so fierce that one of them painfully mauled a Dutchman off the *Duke,* and nearly dragged him to his death in the surf. A large bird that Cooke shot as turkey turned out to be vulture, smelling worse than the seal.[11] However unpleasant, the Lobos provided moorage to fit out the *Beginning* for action. Rogers stepped in a new mast, decked her over, put a well-armed crew aboard, and sent her out to scour nearby waters with the *Duchess.* "She looks very pretty," he thought. Soon the two were back in with a fifty-ton prize. Rogers aptly named this one the *Increase,* and appointed Selkirk her master. The few sick were put aboard her, she was taken in tow by the *Duke,* and the four-ship flotilla sailed north from Lobos.

On April 1 their bows cut through ominous waters of blood-red spawn, but next day they gave — or seemed to give — this omen the lie by capturing two prizes as bloodlessly as one could wish. The *Ascensión,* owned and commanded by the brothers Morel, showed her sail seaward at dawn and struck colors, at a musket shot, before the sun was halfway up the sky. "I saw not so much as a Pistol in her," reported Cooke. A high-pooped galleon of 450 tons, she carried a load of timber and dry goods, some Spanish passengers, and fifty Negro slaves. That evening the *Beginning* took a thirty-five-ton coaster, equally unarmed, with £95 in coin and plate aboard.

11 One of these repulsive carrion-eaters added to Vanbrugh's disgrace. He shot it, gagged on the odor, and ordered a seaman to carry it back to the shore for him. Since Vanbrugh was not an officer, the seaman could, and did, refuse. Vanbrugh loudly threatened to shoot him. For this, and for some abusive language directed at Dover, Vanbrugh was removed from the council. He tried to save himself by a contemptible bit of under-the-table politicking: a whispered promise to Rogers that if allowed to keep his seat, he would thereafter side with the commander on all votes. Rogers declined.

Being themselves caught, the prisoners gabbled eagerly of bigger fish still aswim. A bishop worth 200,000 pieces of eight was coming in easy stages from Panama; the widow of Peru's late viceroy was bound up from Lima with the whole fat treasure of her husband's office. Rogers spread the six ships in a sea net for a week, eyes glued to the horizon, but neither appeared. By April 12 water was in short supply, and their position close in to the coast daily increased the danger of a general alarm.[12] The officers decided that if they must land on the continent they might as well attack it, and resolved to storm the north Peru port of Guayaquil.

The crewmen greeted this decision with sullen murmurs of discontent. They were seamen, they argued, and would fight any ship afloat, but they had not signed on with the intention of storming towns ashore. Rogers thought it best to encourage them a bit more; grumblers would make a poor assault party. The council proceeded to expand its rules on plunder:

> Imprim. All manner of Bedding and Clothes without stripping, all manner of Necessaries, Gold Rings, Buckles, Buttons, Liquors, and Provisions for our own expending and use, with all sorts of Arms and Ammunition, except great Guns for Ships, is Plunder, and shall be divided equally amongst the Men of each Ship, with their Prizes, wither aboard or ashore, according to the whole Shares.
>
> 2. It is also agreed, that any sort of wrought Silver or Gold Crucifixes, Gold and Silver Watches, or any other Movables found about the Prisoners, or wearing Apparel of any kind, shall likewise be Plunder: Provided always we make this Reserve, that Mony and Womens Ear-Rings, with loose Diamonds, Pearls, and precious Stones be excepted.

Booty captured by one party, declared the council, would be

---

[12] Actually, inflated rumors of the expedition were arriving in Lima during that month. From his London spies Philip V of Spain had the news in April, 1708, but his warning did not reach Lima until March, 1709. The elderly viceroy, a Francophile who had built in Lima a hall of mirrors that emulated on small scale the great one at Versailles, posted warnings up and down the Peruvian coast, and specified that cattle and other portable provisions be sent inland, out of the marauders' reach.

shared by all. Every man had free and unhampered right of appeal before an impartial committee if he thought the division of spoil unfair. Should anyone be missing in action, hostages of the enemy would be held until he was accounted for.

These added benefits only strengthened responsibilities, the council warned. Drunkenness, disobedience to orders, cowardice in the face of danger, debauchery with prisoners, or concealment of plunder would, at the very least, deprive a man of his share. "If all the foregoing Rules be strictly follow'd," concluded the council, "we hope to exceed all other Attempts of this nature before us in these Parts; and not only to enrich and oblige our selves and Friends, but even to gain Reputation from our Enemies." Excellent resolve; if wars could be won on paper, the Spanish were already driven to their knees. Heartened, the flotilla moved off on the night of April 14 toward the wide gulf of Guayaquil.

The wind fell to a breeze, the breeze to a calm, and they drifted all night under limp, dew-drenched canvas. Dawn showed a ship miles eastward, as though risen from the glassy sea. Frye and Cooke took the two pinnaces after her. Men rushed gaily over the *Duke*'s side, John Rogers among them, and dug oars for the distant quarry. By nine o'clock the *Duke* pinnace, far in the lead, came within musket range. The Spaniard ran up a fringed white satin banner and fired a warning gun. Frye's crew cheered the white banner — surely the bishop clutching his pieces of eight! — but the gunshot sobered them. They shipped oars to await the other pinnace.

When Frye, Cooke and John Rogers put their heads together to devise a battle plan, they were aghast at their careless departure from the ships. Neither pinnace had bothered to mount its swivel gun or fetch water; both were thinly manned, some of the crew had not even brought muskets, and those who had were short of ammunition. There was nothing to do but board.

A stern-chase swivel gun poked over the Spaniard's taffrail, muskets sprouted from her cabin lights. On the chance that the bow would be more vulnerable, the attackers swung wide around the enemy and dashed for her bow quarter. Frye could see the bobbing heads of the musketeers as they ran through the waist of the ship to the forecastle. Halfway in, he backed oars and steadied to see if a volley from his men would clear the bow deck. Muskets blazed in return; a ball crashing into John Rogers' skull killed him instantly. Frye had another dead and two wounded from the enemy's single burst of fire, Cooke had two wounded in his boat.

The sight of blood running down their floorboards quickly put an end to their foolish attack. While Cooke stood guard out of range, the *Duke's* boat brought back to Woodes Rogers its sad cargo. "To my unspeakable Sorrow," he wrote in his journal, "but as I began this Voyage with a Resolution to go thro it, and the greatest Misfortune or Obstacle shall not deter me, I'll as much as possible avoid being thoughtful and afflicting my self for what can't be recall'd, but indefatigably pursue the Concerns of the Voyage, which has hitherto allow'd little Respite."

By midafternoon a light wind carried the *Duke* and *Duchess* within gunshot. The *Duchess* lobbed two shots over the Spaniard, who struck down her ensign without reply. Cooke ran his pinnace in at once. She was French-built, Captain José de Arizabala told him, still bore the French name *Havre de Grâce,* rated 270 tons, was cargoed with dry goods, plate and pearls, and carried fifty Spanish passengers and a hundred slaves. Although the *Havre* had but six guns aboard, she was ported for twenty-four, and was Lima-bound to fit out as a man-of-war.

Next day Woodes Rogers sat down to make a mournful entry in his journal. "About twelve," he wrote, "we read the Prayers for the Dead, and threw my dear Brother overboard, with one of our Sailors, another lying dangerously ill. We hoisted our Colours but half-mast up: We began first, and the rest follow'd, firing each some Volleys of small Arms. All our Officers express'd a great Concern for the Loss of my Brother, he being a very active hopeful young Man, a little above twenty Years of Age."

Tears would not bring John back; if they would, he could weep an ocean.

To reach Guayaquil they must penetrate an immense gulf, pass the low tangled growth of Puná Island, and make their way 30 miles up the Guayas River. The town was not much to look at — plank and bamboo houses squatting under church spires — and lay on boggy ground, but it boasted 2000 people, and was the foremost shipbuilding center on the Pacific coast. For a small force to take it, secrecy and surprise were essential.

The attack party would have to be reduced in order to secure the fleet, cumbered as it was with captured ships and more than 300 prisoners. Slaves and crewmen inclined to be docile, but the passengers, some of whom Cooke thought "the briskest Spaniards I ever saw," might plot an uprising. Rogers put most of these brisk gentlemen in irons. Don José Arizabala and a few others, too dangerous to leave behind, would go in with the assault boats. A hundred and eleven privateers stayed to work ships and stand guard. They would hold off to sea until the attack was well launched, then anchor at Point Arena, on the north side of the gulf, to await the return.

Rogers, Dover and Courtney split the remaining privateers into three commands of sixty-five men each. Every ten men had a leader, "the best and soberest Man we could pick," and every man pocketed a marked ticket to tell him which squad was his. At midnight on April 17 the ships stood to on a quiet sea, sixty miles from the gulf. Small boats lowered away, pinnaces and barques set oars to locks, men swung down the ropes, and from the decks Cooke and Frye bade them good hunting.

Through the dark early hours and all that day they rowed, until the night tide slowed them to anchor. At four o'clock next morning Rogers and Courtney took two small boats ahead to silence Puná. The barque would follow after a single tide. It was still daylight when they reached the flat, leafy lower end of the island and hid among the mangroves. When darkness fell they crept up the shore to the tiny settlement, pounced on it while it slept, secured its lieutenant, and knocked holes in every canoe drawn to the shallow beach.

The barque did not come up. The noon sun beat down like a white-hot hammer, and still the barque failed to appear. Rogers found it at four o'clock, wandering a dozen miles below Puná, unsure of its bearings. He loaded in what men he had room for and rowed away to rejoin Courtney and Dampier above Puná. The small boats pitched woefully as a fresh wind blew the dirty waters of the gulf into rollers. "I had rather be in a Storm at Sea than here," Rogers moaned. Again daylight had to be worn away batting mosquitoes in the steaming mangrove shallows. At six o'clock on April 21 they thanked God and put out oars for Guayaquil. A hundred and ten men with muskets — rarely had a thriving town been stormed by so few, and so feeble.

Rounding the point, they were dismayed to see all Guayaquil awake. Lights filled the streets, a great beacon fire blazed on the hill, church bells clanged, cannon boomed. A saint's-day fete? An alarm? No one knew. For an hour the boats lay on the dark surface of the river while the officers debated their next move. Rogers argued for going in at once, to take advantage of the confusion. He had little backing; most of the others thought that a night landing into crowded streets would be as confusing to the attackers as to the attacked. They turned for final opinion to the experienced Dampier, who told them that buccaneers never attacked an alerted town.[13] The tide was now

[13] Far from true; Morgan, for one, sacked four cities but surprised only Porto Bello. Dampier was a good navigator, an excellent hydrographer, an observant naturalist, and a poor fighter. On the privateering voyage of the *St. George* his midshipman accused him of abandoning command to lurk, in most cowardly fashion, behind a stout barricade of mattresses. By coincidence, Dampier arrived before Guayaquil under identical circumstances while buccaneering with Davis and Swan in 1684. The buccaneers retreated when they discovered the town alight with torches and candles. In his narrative of that withdrawal, Dampier reported with some scorn that it was only a religious festival, after all. (*Voyages* I, 179).

ebbing, and the barque unable to come up against it, Rogers could only agree to drop downriver, out of sight, for the time being.

Next morning, as the tide turned and the barque came up with reinforcements, Rogers again urged immediate attack. Dover held out for full consultation of all officers in a boat payed out astern of the barque, where they could discuss in private the most reasonable course. Dover was not bred to the iron; by "reasonable" he meant cautious. During the consultation he raised the specter of heavy losses should so small a force assault an alerted town, and argued that they should negotiate for ransom. He remained obdurate when the majority voted with Rogers to go in without delay. Rogers himself, Dover grimly warned, would be responsible for any disastrous results. A minority sided with him, and Rogers saw that a halfhearted landing would be worse than none. He reluctantly agreed to give negotiation a try. Don José and the Puná lieutenant went into Guayaquil for this purpose, armed with the threat that if they had not returned in an hour's time, the attack would proceed. The boats followed and stood off the quay.

Within an hour the emissaries came out with their reply: the governor would negotiate. Not that it was in the slightest degree necessary, the governor had informed them. Was he not Don Jerónimo Bosa y Solis y Pacheco, Knight of the Order of Santiago, and an officer in His Most Catholic Majesty's victorious army? Had he not 1000 horse and foot at his muster in Guayaquil? These invaders, he scoffed, were mere boys; he could sweep them into the river with a brush of his hand. Still, if they had the good sense to refrain from hostilities, he would graciously deign to negotiate.

The governor rowed out that afternoon, and a comfortable discussion went on until five o'clock. It was all immensely promising: the town would ransom itself for 50,000 pieces of eight and would buy the perishable goods of the captured ships. The privateers rubbed their hands in pleasure at this profitable deal. They were going to get more without a fight

17. Alexander Selkirk, probable inspiration for Daniel Defoe's Robinson Crusoe, is rescued by Captain Rogers after four years alone on an island of the Juan Fernandez group off Peru (From *Life Aboard a British Privateer*, Sterling Library, Yale)

18. The Confederate ram *Manassas*, built by private funds as a weapon against the New Orleans blockade during the Civil War. It had a timber-packed bow, a single gun and steam jets to repel boarders. (Naval Photographic Centre, Washington D.C.)

than if they sacked the town. The governor saluted them genially and went ashore with the promise to conclude arrange-
ments at eight o'clock that evening.

Aboard the barque the privateers laid out refreshments,
lighted the candles, and sat down to wait like expectant lovers.
The governor failed to come. After midnight a gentleman
rowed out to them with propitiatory gifts of meat and brandy.
He apologized for Don Jerónimo's absence — a very influential
merchant was away — momently expected — the governor
awaited his return before settling matters finally. True, reinforcements had filled the town with armed men, so it was well
able to defend itself, but since the governor had bound himself
to negotiate, and was a man of the highest honor, he would
continue to do so. Rogers listened to these blandishments in
chill silence. In view of the town's danger, he replied, the governor's absence could hardly be explained away. Rogers would
allow him until seven next morning; at one minute after seven
they would storm the town.

A good negotiator, as Don Jerónimo was, knows in his bones
when to retreat and when to rally. He made it a point to have
his oars in the river before the church bells chimed seven. Yes,
to be sure, he could arrange purchase of the prize cargoes, even
the ships, but 50,000 pieces of eight for the town — ah, that
was beyond reason! By noon he conceded that 40,000 might,
perhaps, be possible; he could make no binding agreement until
leading citizens had discussed it fully. He went ashore at one
o'clock pledged to a prompt reply.

The reply, by messenger, was neither prompt nor pleasing.
It offered 30,000 pieces of eight for the town, and ignored the
prizes entirely. Rogers gave them another half-hour of grace.
The boats moved closer in as men loaded their muskets for the
attack. Three gentlemen, who came to the riverside brandish-
ing white handkerchiefs, raised the ransom by 2000 pieces of
eight. Rogers waved them off. His linguist shouted in Spanish
for everyone in the line of fire to clear out for their lives. The

barque hauled down her flag of truce and trained her cannon on the town, men poured off her deck into boats, and the land-ing party dug oars for the quay.

Militiamen crowded out of back streets to meet them, and a company of horse charged to the riverbank, yanking at their swords. "They made a formidable Show in respect to our little Number that was to attack them," Rogers admitted. His pin-nace grated on the stone landing. Men scrambled out shouting, and fired off a ragged volley toward the militia, who fled back into the town faster than they had come. The cavalry wheeled and pressed after the rout. Pausing only to signal cease-fire to the barque's crew, Rogers marched his little band double-quick after the retreating Spaniards. At the plaza four cannon faced them, the gunners with matches at the touchholes, and the de-fense forces solidly regrouped behind. Rogers and a few men dashed with a whoop straight for the cannon mouths. The guns belched smoke, a blast of shot swept by; then horse, foot and gunners scattered like dust in a gale. While Rogers halted to secure the great church facing the plaza, Dover and Courtney marched their companies unopposed to the far edge of town. A short half-hour had put Guayaquil in their possession. "With a Handful of raw, undisciplin'd Men," was Rogers' contemptuous note, not one of them lost to enemy fire.[14]

But Guayaquil was now hardly worth possessing. The tortu-ous negotiations had bought time for the town's citizens to carry off everything of value. Privateers broke open locked doors, rooted in barren rooms, ransacked cupboards, and were about to tear up the floor of the plaza church. Rogers ruled the

---

[14] Spanish fire wounded one man and, later on, a sniper fleshed another, but in general the invaders were a far greater danger to themselves. During the attack a Portuguese aboard the barque was killed by a case shot exploding as it left the mortar muzzle. Subsequently a nervous sentry shot a privateer dead as a result of misunderstanding the password; one lost an arm in the premature explosion of a grenade; another was wounded in the foot by his comrade; and Lieutenant Stretton's pistol went off in his belt, putting a bullet into his leg. The Spanish fared better: two dead, one of them a renegade Irish gunner who stood by his post behind the plaza cannon a second too long.

church off bounds; too many buried under it had died of a recent plague.

On the hint of an Indian prisoner, Lieutenant Connely and Selkirk took two boats up the river to see if they could lay hands on some fugitives and, literally, did. Houses along the bank were full of Guayaquil women who had not been able to part with all their jewelry, as a few genteel pats by the privateers discovered. "Some of their largest Gold Chains were conceal'd, and wound about their Middles, legs and Thighs, etc., but the Gentlewomen of those hot Countries being very thin clad with Silk and fine Linnen, and their Hair dressed with Ribbons very neatly, our Men by pressing felt the Chains, etc., with their Hand on the Outside of the Lady's Apparel, and by their Linguist modestly desired the Gentlewomen to take 'em off and surrender 'em." This gallantry so impressed the grateful ladies of one house that they spread food for the searchers and broke out a cask of choice liquor.

Spanish men were less cordial. Without ever mounting a counterattack, they kept the English nervously on edge by sniping, feints in force, and night alarms. Strengthened by reinforcements, they might retake the town. At the right moment, Rogers thought, a ransom agreement should be struck, and on April 26 he dispatched his ultimatum: 30,000 pieces of eight, payable in six days at Puná, with sufficient hostages as surety, or he would burn Guayaquil to the ground at three o'clock that afternoon.

An hour before the deadline Spanish horsemen rode in to accept the demand and to exchange written guarantees of the terms. To save his dignity, the governor requested clear statement that the town had been taken by storm.[15] It was agreed that the Puná lieutenant, and three Guayaquil gentlemen already in Rogers' custody, would stand as hostages.

[15] The subterfuge did not prevent Don Jerónimo's disgrace. He lived for twenty years under the shadow of charges against him, until the Council of the Indies, its docket obviously crowded, rendered a verdict. Adverse, of course.

Getting out of Guayaquil was more trouble than getting in. Most plunder was bulky — bags of flour, beans and rice; some cordage and ironware, bales of cloth, a ton of tar — and men fainted under the load in the deadly heat. Rain turned the dirt streets to quagmires. When they tried to carry the Spanish cannon to the riverside, the men sank to their knees, and Rogers had to contrive a huge bamboo frame that sixty men could put their shoulders under. That night the whole company of privateers slept in the plaza church; next day they loaded the barque with plunder, and on April 28, with a loud display of trumpets and drums to announce their departure, dropped down the ebb tide to Puná.

Nor did the ransom money come any easier. The governor was silent, but still negotiating. He sent to Puná 22,000 pieces of eight on the last day of grace. Rogers had heard rumors of pursuit ships readying at Lima, and he wanted to get out of the gulf. Nothing would be worse than to be penned in at Puná with half his fighting force, while Spanish guns sent the *Duke* and *Duchess* to the bottom. He left for Point Arena early on May 3, taking the three Guayaquil hostages along, but released the Puná lieutenant. "A Man we had some Respect for," he explained. The hostages were distressed at the thought that the rest of the ransom might not arrive to redeem them. "It's worse than Death, they say, to be carried to Great Britain," mused Rogers, who himself wanted nothing more. A boat caught them at Point Arena and paid another 3500 pieces of eight — not yet enough. Rogers dispatched away most of his prisoners aboard the *Beginning*, kept the Guayaquil hostages, and on May 8 weighed with the flood for the Galápagos, 500 miles northwest.

Rogers could snort at live Spaniards, but dead ones should be treated with more respect. Rotting coffins of plague victims, stacked beneath church floors, harbored an enemy far more dangerous than snipers from the wood. The landing party sickened almost to a man. Not Rogers; only a bullet could touch him; but by the time they sighted the Galápagos on May 17 the *Duke* had sixty men down and the *Duchess* eighty, all hollow-eyed and tossing with fever.

Narrow channels and fluky winds among the islands scattered the ships, and when they rendezvoused a prize barque with ten men aboard, commanded by the third mate of the *Duchess*, Simon Hatley, was missing. The other ships searched for her in vain, hanging lanterns at mastheads by night, firing signal guns at all hours. Rogers feared that the barque's crew would perish of thirst; but then, so might they all, for not a drop of water could be found on the crusty slopes of islands that they touched. A dozen men died of fever; scores of others were too weak to hoist a sail. The sooner they cleared out of these "unfortunate Islands" the better. With water low and medicine in short supply, they set sail May 27 on a stout wind from the southeast, and made for the continent. Ill fortune had not worn itself out. Rumor drifted to Rogers that prisoners on the *Ascensión* plotted to murder the English aboard and sail off by night. The Spaniards swore they knew nothing of it, and matches lit between the fingers of Negroes drew confession of little more than loose talk. To be safe, Rogers dispersed the Negroes into other ships.

Close to the mainland the *Duchess* captured the *San Tomás* of ninety tons, Juan Navarro, master, carrying a bit of cargo, which the privateers wanted, and forty passengers, which they did not. Young Don Juan Cardozo, bound for his new post as governor of Valdivia, took the capture with aplomb — he had already been made prisoner once, by a Jamaica privateer, on the Caribbean leg of his journey. A young married couple was more upset. The husband suffered from what Rogers called "the *Spaniards* Epidemick Disease" — jealousy. The man's fear for his wife's virtue was prodigious, and to calm him Rogers secluded the two in the *Ascensión* cabin. Lieutenant Glendall, a doddering oldster of fifty, whose fires were surely banked, stood guard over their door like a Nubian eunuch at a seraglio. Burdened by these additional mouths to feed, the fleet ran up the east side of Gorgona Island and anchored in a sandy bay on June 7. The place was risky; any pursuit ship would look for them there; and Rogers had a moment of gloom: "Our Men being very much fatigued, many of them sick, and several of our Good Sailors dead, we are so weak, that should we meet an Enemy in this Condition, we could make but a mean Defence. Everything looks dull and discouraging . . ."

Gorgona had the thickest jungle, noisiest monkeys, fattest guinea pigs, laziest sloths and most poisonous snakes on all that coast. Its sun burned straight overhead by day, its sky brimmed rain by night. "It's in vain to look back or repine," Rogers confided to his journal, and plunged into the task of recuperating his forces. Within two weeks the *Duke* and *Duchess* were scraped, caulked, re-rigged and re-stowed, to the loud amazement of the Spaniards, who cried that a single ship took six weeks in Lima. "Puny mariners," sniffed Rogers. He converted the *Havre de Grâce* to a fighting ship: new mast, yards and cordage, twenty guns, a crew of eighty, Cooke as her captain, and a name in the proper rank of peerage — the *Marquis*. "We saluted each of the other Ships with 3 Huzzas from on board her, distributed Liquor among the Company, drank her Majesty's and our Owners Healths, and to our own good Success. The Ship look'd well . . ." She never sailed as well as she looked, however: heavy on a wind, cranky in all weather.

Leisure on that wet, green isle gave Rogers a chance to rummage the deep holds of the larger prizes. The *Marquis* yielded 500 bales of smudged papal indulgences which the Spanish king sold to his subjects for a neat profit. Out of the *Ascensión* came myriad boxes of bones, "ticketed with the Names of *Romish* Saints, some of which had been dead 7 or 800 years; with an infinite Number of Brass Medals, Crosses, Beads and Crucifixes, religious Toys in Wax, Images of Saints made of all sorts of Wood, Stone and other Materials." By chance, a wooden image of the Virgin fell over the side and drifted about the bay until prisoners found it washed up ashore. They marveled that however often they wiped the wood dry, moisture still came out. Rogers smiled his faint smile at this miraculous sweat. The Spanish protested far greater wonders; how, for example, the Virgin's jewel-bedecked statue in the Lima cathedral had seized a thief and held him fast until morning brought the guards. Rogers chuckled, but he maintained at all times tolerance for the Spaniards' right to worship as they pleased. Each Sunday, services were held on the *Ascensión,* the Protestants on the quarterdeck, the Catholics beneath in the cabin. "The Papists here were the Low Churchmen," Rogers made note.

Leisure bred trouble, too, as Rogers discovered when the men clamored for a division of plunder. He dreaded it, "for Disputes about Plunder is the common Occasion of Privateers Quarreling among themselves, and ruining their Voyages." He did his best to keep the business manageable. An order of council clarified, and further liberalized, what constituted plunder. Four officers, honest men all, were appointed appraisers, and worked three exhausting days over booty spread out between decks in the *Ascensión.* The men did not even wait for the result; whatever it was, they didn't intend to like it. As the appraisal ended, sixty hands of the *Duke* agreed among themselves to accept no shares, nor stir from Gorgona, until satisfied that they were honorably dealt with. Rogers seized the ringleaders, and soothed the rest with "healing Arguments."

Officers, too, were grating on each other's nerves in Gorgona's tedious, unending summer. They refought the Guayaquil fiasco among themselves and stalked off fuming. Rogers considered it not beyond possibility that the expedition would break up if the bickering continued. "I long for a Reconciliation and good Harmony amongst Us," he sighed. To promote it, he drew up an oath that in battle or misfortune each ship would aid and defend the other, and had each officer swear to it with his hand on the Holy Scriptures.

If a man lost his sword he could fight with fists or teeth; if he lost his spirit, no arms would defend him. Morale, Rogers meditated, was the essential. Perhaps a passage of arms in realistic battle practice would stir the men up. He arrayed the ships off Gorgona with the *Duchess* posed as the enemy. When she suddenly ran up a Spanish flag, an excitable Welshman on the *Duke* loaded his musket with shot, and Rogers was pleased to observe that even a chucklehead could be valiant. Gunners swabbed cannon and boomed off blank charges, surgeons laid out their instruments in gleaming rows. Rogers had a pair of men carried below dripping red paint and writhing with mock pain. Spanish prisoners shrank back horrified at the sight of them, while the surgeon sprang to dress their wounds before they bled to death. "A very agreeable Diversion," 'was Rogers' dry comment.

Still, if the fleet was to trim down to a lean fighting force, prisoners and prizes must be gotten rid of. In the nearby mainland bay of Tacames, the Morel brothers dug up 3000 pieces of eight to redeem the *Ascensión,* and Juan Navaro got his *San Tomás* back on promise to pay 1200 pieces of eight at Porto Bello. One Guayaquil hostage went ashore under solemn oath to return with 15,000 pieces of eight in fulfillment of the town's ransom and to purchase one of the prizes; seventy prisoners were released outright; and thirty-two Negro slaves joined the privateer crew as free men. A priest who had smoothed the way for trade with mainland Indians was rewarded with some cloth and a pretty Negro slave girl. "The young Padre parted with us extremely pleas'd, and leering under his Hood upon his black Female Angel," it appeared to Rogers; "we doubt he will crack a Commandment with her, and wipe off the Sin with the Church's Indulgence." On August 29 the council voted to replenish meat at the Galápagos, and then cruise north for the big game of the voyage — the Manila galleon.

Waterless as they were, the harsh, satanic Galápagos supported an astonishing variety of edible creatures. Spiny iguanas crawled on the lava rocks, seal sported along the shore, boobies clung to sea ledges, and turtles dozed by the hundreds in the cactus shade. Unused to man, all were quite tame, except a vicious sea lion "as big as a large Bear," who considered Rogers an affront. "Had I not happen'd to have a Pike-staff pointed with Iron in my Hand, I might have been kill'd by him," Rogers recalled. "I was on the level Sand when he came open-mouth'd at me out of the Water, as quick and fierce as the most angry Dog let loose. I struck the Point into his Breast, and wounded him all the three times he made at me, which forc'd him at last to retire with an ugly Noise, snarling and shewing his long Teeth at me out of the Water."

On September 14, their meat restocked, and a few forlorn guns sounded for the missing Hatley, the ships rowed and towed out of the calm channels, northward.[16] Somewhere above them, they hoped, the unsuspecting Manila galleon bore eastward on a stiff September breeze. Patience, that was all; they would spin a web for her.

---

[16] With only two days' water aboard, Hatley had to run for the continent. He and his men suffered torments on the way, one died, the survivors fell into Spanish hands, and Hatley did not get out of his Lima dungeon until the peace of Utrecht was signed in 1713. He is remembered far less for these pains than for an unwitting contribution to literary history. Again at the Horn, under Captain George Shelvocke in 1719, dreadful storms threw Hatley into a fit of melancholy. Offended by "a disconsolate black albatross" that haunted their masthead, he shot it, an incident mentioned by Shelvocke in his *Voyage Round the World*, 1726. Seventy years later Coleridge and Wordsworth set out on a walking tour through the Quantock Hills. As they trudged along, Coleridge sketched the rudiments of a sea-ballad: a ship manned by the shadowy dead, save for one mariner doomed to life among them. But why should the mariner be sentenced to this ghastly company? "I had been reading Shelvocke's Voyages, a day or two before," Wordsworth recalled. "'Suppose,' said I, 'you represent him as killing one of these birds on entering the South Sea, and that the tutelary spirits of these regions take upon them to avenge the crime.'" This suggestion gave Coleridge the moral pivot upon which the "Rime of the Ancient Mariner" turns:

> "God save thee, ancient Mariner,
> From the fiends, that plague thee thus! —
> Why look'st thou so?" "With my crossbow
> I shot the Albatross."

The *nao de China*, as the Spanish called her, was worth waiting for; was, in fact, the richest prize afloat, crammed with spices, silks, porcelain, gold and exquisite artifacts brought to Manila by seagoing junks from the China coast. Spaniards in the Philippines did little else, in a business way, than cargo the galleon in June and bite their nails until she returned a year later. She was always a huge vessel, broad-beamed, incredibly slow, with gilded woodwork blazoned over a poop four stories high, framed in teak to survive Pacific storms, and planked with tough native wood in which the largest cannonballs harmlessly buried themselves. "Each one is a strong castle in the sea," breathed an awed admirer, but negligence and greed made them vulnerable. Guns often went into the hold to provide room for merchandise, and native crews were both cowardly and incompetent in a fight. Usually one, sometimes two galleons left Manila each year for a voyage lonely as a journey to the moon and harrowing as a descent into the maelstrom. Fireworks saluted her departure from Manila, the governor ceremoniously handed over her papers and royal ensign, friars chanted, an image of the Virgin was put aboard, and the archbishop blessed her as to a sacrifice. Mortality was always high as she plowed a great circle far north to catch the prevailing westerlies; indeed, on the 1656 ship every person aboard died and she drifted rudderless, silent as a floating charnel house, to the Mexican shore. Most galleons made landfall in California and struck down along the coast, past Cape St. Lucas, to the fetid Mexican port of Acapulco.

Across this course Rogers' ships laid their net on November 3. The *Duke* rode off the Cape in the most likely passage, the *Marquis* westward, the *Duchess* still farther beyond with a little prize barque serving as courier between. The clear, dry air gave them visibility of ninety miles to sea.

No galleon hove down on them. Day after day the same blank sky, the same vacant horizon. A Negro slave woman, who served as laundress on the *Duke*, provided the only excitement. As the ships approached their stations she let out a wail of pain. Dr. Wasse diagnosed her ailment and rushed her into the cabin, where she eagerly gulped anesthetic in the form of thick Peru wine, and in a short time gave birth to "a Girl of tawny Colour." The tawny color set Rogers to reckoning, but since the woman had been only six months on the ship he had no grounds for a paternity case. However, he took occasion to warn the other Negress aboard "to be modest," with the reminder that one on the *Duchess*, failing in that respect, "was lately whip'd at the Capston."

November passed, and no galleon. Two weeks of December went by — the galleon was a full month overdue. Now their situation, which had been only depressing, became desperate. On December 19 the council reckoned that even if they gave up the patrol at once, they were in grave danger. Provisions were down to a seventy-day supply. Nine days to refit, and fifty more for the westward voyage, left them a margin of but eleven days' food and water. Calms or storms, faulty navigation or unforeseen mishap would reduce them to starvation. "We all looked very melancholy and dispirited, because so low in Provisions, that if we did not reach *Guam* in the limited Time, or accidentally miss it, we shall not have enough till we shall arrive at any other Place."

Rogers took defeat quite sensibly; he took everything sensibly. To win with honor was much desired, of course, but someone must lose, and that could be with honor, too. Shortage of food, and worms in the sheathings dictated only one prudent course: hasten westward. The leaky *Marquis* was already ashore, making repairs for the long voyage. On December 20 the council voted that the *Duke* and *Duchess* should join her there and do likewise.

Next morning, as the two ships beat slowly landward in the face of contrary winds, the watch let out a whoop and waved his arms. Sail!

Was the distant patch of canvas only the *Marquis* out of
port? Very likely. The wind died to a whisper, and both pinnaces put out, hoping to make better way. The *Duke*'s was still
within hail when the watch shouted down that the stranger
lacked a fore-topmast, as did the *Marquis*. She had come for a
cap to set her mast. Rogers called the pinnace back and put
one aboard. It was now noon; the ships sat in their shadows on
the placid sea, with drooping sails.

But the pinnace did not return. Rogers swung into the
shrouds to get her in his glass. She had stopped far short of
the stranger, and lay in gunwale-to-gunwale consultation with
the *Duchess*'s pinnace. Then the latter rowed back, leaving the
Duke's on guard. Frye took the yawl to the *Duchess* and hurried back with good news: the stranger was the Manila galleon.

Before nightfall Rogers had the *Duke* in battle array. The
carpenter's gang downed bulkheads to reduce splintering, and
readied mauls and shot-plugs to repair leaks at the waterline.
Hammocks were strung in the netting to shield the men from
enemy musket fire; gunners racked their rammers, sponges,
wads, priming-irons, set water tubs handy and notched slow
matches to linstocks. Port lids were hung up, guns run out at
point-blank range; spare rigging was coiled in the scuppers,
hatches battened, boarding grapnel posted fore and aft, muskets passed around to the men.

Guided by flares from the pinnaces, the ships spread all sail
to the night breeze, and daybreak showed the galleon three
miles off the *Duke*'s bow. Rogers ordered up the best substitute
that he had for liquor — a tub of hot chocolate. All went to
prayers, and before the last amen was said the galleon's guns
were trying the range.

A mile to leeward of the quarry, having overrun her in the
dark, the *Duchess* was laboring back in the face of a scant
breeze. Rogers prepared to go in alone. He ordered the main
courses brailed up to slow ship, and bore down on the galleon's
stern under tops. Her stern-chase let off a charge of small shot

that whipped the water in front of him like hailstones. The gap closed; the *Duke* edged athwart the high poop, then gradually worked abeam. On his quarterdeck, Rogers coolly gauged the distance.

The *Duke* rolled as her guns boomed in rapid succession. Through the curtain of smoke that billowed up her side, yellow spurts of flame leaped from the galleon's ports as she replied. Muskets barked from her waist, and Rogers spun heavily onto his side, a ball through his left cheek. Frye ran to prop him up. He choked, spat blood and teeth down his shirt, and squinted in a half-daze at the side of the galleon gliding past. They had almost run down her beam now; through wisps of smoke Rogers could see the rise of her forecastle at his midships. He tried to speak, but had no idea if his mouth opened or if there was still a tongue in it. He motioned vaguely: starboard helm across the galleon's bow. Frye shouted the order, the *Duke* swung about with guns thundering in a raking fire, and Rogers hauled himself to his feet in time to see the enemy strike her colors.

Frye took the *Duke* pinnace to bring off the galleon's chief officers for questioning. Rogers hunched in his bunk, spitting blood into a bucket and jotting notes for Frye, who did the talking. The prize was the *Incarnación*, twenty guns and 193 men, her commander a French chevalier, le Sieur Jean Pichberty. She had nineteen killed or wounded and Rogers, with his usual generosity, sent surgeons to care for them. Besides Rogers himself, only one of the *Duke's* men had been hurt, and in a place no hero could boast of — the buttocks.

The Spaniards prattled as though their tongues were hinged in the middle. The *Incarnación* was not the great galleon, after all, only the lesser. The *Begoña*, larger, richer, better armed, left Manila at the same time, but they had lost each other in heavy weather. A faster sailer, the *Begoña* was no doubt long since snugged down in Acapulco.

Rogers was not so sure. For nearly two months he had

thrown a barrier of ships across the coastal passage. The lumbering galleon would have to turn into a shimmer of moonlight to slip through. Back in the mainland port he scribbled his recommendation that the *Duke* and *Duchess* return at once to patrol. His men balked, angry that the *Duchess* had potted off a few shots only when the prize lowered her flag. Any terrier, they grumped, can worry the kill after the hounds have brought it down. Since the crew sulked, and Rogers lay disabled, the council kept the *Duke* in haven, while the *Duchess* and *Marquis* put to sea. Rogers did not relish being left out of it. He sent watchmen to a nearby hilltop, with instructions to signal three "waffs" of a flag if any strange sail hove into sight.

He was in dismal shape — hardly able to get liquids down his swollen throat, and talking only in tortured whispers — but when the watchmen waved from their hilltop on Christmas afternoon he brushed aside all pleas that he lie quiet. He ordered the prisoners into the barque, took away its rudder, sails and boat, and moored it a full mile from the galleon. By seven o'clock the *Duke* beat out of harbor against a bow wind, following cannon flashes of the seaward battle. Next morning, still ten miles from the quarry, Rogers got her in his glass. The *Duchess* was close in to her, the *Marquis* crowding all sail to come up.

Battered by the night cannonade, the *Duchess* soon lay by to await the *Marquis,* who beat slowly into range. All through the late afternoon the *Marquis* abeam and the *Duchess* astern poured six-pound shot into the galleon. The recoil of the *Marquis*'s guns drove her steadily leeward until she was out of effective range. She wore to get the wind, and the *Duchess* replaced her abeam for a half-hour exchange, then stretched ahead, fearfully mauled by accurate fire from the galleon's twelve-pounders. Now the *Marquis* crossed the enemy's bow, starboard guns booming in rapid order, wore under the high stern, and let off a barrage from her port row. The galleon sailed on, unhurt. As darkness fell, the *Marquis* dropped back to replenish ammunition from the *Duchess.* The latter had shot-holes gaping at her waterline, and seven of her men were killed or wounded. All night the two ships hung in the enemy's wake, swinging lanterns aloft and firing signal guns to guide the *Duke.*

Rogers got up to them at dawn. The galleon set studding sails to the early breeze and wheeled ponderously away for the coast. Clapping sail after her, all three ships poured shot down her length, and stretched ahead. The *Duke* and *Duchess* wore about and ran close alongside to board; men armed with grapnel, poleaxes, cutlasses and grenades swarming the shrouds. As the gap of water closed and the great hull loomed over them, a flying splinter cut into Rogers' heel. It broke away part of the bone and ripped the flesh to his ankle. He lay where he fell, clutching the foot in agony. At the same moment a fireball from the Spaniard burst a chest of ammunition on the *Duke's* quarterdeck. Smoke shot up, the *Duchess* bore off in haste, and the boarding attempt was over.

The *Begoña* sailed on, impervious as a whale among minnows. False decks jutted from bow and stern to hamper boarding, stacked bales of goods shielded her bulwarks and gunports. Her twelve-pounders had made a shambles of the attack ships. The *Duchess's* rigging flapped in shreds, and a quarter of her crew groaned under the surgeon's hand, or were forever beyond need of it. The *Marquis* had thirty shot-holes in her sails, the *Duke's* shattered mainmast threatened to go overboard. "To give the enemy their due," Cooke grudgingly admitted, "they defended themselves very well." [17]

So well, indeed, that the attackers were now on the defensive. The enemy could close in on a disabled ship and blow her

[17] In Holland a Spaniard who had been aboard the *Begoña* described the galleon's chief gunner as a Genoese, and her gun captains as English and Irish brigands sailing home with their booty. This may explain their marksmanship. The Genoese, said the Spaniard, perched himself on some powder kegs with a lighted match in his hand, and swore by the sacrament that if the gunners allowed the galleon to be taken he would blow her to splinters. Cf. Rogers, p. 242.

to scrap. Prisoners taken might reveal where the *Incarnación* lay hidden, and the great galleon could easily take her back. The privateers had better be content with what they had. Where Rogers stretched out on his quarterdeck, pale from loss of blood and grimacing with stabs of pain, the officers gathered in dejected council. A glance after the galleon showed her enjoying the fight: aloft men hung fresh powder kegs from yardarms, below ports opened to let out a row of unused cannon. They watched her depart with some relief. Only when she neared the horizon did they dare to limp back to their harbor of refuge.

A week was consumed in repairing damage to the ships, and sending off all the prisoners in the barque. The privateers gleefully ferreted in the prize galleon's cargo. She was loaded to the hatches with cloth, spices, jewels and plate, thousands of ladies' fans, cotton stockings by the hundreds, a set of chinaware intended for the Queen of Spain and, more practically for present needs, a good supply of bread.

But who should command this rich prize on its journey halfway round the world to England? None other, thought Dr. Dover, than himself. He stirred up council support, and bludgeoned most of the officers into signing a statement that made him their choice. The statement, handed to Rogers in his bunk, contained a pointed reminder that the majority of the council ruled.

Rogers was appalled. " 'Twas our great Unhappiness, after taking a rich Prize, to have a Paper-War among our selves," he lamented, but there was no help for it if Dover was going to be stopped. Rogers marshaled the *Duke*'s officers in reply. They declared Dover "utterly uncapable of the Office," both for lack of experience in seamanship and because "his Temper is so violent that capable men cannot well act under him." Let the doctor be aboard to oversee cargo if he chose, but he must have no part in sailing the galleon or in directing her defense if attacked. After heated debate the council muddled to a compromise. It salved Dover's vanity by naming him Chief Captain, with Frye, Stretton and Selkirk to actually run the ship.

The westward rendezvous was set for "*Guam*, one of the *Ladrones* Islands, where we design'd to touch at, God willing, to get Provisions." [18] They would be lucky to touch before they had to chew leather. Every mess of five men was rationed to a daily pound-and-a-half of bread and one small morsel of salt meat. Each man received three pints of water a day — too little for the tropics. Negroes who had joined the crew got less, just enough, Rogers supposed, "to keep those that are in health alive." Hoping for the best, fearing the worst, the four ships weighed anchor on the night of January 10, 1710.

They fought starvation all the way. A Negro addicted to stealing food died, and they were not sorry to slip him over the side. "His Room was more acceptable than his Company," was Rogers' cool comment. Others caught pilfering got the cat across bare backs from every hand of the watch. Men began to collapse at the pumps or helm, and the food ration had to be increased. But the westerly trades held fair. In fifty-eight days they were coasting Guam, escorted by outriggers that flitted over the sea swift as flying fish.[19]

In the harbor of Port Umatta the fleet ran up Spanish flags. Two gentlemen of the town came out in a *proa* and lay under the *Duke's* stern. What ships were these, and where from?

[18] The Ladrones, or Isles of Thieves (present Marianas), so named by Magellan for the native habit of leaping over the ship's side with anything that they could snatch up. Guam was maintained by the Spanish as a way station for the galleons returning from Acapulco to Manila. Its isolated position removed it, however, from Spain's wars, and it had the reputation of cooperating with the enemy whenever the island's weakness, and the enemy strength, made this prudent.

[19] Rogers was intrigued with these red-painted *proas*, which "passed by us like Birds flying." Each carried a triangular lateen sail, its peak fixed in the bow. By means of a steersman at each end they never came about, but simply reversed bow and stern, so as to keep the single outrigger always to windward. Struck by the idea that such a curious craft would be a novelty on the canal of St. James park, Rogers took one home on the *Duke's* deck.

Friends, from New Spain. Had they a message for the governor? Indeed they had, come aboard.

Their message for the governor was friendly, up to a point. The privateers' intentions, it said, were entirely peaceful. They wanted only provisions, for which they would make generous payment. However, should this amiable request be denied — slipping the dagger from its velvet sheath — "you may immediately expect such Military Treatment, as we are with ease able to give you." Officials ashore took a brief look at the rows of gunports and became the soul of cordiality. They sent out corn by the sack, eggs by the basket, piles of yams, jugs of nipa wine, and 800 coconuts. Fowl, hogs and cattle turned decks into farmyards. Ships' officers went ashore, amid a great show of provincial pomp, to a sixty-dish feast; in return, the Spanish gentlemen enjoyed an afternoon of music and sailors' jigs on the galleon's broad quarterdeck. Then it was time for the fleet to move on; many a sea lay between them and home. At break of day on March 21 they weighed on a fine breeze for the Dutch East India station of Batavia.

For three months the ships wandered through the baffling islands of east Asia. All charts were unreliable; even Dampier had no idea where they were. Adverse currents and contrary winds drove them from channel to channel; storms as bad as the Horn (but blessedly warmer) split their sails; waterspouts pursued them; the galleon and the *Marquis*, both sluggish, slowed their pace, and the *Duke* leaked so badly that four men worked the pump at all times. By May 10 the crews were back on rations. Rats became a delicacy: "I have known the men to give a Groat or six Pence a-Piece for Rats, and eat them very savourly," said Cooke.

At Bouton Island Dampier and Vanbrugh waited on the native king to obtain provisions and a pilot. He received them in state — spangled headdress, bodyguard armed with gleaming scimitars, and four slaves at his bare feet, "one of them holding his *Betele*-Box, another a lighted Match, another his Box to smoke, and the fourth his Spitting-Bason." The visitors presented his majesty with "a Bishop's Cap, being of little or no Value to us." It softened the monarch not at all. He charged the dearest prices for rice, beans, fowl and arrack and, with a shrewd eye to the Dutch dislike for intruders, refused a pilot to Batavia. "We resolv'd to stay no longer," Rogers recorded, "and to trust wholly to Almighty Providence for our future Preservation."

Providence responded in the form of a small trading boat which they drove ashore. The owner consented to pilot them to Batavia if they would not tell the Dutch, and at sunset of June 20 brought them to anchorage in Batavia road. The *Duchess* saluted the fort with thirteen guns. The fort was silent, and next morning the commander hurried out to explain that he did not customarily reply to salutes after nightfall. If they wished — but of course! The *Duchess* fired a second round of thirteen guns, which the fort acknowledged, and all sighed with relief.

In fact, for unwelcome strangers, protocol was the curse of Batavia. The alliance of England and Holland since Dutch William ascended the English throne removed Holland from her old role of enemy, but made the Dutch East India Company no more hospitable to unauthorized vessels in its trading area. Rogers approached this delicate situation with studied care. A council decree, forbidding any crewman to deal privately ashore, was nailed to the masts. Diligent efforts to provision and careen ship were blocked by the governor's snappish factotum, until Rogers obtained audience by bribing a guard. The courtly governor assured them that they could provision as they wished, and could careen ship on one of the beaches, with a sampan to heave down by and a dozen Malay caulkers to pitch their seams. Charged with carrying out these orders, the factotum delayed, excused himself, shuffled papers, scolded their impatience, and finally shunted them off to careen on a wretched shore exposed to the full blast of the wind. All but the single-bottomed *Marquis* managed to refit in this difficult spot; worms had honeycombed her planks, and she was sold for junk.

The four tedious months at Batavia were necessary to their recruitment, but not in all respects beneficial. The handsome city, its tree-lined canals, tropical gardens, and arrack houses at every corner, were tempting to seamen worn out with the rigors of shipboard. Some deserted, others died of fever; one rash fellow went swimming off the *Duke's* anchor cable and was bitten in two by a shark. Rogers signed on seventeen men, mostly Dutch, to make up his losses. A doctor pried the musket ball out of his jaw, and removed bone fragments from his heel, but he remained weak and thin.

On October 24 the three ships cleared Java Head into "an ugly swelling sea" for a run to the Cape that was ugly in more ways than weather. Rogers pottered about in the cabin, nursing his wounds, too miserable to do more than keep his log. The *Duke* leaked so furiously that when the pump clogged the officer on watch hoisted distress signals in a panic. Surgeon James Wasse died, mourned by all, and a seaman who fell from the yardarm sank before a boat could get to him. However, all bad things, like good ones, must come to some end. On December 29 the ships saluted Cape Town, lowered yards and topmasts to rest more tranquil under quick flaws from the tableland, and sent sixteen men to the shore hospital.

They fretted away three months waiting for convoy ships to gather from Mocha, Bengal and the Indies. Rogers thought the neat Dutch town a fine place to be "out of the Noise of the World," but his health failed to improve, and he came aboard at the sailing gun on April 5 feeling no stronger than when he went ashore. Twenty-five ships sailed out, the *Duke* leaky as ever, and the galleon so slow that she was permitted to forge ahead of the convoy by night and go in tow by day. They skirted Ireland to avoid French privateers in the Channel. Ten Dutch warships took them in escort at the Shetlands; on July 23, 1711 they sighted the low dunes of Holland; and by evening had come on the flood to anchor at the Texel.

Choppier seas than the Channel now pitched up ahead of the voyagers. A message from the owners warned them that the English East India Company was "incens'd against us" for trespassing on its monopoly of Asiatic waters. The ships idled for weeks in the Zuyder Zee, hoping that the legal tangle would unsnarl. Two hundred resentful crewmen signed up with a cunning lawyer named Creagh, who promised to defend their interests for a 5 percent fee. Owners and council agreed that anything was better than a winter in Holland. On October 14, 1711, a guard of four British men-of-war brought the weary flotilla up the Thames to Erith. "Which," sighed Rogers, "ends our long and fatiguing Voyage." [20]

If only it were the end. As their anchors hooked bottom at Erith, East India Company agents rowed out to toss declaration of seizure onto the decks. Next the Company of Silk Throwers brought suit charging that illegal importation of East Indian silk from the galleon snatched the very food from their childrens' mouths. Creagh carried the men's case to the Lord Chancellor, and the owners retaliated by suing officers and crew. For five years the wrangling went on. Twice crew members petitioned the House of Lords for relief. They were "perishing for want of bread and daily thrown into gaol," they protested, while owners and officers fraudulently clung to booty worth three million pounds.

The actual sale of ships and cargoes came to £147,975 and a few shillings. The owners' two-thirds was cut in half by an exasperating medley of court costs, bribes, custom duties and storage fees. Few seamen received more than £50; Dampier

---

[20] Only a handful of Englishmen had been around the world since Drake (1580) and Cavendish (1588). Dampier (1691 and 1707) and William Cowley (1686) used more than one ship, and were not always in command. In the decades immediately after Rogers, Shelvocke (1722) and Anson (1744) succeeded in circling the globe, without matching Rogers' extraordinary preservation of ships and men. Anson, an able naval commander of a well-equipped expedition, started with eight ships, came back with one, and lost half his men by the time he had doubled the Horn. It was Rogers' remarkable feat to bring home both his original ships, and the prize galleon, while losing no more than fifty men on the whole voyage.

was never fully paid. Canny Dr. Dover piled up a small fortune
on invested shares, physician's salary, "storm money" as commander of the Guayaquil attack (which he opposed) and a bonus
as chief captain of the galleon (for which he did nothing).[21]
Rogers ended up with a niggardly £1530. He brought home
a shattered jawbone and broken heel, his powerful physique
had suffered permanent damage, and when three years of accu-
mulated family bills were paid he was financially cleaned out.

During the winter of 1711 Rogers brushed up for the printer
his detailed notes of the voyage. He disclaimed any pretensions
to literary gloss, preferring "to keep to the Language of the
Sea." [22] *A Cruising Voyage Round the World* that appeared in
1712 was as humane as Rogers himself, generous to friends and
gracious toward opponents, lightly touched with humor, and
valuable enough in its seamanly hints for Shelvocke and Anson
to carry it with them on later voyages west of the Horn.[23] In

[21] Though Dover was far from a bad man, no one in all the record, comments
a biographer, expressed a liking for him. His boasting (he would recall, "when
I took Guayaquil . . .") and his biting scorn of medical colleagues won him
distinction, in later years, as the most unpopular man in his profession. He
prescribed mercury so indiscriminately that scoffers dubbed him the "quicksilver
doctor," and delighted to relate how an actor who adopted this remedy, on
Dover's assurance that it would put an end to all his complaints, found that
it served perfectly — he died in a fortnight. Dover's famous concoction of
opium and ipecac fared better, and is still sold today. Stanley, crossing the
Makata swamp in search of Livingstone, cured himself of near-fatal dysentery
by "a judicious use of Dover's powder." At age seventy-three Dover wrapped
up his lifetime store of misinformation, common sense (for he had a good
deal of it) and spleen in *The Ancient Physician's Legacy to his Country*
(1733), a housewife's compendium that quickly ran through seven printings.
Jealous cries of "charlatan" from colleagues hardly seem justified. Dover can
be accused of much, but not dishonesty. He was simply one of those gusty
fellows who are as offensive as the itch: everyone dislikes them, but no one
can ignore them.
[22] Still, thought the printer, the rough mariner's style could stand dressing up.
He paid £ 10 to a "Mr. Ridpath for correcting Rogers's voyage."
[23] Eager to beat Rogers into print, Edward Cooke, second captain of the
Duchess, rushed out a first volume of his narrative early in 1712, and followed
it with a second volume a few months later, as Rogers' book appeared. Cooke's
more pedestrian record of the voyage was dedicated, in the florid fashion then
current, to the Tory leader, Lord Oxford. Rogers was not used to fawning on
the great. With characteristic loyalty he dedicated *A Cruising Voyage* to the

addition, the book had two remarkable effects. It inspired one of the great classics of our literature, and contributed to the worst financial crash in English history.

Three pages devoted by Rogers to Alexander Selkirk offer the most explicit description ever printed of his lonely life on Juan Fernández. Certainly Daniel Defoe read it, and he may have been reminded of the story again when a second edition of *Cruising Voyage* appeared in 1718. Though the theme of solitary island existence was old, Rogers' recital of Selkirk's story had the solid factual quality needed to stir Defoe's gift for fiction that reads like biography. In 1719 *The Life and Strange Surprizing Adventures of Robinson Crusoe of York, Mariner*, appeared on the stalls. Crusoe's island was a different one, his stay longer, the cause of his exile shipwreck rather than marooning, and the man Friday supplied human company, but in the many practical details of his survival, and in his religious preoccupation, Robinson Crusoe was simply Selkirk amplified.[24]

Rogers' small part in the South Sea Bubble disaster was less direct and more unhappy. His introduction to *A Cruising Voyage* urged England to move aggressively into the whole Pacific area, especially temperate, thinly settled Chile. A third of the book described coastal territories of South America, and such way stations for traders as Juan Fernández, Gorgona, Guam and Batavia. He was sure that the immediate gains of the voyage were quite dwarfed by the glittering prospects of empire which it unfolded. "The Wisdom of the Nation has now agreed to establish a Trade to the South-Seas," he stated in his dedication, "which, with the Blessing of God, may bring vast Riches to Great Britain." The nation's wisdom, in this respect, rested

---

"surviving Owners, who had the Courage to adventure your Estates on an Undertaking, which to Men less discerning seem'd impractible."

24 Cowper's poem, "The Solitude of Alexander Selkirk," which has fixed in popular memory only its stately opening line, "I am monarch of all I survey," pictures Selkirk gladly surrendering his lonely sovereignty for the sound of a human voice. The outcome of Selkirk's return to civilization was not so happy. He was soon in court for brawling, later ran off with a poor country girl and abandoned her to marry a Plymouth jade, then died in 1721, aboard H.M.S. *Weymouth*, in an epidemic that swept the ship near the African coast.

on the unsound foundation of the South Sea Company, a Tory answer to the powerful whiggish combination of the Bank of England and the East India Company. Organized in 1711, the young Company seized upon Rogers' voyage as evidence that a South Sea empire was anything but airy delusion.[25] That, however, is exactly what it proved to be. To enlarge its charter powers, and gain a dominant place in British finance, the Company assumed management of the soaring national debt in 1720. The move triggered months of reckless speculation as the bubble blew to gigantic proportions. Companies sprang up to import asses from Spain, make square cannonballs, manufacture perpetual motion machines or, in one instance, for no stated purpose. They all got money from investors that packed Change Alley thick as herring in a barrel. When the inevitable reaction set in, and the value of shares plummeted, thousands were ruined. The ministry collapsed amid general misery, and England's dream of a South Sea trading empire fell with it.

A disappointment to Rogers, of course, but he was already tutored in great expectations unfulfilled. Soon after his return he had agitated for a Madagascar colony that would serve England as the Cape served Holland. It could easily be done, he thought: just clear out a few unwashed pirates, and send in some true Englishmen. He took an East Indianman around the Cape in 1713, ostensibly to deal in slaves, but covertly to have a closer look at the island; he collected religious tracts for the "English inhabitants of Madagascar" — as yet, pirates and their half-breed bastards — and wrote to the naturalist Hans Sloane for information on the island, explaining that he was "ambitious to promote a settlement." Somehow nothing came of it.

Soon he fixed his eye on the slovenly, piratical Bahamas, and pictured them green as Eden. He drew up grandiose plans for

[25] "I might, perhaps, go too far should I assert that this voyage gave rise to the South Sea Company, but this much I can safely say, that the success of this voyage was what the patrons of that company chiefly insisted upon in their defense, when the plan of it was attacked as insufficient and chimerical." Callander III, 379.

them — cutting dyewood, reaping great crops of cotton and sugar, harpooning whales, fishing baskets of gold from sunken galleons and, incidentally, controlling the strategic sea routes to all the middle Americas. In 1717 he and six copartners acquired from the neglectful Lords Proprietors a twenty-one-year lease of the islands, and next year Rogers arrived as unsalaried governor. Unfortunately, it was his duty to stamp out the only source of income that the islands had: piracy. When he had accomplished this by pardoning those who submitted and stringing up those who did not, the shiftlessness of the islanders and the infertility of the soil drove him to ruin. He emptied his own pockets to shore up the rickety structure of government and pay the garrison. By 1721 his credit was being refused, and he sailed for England, worn out with the "dangers, troubles and fateagues" of his post, to put his affairs in order.

Neither the government nor the copartners would make good his losses. Rogers was the stuff that martyrs are made of, but instead of going to the stake — and blessed immortality — he went through the humiliation of bankruptcy. He saw the inside of a debtor's prison. Weary of unstable dreams, his wife seems to have left him. Not until 1726 did the sad condition of one who had served England honorably draw sympathetic attention in high places. The king granted him a modest pension, and in 1728 he was again commissioned to the Bahamas, this time on salary. On the eve of their departure Hogarth painted the little family as it might have gathered in the shade of the Nassau fort at teatime: father sitting bolt upright, wearing his perpetual look of mild surprise, his son exhibiting a map of Providence Island, his pretty daughter with chin lifted in aloof pride, and on the wall a cartouche that read: *Dum Spiro Spero* — while I breathe, I hope.

For three more years, often harassed but always hopeful, Rogers labored to mold the scattered islands and their ragtag population into a respectable colony. Then his breath forsook him. On July 20, 1732, the Bahama Council wrote to the Secretary of State: "Whereas it pleased Almighty God to take unto himself the soul of Woods Rogers Esq. our late Governor on the 15th inst. We acquaint Yr. Lordship therewith." Brief, all too brief, for the man who never failed his duty. Brief, too, his place of burial. The restless sands soon covered it, and no man knows where he lies.

EPILOGUE

DUSK OF THE "SWEET TRADE"

". . . he which hath no stomach to this fight,
Let him depart;
his passport shall be made."
Shakespeare, *Henry V*, Act IV, Scene 3

"THE PRIVATEERS in our wars," said an Admiralty judge comfortably, "are like the *mathematici* of old Rome: a sort of people that will always be found fault with, but still made use of." England and France continued to make use of them in wars that punctuated the eighteenth century. Their ships increased in size, flew an official flag, drilled at gunnery, carried chaplains and surgeons, turned their ragged fiddlers into small orchestras, and mounted enough firepower to battle yardarm-to-yardarm with naval vessels of modest rating. Still, such respectability chafed English seamen like a starched shirt. Whenever the Admiralty dozed, fishing smacks forsook their nets and coasters their cargoes to whoop off in chase of anything afloat. The neutral Dutch suffered most. During the Seven Years War (1756–1763) one Dutch captain reported that off Dover his trader was robbed by a nine-man fishing smack in the morning; within minutes another crewed by twelve was alongside; a mile further, a third, the boarders armed only with clubs and pistols; at midnight, still another. Next morning a small privateer took more plunder; an hour later, a second; and at noon two arrived at once. That afternoon a large privateer rifled him of goods that filled a pair of longboats to the gunwale. A few days later he was held up for the tenth and last time, but was not robbed — there was nothing left to take.

At worst these rascals were piratical; at best they constituted no more than auxiliaries to Britain's growing naval power. It was left to the Americans to revive the Elizabethan tradition by fighting two wars with little but privateers at their command. The War of Independence caught the American colonies with a sea arm that consisted of thirteen moldering frigates, a number that steadily dwindled as the war progressed. Britain already had more than a hundred naval vessels in American waters, backed by a vast reservoir at home, and the Continental Congress recognized that any direct clash with her sea power was as foolish as "an infant taking a mad bull by his horns." But the smoke of Lexington Common had hardly faded before a New Bedford privateer scooped up the royal sloop *Falcon* off Martha's Vineyard, and thereafter the struggle at sea belonged to the private fighting ships.

The Americans commissioned anything that would float — longboats, whalers, ferries, pilot boats, traders — and launched the largest privateering operation in history. One Chesapeake cockleshell cruising the Irish Sea was so small that the captain of a prize asked the crew where they had left their ship. In all, Congress and the states issued more than 2500 letters of marque, to 120 issued by the British. With greater opportunity for plunder, and many more ships at sea for the purpose, the Americans were able to capture 2300 enemy prizes while losing only half that number. Fast, light-armed cruisers roamed recklessly from the Shetlands to Gibraltar. In American waters they reduced food and munitions available to the redcoat army by intercepting supply ships. In the Caribbean they sailed from Martinique with French crews and French papers, and George Washington dined off china snatched by these masqueraders from the solicitor-general of the British West Indies. Minister to France Benjamin Franklin further exacerbated Anglo-French relations by commissioning Dunkirkers that drove Channel shipping to cover.

"A short, easy and infallible method of humbling the English," crowed John Adams from his Amsterdam station. In England prices rose, marine insurance climbed steeply, food shortages threatened. A West Indian merchant wrote home: "God knows, if this American war continues much longer, we shall die of hunger." Harbor dues fell to half in West-of-England ports. Liverpool's trade was so paralyzed that charity rolls jumped by 10,000 and London goods moved largely in French bottoms for safety.

Yet injury to British commerce by privateers could not humble the mother country's armed might. That demanded professional fighting ships whose aim, and power, was to destroy the enemy's naval force. Not until thirty-six French warships blocked the British relief fleet, and cut off Cornwallis' retreat by sea from Yorktown, did the War of Independence end in an American victory.

Failing to learn this lesson, the brash young republic pitted itself against Britain thirty years later in a war that the Americans were lucky to get out of with a whole skin. During the conflicts arising from the French Revolution *flibustiers* had seized 2100 English vessels between 1793 and 1796, spreading their depredations to American waters, where they took any ship suspected of trading with a British port. American merchantmen bound for the West Indies were confiscated with the utmost arrogance — passengers robbed, crews beaten and stripped of their clothing, officers thumbscrewed. In retaliation, Congress authorized seizure of any French ship caught in the Americas, and this harsh order resulted in a Franco-American accord to pass all neutral shipping except contraband of war. However, the situation only grew worse. Napoleon's "Continental System" attempted to cripple England economically, and in reply England imposed a blockade upon the ports of the continent with the object of forcing them to trade with Britain. No neutral ship was safe in European waters. The United States, whose trade was hardest hit, was further angered by England's insistence on the right of search at sea, and her practice of impressing from on board American ships seamen suspected of being British citizens. June 18, 1812 the United States declared war on Great Britain.

At sea, the combatants were more unequally matched than

ever. The United States had but a score of ships, not all fit for action, to throw against 800 British warships in fighting trim. American officers gloomed that they were expected to be pillars in war after being scorned as caterpillars in peace. Congress knew where its martime strength lay; the same Act that declared war also authorized the issuance of privateering commissions.

The contest at sea opened in the atmosphere of a tilting tournament, where someone might get hurt, but all were knights of the same realm. The courtesies prevailed. When the American *Dash* captured the British *Whiting* before the latter knew that war was declared, she let the prize go as the only sporting thing to do. The captain of the British frigate *Guerriere* challenged any American warship of equal firepower to what he archly called "a social *tête-à-tête*." Meanwhile American shipwrights worked double shift to turn out some of the deadliest marauders that ever stalked a sea lane: the "Baltimore clippers." Long, low in the water, tall masts raked aft and canvas piled high, these beauties were built to chase or run, and Britain had nothing that could catch them. They cut merchantmen out of a convoy as neatly as a cowpoke cuts heifers out of a herd. Light-armed, but manned by large crews, they preferred to sweep down on a victim for one point-blank broadside and then board with a rush. During two and a half years of war, they bagged 1300 British vessels to Britain's 900.

Britain could not contain these swift cruisers until freed from the Napoleonic struggle in the spring of 1814. Then she swung westward like a massive door to shut up American ports with a tight blockade. Land sorties on both sides had been ill-managed and inconclusive. Stalemated in a war that few wanted and neither could win, the belligerents made peace at Ghent in December, 1814.

As though a hidden bell had tolled, privateering by European nations ceased with the Treaty of Ghent. For five centuries the privateer had served to expand the seapower of every maritime nation. He had crushed the Armada and saved England. He had safeguarded colonies, fought sea wars, trained seamen for battle, despoiled the enemy, fetched home rich treasure. Abruptly, the private fighting ship disappeared from European waters, and was seen no more.

The departure was startlingly sudden, but the reasons for it are easy to find. By the time Napoleon had surrendered after Waterloo, all the major causes that led to privateering had disappeared. Its existence depended on frequent wars, weak navies, and private vessels easily converted to military use. Now Europe entered a century of comparative peace. The British navy, a match for all other sea forces in the world combined, had no further need of its unruly auxiliaries. The professionalization of the naval service and the construction of vessels designed solely for battle made the conversion of merchantmen to war service less and less practicable. Costly steam power replaced sail, corporations replaced individual shipowners. As trade grew and peace held, neither merchant vessels nor merchant crews were prepared to go onto a war footing. The privateer simply became obsolete.

During the eighteenth century, more humane treatment of noncombatants in land fighting had produced a change in military ethics. Unrestrained pillage of civilian property had greatly diminished, although the levy of ransom, as a substitute, fell chiefly on civilian shoulders. Captured soldiers no longer were the personal property of their captor, but were exchanged by the belligerent governments through regular channels. National armies held roving bands of mercenaries in disrepute. More and more, wars were fought between professional soldiers wielding specialized weapons, and noncombatants were not harmed in their persons or property if they kept out of the way.

The theory of warfare slowly caught up with these realities. Until mid-eighteenth century, writers on the subject had placed whole populations at the mercy of the victor. From the Roman Cicero to the Dutch jurist Bynkershoek in 1737, all property of the vanquished was considered confiscable. But the growth of national states, coupled with a romantic view of man's nature, evoked the curious theory that noncombatants are not involved in war at all. In his *Contrat Social* (1762) Rousseau gave this idea its most influential statement: "War is not at all a relation of man to man, but a relation of state to state, in which individuals are enemies only accidentally — not as men, not even as citizens, but as soldiers, not as members of their states, but as its defenders."

This detachment of citizens from their government's warlike actions had its humanitarian side, and appealed to those eager to humanize war and encourage peaceful pursuits. Soon its logic was transferred to the sea. "We should regard with horror," said a French writer in 1754, "an army which made war on citizens and robbed them of their goods . . . How, I ask, can that which is infamous on land be just or at any rate permissible at sea?" The French championed this point of view vigorously, joined by a chorus of voices from Holland, Germany, Italy, Belgium and Russia. England, her all-powerful navy in control of trade lanes, would not agree. Nor, in a pinch, would the United States, although she had given lip service to the outlawry of private seizure. Wars, said Jefferson bluntly, as his country grappled with England in 1812, are fought by whole nations: "Who carries on the war? Armies are formed and navies are manned by individuals. How is the battle gained? By the death of individuals. What produces peace? The distress of individuals . . . By licensing private armed vessels the whole naval force of the nation is truly brought to bear on the foe, and while the contest lasts, that it may have the speedier termination, let every individual contribute his mite in the best way that he can — to distress and harass the enemy and compel him to peace."

However, in many quarters, American and British as well as

continental, sentiment continued for the protection of neutral shipping and nonmilitary cargo in wartime. When England and France allied against Russia in the Crimea (1854), both sides disclaimed any intention of commissioning privateers. This was easily done, for Russia had virtually none to commission, and the allied fleets did not need any. At the Paris peace conference of 1856, when its main business had been concluded, the president, Count Walewski of France, had a suggestion to make. Should not the distinguished delegates do something memorable before they disbanded? Could they further the progress of humanity "by laying the foundations of a uniform maritime law, in time of war"? Why not bring about widespread, even universal, agreement that seizure of private nonmilitary goods at sea should be henceforth outlawed?

He set forth four propositions:

1. Privateering is and remains abolished.

2. The neutral flag covers enemy's merchandise with the exception of contraband of war.

3. Neutral merchandise, with the exception of contraband of war, is not capturable under the enemy's flag.

4. Blockades, in order to be obligatory, must be effective — that is to say, maintained by force sufficient to really prevent access to the coast of the enemy.

The British were feeling relaxed. Their delegate, Lord Clarendon, thought that "our state of civilization and humanity required that an end should be put to the system which no longer belongs to our time." Representatives present at the treaty conference cleared with their home governments and signed, although the Russian muttered a few doubts before he took up the pen. Most great powers ratified, and many small ones, even those without ports or marine, such as Switzerland.

The United States, Spain and Mexico did not ratify. Although Americans had defended the policy that "free ships make free goods," they were not yet ready to surrender the privateer and become helpless before an effective blockade. This made the liberal republic seem to repudiate a humanitarian step, and Secretary of State William Learned Marcy recovered with a neat diplomatic ploy. He declared that the peace conference had not gone far enough in advancing human welfare, and he proposed as an amendment that *all* private property (except materials of war) be exempted from seizure, even if carried in belligerent ships. This, of course, was going too far, since nations at war would then be unable to attack the private commerce of each other in any degree, and the amendment quietly died.

Within less than a decade the United States had reason to regret its stand. If the Declaration of Paris had little persuasive power on the government at Washington, it could have even less on the secessionist South, and as soon as the Confederacy was formed in the spring of 1861 President Jefferson Davis invited privateering applications. Two days later President Lincoln announced that since the Confederacy was not a legitimate government, its privateers would be treated as pirates. He soon had a test case. By November captured southern privateers were on trial in New York and Philadelphia, with the war press howling for their necks. The defense argued that Britain had recognized Revolutionary War commissions with far less reason than in the present case. The New York jury refused to convict, and a new trial was set for the next term, but prisoners in the Philadelphia court were condemned. At once Davis selected by lot the same number of high-ranking Northerners who were in his custody, and promised that they would suffer the same fate as the privateers. Rough justice, but effective; the privateers were packed off to military prison, and no more was heard of piracy trials.

The South's lack of ships, and those few hemmed in by what the Charleston *Mercury* admitted to be "the very efficient blockade of Abraham I," reduced conventional privateering to a rather scrubby affair. Inventive Southerners hoped to even the balance with ingenuity. The first product of this strategy was an iron-clad ram, the *Manassas,* built at New Orleans in the summer of 1861. A thick, convex, housing, sheathed with iron plates and surmounted only by a smokestack, was set onto the cut-down hull of a former icebreaker. Solid timber filled twenty feet of her prow. A 32-pound gun could poke from an automatic port forward; steam jets would repel boarders. "Something very like a whale was seen yesterday morning up and down the river," ran the discreet notice in the New Orleans *True Delta* on September 11. Secrecy during the *Manassas*'s construction only spurred fevered rumors in the North: New Yorkers pictured her with an augur in her snout to bore holes in enemy bottoms.

This melon-shaped monster was too promising for the feeble Confederate naval force to lose. Although the *Manassas* was built with private funds, and regularly commissioned as a privateer, the New Orleans commodore took possession of her a month after she appeared on the river. Two nights later he sent her downstream, in advance of his shabby flotilla, to attack Union warships anchored at the Head of the Passes. In the dark of early morning, under cover of a sky moonless and overcast, the *Manassas* glided noiselessly among the four blockaders. The watch on the stout flagship *Richmond* cried alarm too late as the *Manassas*, under a full head of steam, crashed into her midships. Planks splintered at the *Richmond*'s waterline, but the shock did more damage to the rammer than to her victim. Both her engines shook loose, one ceased to function entirely; the smokestack toppled and poured fumes over the choking crew. She limped away under a hail of enemy fire. The *Manassas*'s brief dream of ramming the North into submission was over.

Then why not a submarine? Private capital in New Orleans soon launched the *Pioneer,* an underwater midget crewed by four, and propelled by a pair of hand cranks. Her attack plan: run under the enemy with a contact-fused torpedo in tow. After blowing up a practice barge "so that only a few splinters were heard from," the *Pioneer*'s future looked auspicious. She

R

was commissioned as a privateer on March 31, 1862. Plunder was out of the question, but rewards as high as $100,000 were being offered for the destruction of a strong Union ship. As it turned out, the *Pioneer* never met her test in action. When Farragut's fleet took New Orleans in April, the world's first privateer submarine was sunk to keep her from enemy hands.

In Mobile, her builders put together a somewhat more sophisticated *Pioneer II*, which foundered in choppy seas. A third, made from a steam boiler, was double the length of her predecessors, and carried twice as many men. She had a fatal habit of diving her nose into the mud and sticking there while her crew asphyxiated. Turned over to the military, she was shipped by rail to Charleston, but the change of auspices cured none of her faults. In October, she trapped one of her builders, Robert Hunley, in a dive beneath the surface of the harbor, and when the submarine was fished up and the hatch opened, his dead face stared out with an expression of despair.

A kinder snipper of threads would have spared poor Hunley for one more voyage. The submarine was now named in his honor, and a new crew enlisted, although the men called their craft the "Peripatetic Coffin." A rigorous period of drill and maneuvers aimed at avoiding further disaster. The towed torpedo had a dangerous tendency to drift on the current faster than the *Hunley* could navigate, so the charge was fixed to a twenty-foot spar in her nose. At dusk of February 17, 1864, the *Hunley* proceeded out of Charleston Harbor through a sea "smooth as a small pond." South of the harbor lay the blockade ship *Housatonic*, a wooden corvette of 1800 tons and twenty-three guns. A few hours later the *Hunley* rammed the torpedo spar against her side, a tremendous explosion blew out the *Housatonic*'s bottom, she rolled over, settled by the stern, and sank in seconds. Caught in her rigging, like Ahab clenched to the side of the white whale, the *Hunley* went down with her prey.

It was premonitory that by 1863 the Confederacy had gathered its privateers under government control as a Volunteer Navy, complete with uniform dress. Plainly, privateering was obsolete. No Declaration of Paris was necessary to banish it. That rude magistrate, time, banished it. Specialized armed services banished it; strong government banished it; public opinion buried it deep. It ceased, as things will, when they are no longer useful. One can hardly imagine its return, but man is a pragmatic creature who must, above all, survive. If privateering is ever needed, it will be back.

GLOSSARY OF SEA TERMS
SOURCES
BIBLIOGRAPHY
INDEX

GLOSSARY OF SEA TERMS

ABACK: said of sails when they are faced to a head-on wind, and the ship's forward progress halts.

ARRACK: various oriental liquors, usually brewed from rice or coconut.

BARQUE: a small three-master, the sternmost rigged fore-and-aft.

BARKENTINE: a small three-master, square-rigged forward, fore-and-aft on the other two masts.

BEAK-HEAD: a small raised platform over the bow.

BEAT: to sail against the wind, especially on alternate tacks.

BIGHT: a loop in the body of a rope, formed accidentally or for purposes of knotting.

BILBOES: two bars of iron, with shackles sliding on them, to bind the prisoner's feet in a sitting posture.

BINNACLE: a wooden box at the tiller, holding the compass, log glasses, and lights for night readings.

BRAIL UP: furl sail by tying securely to yard or mast.

BULKHEAD: any of the partitions throughout the ship.

CASE SHOT: a cylindrical tin container filled with small shot and scraps of iron for scattered fire.

CAP: a large block of wood by which the base of an upper mast is fitted to the top of the next lower one.

CAPSTAN: an upright circular winch turned by handbars, for heavy work.

CAULK: to drive strands of oakum or old rope into a ship's seams and cover with pitch or resin, to prevent leaking.

CRANK, CRANKY: said of a vessel that lacks stability, and is easily heeled over by sea or wind.

DINGHY: a small ship's boat without sails.

DRIVE: to be carried by wind or current, with or without sails.

FLAW: a sudden gust of wind.

FLIP: small beer, brandy and sugar — a seaman's favorite.

FORE-AND-AFT–RIGGED: as in the case of virtually all modern sailing ships the inside (luff) edge of the sail is secured to the mast, and its lower edge to the boom, by which latter the sail is swung from one side of the ship to the other.

FRIGATE: has a distinct rise of four or five steps from the waist to the forecastle and quarterdeck; in naval parlance a fast-sailing man-of-war, usually mounting twenty-eight to thirty-six guns on a single gundeck.

FUSEE: a light musket.

GAFF-RIGGED: has rectangular, assymetrical sail, fore-and-aft, the upper edge fixed to a spar called the gaff.

GALLEY: in England, a level-decked vessel, stem to stern, relying primarily on sails, but fitted with auxiliary sweeps; in the Mediterranean, a vessel primarily or solely oar-driven, and worked by slaves or convicts.

GRAPNEL: light anchor with sharp flukes, used to hook the enemy in boarding.

KEDGE: small anchor thrown out to keep a ship from riding over its bow anchor in a change of tide or wind; also carried out by boat and the ship drawn up to it on the capstan, to move ship in harbor.

KEELSON: heavy timber set above the keel and over the floor timbers, to secure the latter.

KETCH: small two-master, fore-and-aft rigged, the mizzen set well aft.

LATEEN SAIL: triangular, slung on a long yard, the narrow point of the sail set low to the mast.

LIE TO, HEAVE TO: set sails so as to counteract each other and hold ship stationary.

LIFT: rope strung from masthead through the yardarm to steady the latter.

LINSTOCK: long metal stick for holding the gunner's match.

MATCH: slow-burning rope-end used to ignite the cannon charge.

MAUL: large iron hammer for heavy work.

MIZZEN: the sternmost mast of a two- or three-masted vessel.

MORTAR: short, wide-mouthed cannon, used to discharge fused bombs which exploded after reaching the target.

OUTRIGGER: pontoon, extended by two arms from the side of a small sailboat, to give it stability.

PINNACE: ship's boat, usually equipped with a single sail, eight oars.

PIRAGUA: canoe hollowed from a single log; sometimes large boat, plank-built, flat-bottomed, with one sail.

POLEAX: large hatchet armed with a sharp point at the back of the head; by driving a series of them into a tall ship's side, boarders made themselves an impromptu ladder.

PRIMING-IRON: thin iron rod pushed down a cannon's touchhole to pierce the powder bag for firing.

QUARTER: used alone, always off the stern, the port or starboard quarter circle between keel and beam.

RAKING FIRE: down a ship's length, either from bow or stern.

RAMMER: wooden cylinder on a staff, to drive the powder bag down the cannon barrel.

REEF: to reduce or shorten sail by hauling part of it up to the yard.

RUNG: upper end of a floor timber, where it joins the side timber.

ROW AND TOW: to move ship in calm weather by using sweeps, and by towing with small boats.

SCUPPER: channel cut through the ship's side at the deckline, to drain off water.

SHOT-PLUG: conical piece of wood to hammer into holes made in the ship's side by enemy fire.

SHROUD: rope from masthead to side of ship to steady mast.

SLOOP: single-masted sailing vessel, gaff-rigged.

SPONGE: cylindrical piece of wood, covered with lambskin or coarse wool, to clean cannon after firing.

SQUARE-RIGGED: rectangular sail set before the mast, its normal position across the ship's width.

STAY: strong rope fore-and-aft to support mast.

STEERAGE: fore part of stern cabin, under quarterdeck.

STERN CHASER: small cannon placed in stern of ship to fire on pursuer.

STRETCH: to run before wind under full sail.

STUDDING SAIL: light sail extended beyond usual one, to catch moderate breeze.

SWEEP: long oar used on ships of war to make way in calm, or assist in turning about when the wind was light.

TACK: to set sails at an angle and make way off, but against, the wind, to port or starboard of its direct force. Also rope and hook used to secure windward corner of mainsail close to wind.

TAFFRAIL: curved upper works of ship's stern.

THWART: boat bench on which rower sits.

TRADE WIND: steady wind, either perpetual or during a known season, in or near the tropics, N.E. to S.W.

WAD: ball of rope yarn, tow or hay, pressed down cannon barrel to keep ball and charge in place.

WAIST: middle deck, lower than either forecastle in bow or quarterdeck aft.

WEAR: to reach opposite tack not by swinging across the wind, but by turning away from it and coming about in a three-quarter circle.

WHERRY: light, two-oared riverboat, used especially to carry passengers on the Thames.

YARD: crosspiece on mast from which square sail hangs.

YAWL: small ship's boat with single sail, usually six oars.

SOURCES

(For complete titles and authors, see Bibliography, pp. 251–257)

Prologue

Page
4   "The conduct of all privateers" Statham, p. 12.
5   "almost attained the dignity" Oppenheim, p. 177.
10 "should violate the peace" Hakluyt, p. 136.
10 "that he, in the faith" Hakluyt, p. 137.
11 "cook, brewer" Kendall, p. 33.
11 "God would be pleased" Kendall, p. 25.
12 "deare Pyrat" Kendall, p. 2.
12 "the master thief" Gosse, p. 115.
12 "flogged, tortured" Kendall, p. 17.
14 "Your mariners rob" Kendall, p. 21.
14 "James was made up" Kendall, p. 54.
15 "Their North Pole" *State Papers*, J. Thurloe Collection, London, 1742, VII, 525. Quoted Means, p. 146.
15 (*fn. 9*) "whole, entire" Hurd, p. 38.
16 "above all in humbling" Means, p. 146.
17 "a Colossus" Cambridge, I, 228.
18 "sold, spoiled" Jameson, p. 349.
20 "outdo the Dutch" Part of the title of Andrew Yarranton, *England's Improvement by Sea and Land*, 1677. Quoted Clark, p. 59.
20 "What matters this reason" Moorhouse, p. 89.
26 "Corbleu!" Roberts, p. 43.
27 "Your past is nothing" Kendall, p. 112.
27 "from strict saints" *CSP*, November 6, 1665, no. 1085.
30 "People have not married" *CSP*, 1669–74, no. 697.
30 "sickness of Jamaica" *CSP*, 1669–74, no. 777.
33 "They only permit him" Johnson, p. 185.

Page
34   "All the persons"   *CSP*, June 6, 1699, no. 495.
36   (*fn. 15*) "at the Desire" *London Stage*, Carbondale, Ill.,
        Southern Illinois University Press, 1960, pt. II, vol. II, p. 290.

Morgan

Page
39   (*fn. 17*) "was that the Tories" *Lives*, p. 8.
45   "was a rich yeoman"   Esquemeling, p. 120.
45   "Gentleman's Son"   Lindsay, p. 281.
45   "went at first out"   P.A. Esq., Preface.
45   "the good old Colonel"   *CSP*, 1661–8, no. 1085.
47   "the old privateer"   *CSP*, 1661–8, no. 1085.
47   "There is no profitable employment"   *CSP*, 1661–8, no. 1265.
47   "first felled the trees"   *CSP*, 1661–8, no. 1851.
48   "died very poor"   *CSP*, 1661–8, no. 1085.
48   "of good estate"   *CSP*, 1661–8, no. 1085.
48   "very well"   (Morgan's will); Roberts, p. 275.
48   (*fn. 4*) "having no clothes"   *CSP*, 1661–8, no. 1851.
49   "The Spanish look on us"   *CSP*, 1661–8, no. 1246.
49   "Had my abilities"   *CSP*, 1661–8, no. 1537.
49   "gentle usage"   *CSP*, 1661–8, no. 1264.
49   "who upon serious consideration"   *CSP*, 1661–8, no. 1264.
50   "to draw together"   *CSP*, 1661–8, no. 1838.
51   "if you surrender not"   Esquemeling, p. 135.
52   "But Captain Morgan"   Esquemeling, p. 140.
53   "If our number is small"   Esquemeling, p. 141.
57   (*fn. 9*) "This they performed"   Esquemeling, p. 146.
57   (*fn. 9*) "and one that was sick"   *CSP*, 1669–74, no. 138.
57   (*fn. 9*) a person of quality" etc.   *CSP*, 1661–8, no. 1838.
58   "that in case he departed not"   Esquemeling, p. 147.
58   "he desired him to accept"   Esquemeling, p. 148.
59   "Being arrived"   Esquemeling, p. 149.
59   "questionless either murdered"   *CSP*, 1661–8, no. 1850.
59   "It is most certain"   *CSP*, 1661–8, no. 1850.
61   (*fn. 13*) "that she was abroad"   Dampier, I, p. 72.
63   "We must make one meal"   Esquemeling, p. 159.
63   "but the fears"   Esquemeling, p. 165.
64   "My intent is to dispute"   Esquemeling, p. 168.
64   "they had rather fight"   Esquemeling, p. 169.
67   "not doubting"   *CSP*, 1669–74, no. 103.

Page
67   "their ships will wear out"   CSP, 1669–74, no. 129.
67   "absolutely and forthwith"   CSP, 1669–74, no. 193.
68   "cause war to be published"   CSP, 1669–74, no. 149.
68   "The Spanish begin"   CSP, 1669–74, no. 162.
68   "to perform all manner"   CSP, 1669–74, no. 211.
68   "then with all expedition"   CSP, 1669–74, no. 212.
68   "loathness to spill" etc.   CSP, 1669–74, no. 212.
69   "I Captain Manuel Rivero Pardal"   CSP, 1669–74, no. 310, II.
70   "To advise his fleet"   CSP, 1669–74, no. 212.
71   "unless he were assured"   CSP, 1669–74, no. 237.
71   "intimating that though"   CSP, 1669–74, no. 359.
72   "for the good of Jamaica"   CSP, 1669–74, no. 504.
77   "Dogs! we shall meet you"   Esquemeling, p. 217.
79   "The enemies' retreat"   CSP, 1669–74, no. 504.
79   "Thus was consumed"   CSP, 1669–74, no. 504.
79   (fn. 17) "About noon, he caused"   Esquemeling, p. 223.
79   (fn. 17) "instead of fighting"   CSP, 1669–74, no. 504.
81   "he came not thither"   Esquemeling, p. 234.
81   "a man little given"   Esquemeling, p. 235.
82   "having designed in his mind"   Esquemeling, p. 238.
82   "who gave him many thanks"   CSP, 1669–74, no. 542, I.
82   "It is impossible"   Roberts, p. 184.
83   "Whereas Sir Thos. Modyford"   CSP, 1669–74, no. 405.
84   "that his life and fortune"   CSP, 1669–74, no. 604.
84   "answer for his offences"   Roberts, p. 187.
84   "to speak the truth of him"   CSP, 1669–74, no. 697.
84   "they would take it"   CSP, 1669–74, no. 580.
85   "very much tired"   Roberts, p. 189.
86   "a very high and honourable"   CSP, 1669–74, no. 789.
86   "and all good men"   Roberts, p. 198.
86   "particular confidence"   CSP, 1669–74, no. 1379.
87   "one of the lewdest"   Pepys, VIII, 464.
87   (fn. 22) "A person of as ill fame"   Pepys, VIII, p. 464, note.
88   "In the Downs"   Lindsay, p. 192.
88   "73 dishes"   Lindsay, p. 191.
89   "I am perfectly weary of him"   CSP, 1675–6, no. 566.
89   "has made himself"   CSP, 1675–6, no. 673.
89   "what I most resent"   CSP, 1675–6, no. 912.
90   "if ever I err"   CSP, 1675–6, no. 1129.
91   "a perishing condition"   Lindsay, p. 205.

Page

92 "he asked nor desired nothing" Lindsay, p. 212.

92 (*fn. 24*) "with his generous humor" *CSP*, 1681–5, no. 85.

93 "not above four thousand whites" *CSP*, 1677–80, no. 815.

93 "many of them were weak" Haring, p. 224.

94 "dangerous pestilence" Lindsay, p. 227.

94 "privateers in the West Indies" *CSP*, 1681–5, no. 73.

94 "I have put to death" *CSP*, 1681–5, no. 73.

95 "When any of the pirates" *CSP*, 1677–80, no. 159.

95 "I abhor bloodshed" *CSP*, 1681–5, no. 431.

95 "nothing can be more fatal" *CSP*, 1681–5, no. 1425.

95 "God forgive 'em" *CSP*, 1677–80, no. 73.

95 "an absolute averseness" *CSP*, 1681–5, no. 115.

95 "contemptuous toward" *CSP*, 1681–5, no. 77.

95 "I wonder that notwithstanding" *CSP*, 1681–5, no. 176.

96 "A little, drunken, silly party" *CSP*, 1681–5, no. 1348.

96 "one of the worst" *CSP*, 1681–5, no. 1573.

96 "an ill man" *CSP*, 1681–5, no. 963.

96 "more trouble" *CSP*, 1681–5, no. 1573.

97 "a virulent, base-natured fellow" *CSP*, 1681–5, no. 1249.

97 "Do you say" *CSP*, 1681–5, no. 1249.

97 "By chance, Sir Henry Morgan" *CSP*, 1681–5, no. 1249.

98 "loyalty to him" *CSP*, 1681–5, no. 1302.

98 "disorders, passions" *CSP*, 1681–5, no. 1302.

98 "God damn the Assembly!" *CSP*, 1681–5, no. 1294.

98 "malicious disturbances" *CSP*, 1681–5, no. 1311.

99 "I would not live" *CSP*, 1681–5, no. 1348.

99 "so haughty" *CSP*, 1681–5, no. 1348.

99 "in his drink" *CSP*, 1681–5, no. 1348.

99 "these men are of great violence" *CSP*, 1681–5, no. 1348.

100 (*fn. 29*) "All those Cruelties" etc. Preface.

101 "and whereas also" Roberts, p. 298.

101 "the aforesaid Henry" Roberts, p. 303.

102 "Let the great Morgan" Lindsay, p. 258.

102 "History of ye Buccaneers" Roberts, p. 263.

103 "he is said" *Complete Peerage*, London, St. Catherine Press, I, 90.

103 "One thing I have omitted" Roberts, p. 273; cf. *CSP*, 1685–8, no. 1567.

104 "was an honour" Edwards, I, 177, note.

104 "utterly undone" Lindsay, p. 267; cf. *CSP*, 1685–8, no. 1941.

Page
105 "But the name of the wicked" Lindsay, p. 292.
105 "I am afraid" *CSP*, 1685–8, no. 1858.
105 "Lean, sallow-coloured" Sloane, I, p. XCVIII.
105 "falling afterwards" Sloane, I, p. XCIX.
106 "my very well" Roberts, p. 275.
106 "sixty pounds per annum" Roberts, p. 275.
106 "having black ribbands" Lindsay, p. 273.
106 "This day about 11 hours" Roberts, p. 278.
106 (*fn.* 32) "he has seized" Leslie, p. 48.
106 (*fn.* 32) "he died soon after" Gardner, p. 68.
106 (*fn.* 32) "he was a ruffian" Bancroft, VII, p. 515.
106 (*fn.* 32) "in the Tower of London" Pyle, p. 31.

Kidd

Page
112 "never disbursing six pence" *Docs. Rel. Col. Hist. N.Y.*, IV, 251.
113 "He was a mighty man" Howell, p. 208.
113 "the many good services" Hinrichs, p. 145.
113 "On the whole" *Manual of the Corporation of New York City*, D. T. Valentine (ed.), 1858, p. 514.
113 (*fn.* 2) "You have caused" Doc. Hist. N.Y., II, 215.
114 "lovely and accomplished" de Peyster, p. 29.
114 (*fn.* 3) "about 56 years old" Paul Lorrain, "Ordinary of Newgate his account of the Behavior, Confession and Death of Captain William Kidd . . . ," London, 1701; cf. Wilkins, p. 4.
115 "He is a stranger" Blathwayt Papers, X, Col. Wmsbg., May 29, 1695. Cf. Leder, p. 109. The writer is indebted for the full text of the quotation to a personal letter from D. M. Hinrichs.
115 "We have a parcel" *CSP*, 1693–6, no. 1892.
115 "wild worldly" Jasper Danckaerts, *The Journal of Jasper Danckaerts, 1679–1680* (New York: Charles Scribner's Sons, 1913), p. 44.
116 "be always present" E. Keble Chatterton, *The Old East Indiamen* (London: T. Werner Laurie, 1914), p. 122.
116 "I send you" Macaulay, IV, 498.
117 "We can make it" See Burnet, IV, 433.
118 "liv'd regularly" Wilkins, p. 28.

Page

118   "I was without my knowledge" *Hist. MSS. Com.*, VIII, 79.
118   "told him he had enough" Howell, p. 208.
118   (*fn. 5*) "emphatically a bad man" Macaulay, III, 307.
118   (*fn. 5*) "He gave me" *Hist. MSS. Com.*, VIII, 69.
119   "I hope by this" Livingston Journal, Van Laer typescript, p. 80; cf. Leder, p. 109.
119   "the Earl of Bellomont" Brooks, p. 8.
120   "to apprehend seize and take" Brooks, p. 13.
120   "To our Trusty" Brooks, pp. 15–16.
120   "as far as the said Premises" Brooks, p. 192.
122   "broke articles with us" *CSP*, 1700, no. 850.
122   "Many flocked to him" *CSP*, 1697–8, no. 1098.
123   "so few" Hinrichs, p. 155.
124   "Come, boys" Howell, p. 164.
126   "I am not come" Cf. Kidd's "Narrative," Brooks, p. 196; also Hugh Parrott testimony, Howell, p. 142.
127   "How could you have put me" Cf. Howell, pp. 134–142, *passim*.
128   "By God, have I catched you?" Howell, p. 158.
130   "before I would do you any harm" Howell, p. 167.
131   "obnoxious pirate" Dow-Edmonds, p. 74.
131   "Take particular care" *JHC*, XIII, 16.
132   "received him" *A Brief Historical Relation of State Affairs*, Oxford University Press, 1857, IV, 544.
132   "an honest man" Hinrichs, p. 114.
133   "with folded hands" Hinrichs, p. 118.
133   (*fn. 11*) "my loving brother-in-law" *Abstracts of Wills on File in the Surrogate's Office*, City of New York, Vol. 1, 1665–1707, published in *Collections of the New York Historical Society*, 1892 (New York: New York Historical Society, 1893), p. 366.
134   "menacing him" *CSP*, 1700, no. 983.
134   "are of the opinion" *JHC*, XIII, p. 22.
134   "When I heard people say" *CSP*, 1699, no. 621.
135   "I doubt not" etc. *JHC*, XIII, p. 22.
136   "fancied he looked" *CSP*, 1699, no. 680.
137   "seven of the buttons" Wilkins, p. 113.
137   "the said Ship" Jameson, p. 212.
138   "What a knave" *CSP*, 1699, no. 1016.
138   "to acquaint me" *CSP*, 1700, no. 14.

Page
138 "there never was a greater liar" *CSP*, 1699, no. 680.
138 "Your Lordships" *CSP*, 1699, no. 890.
139 "perishing" *CSP*, 1699, no. 850.
139 "Send hither" *Docs. Rel. Col. Hist. N.Y.*, IV, 603–4.
140 "these seemed to be" Stock, II, 311.
140 "What would become" Stock, II, 311.
140 "That the letters patent" Stock, II, 316.
140 "be gagged" Stock, II, p. 326.
141 "when I am clear" *Hist. MSS. Com.*, VIII, 78.
141 "not be tried" *JHC*, XIII, 286, March 16, 1700.
141 "if this fellow" James, III, 6.
142 "fitt" Wilkins, p. 151.
142 "two Deale Boxes" Wilkins, p. 150.
142 "Capt. Kidd was troubled" Wilkins, p. 158.
142 "I have had a great fit" Hinrichs, p. 166.
143 "he could not see" Wilkins, p. 155.
143 "I am wholly unprepared" Hinrichs, p. 166.
143 "according to law" Wilkins, p. 163.
143 "Capt. Kidd is now" Wilkins, p. 164.
144 "I had thought him" Brooks, p. 40.
144 "illegal and void" *JHC*, XIII, 446.
144 "be proceeded against" *JHC*, XIII, p. 446.
144 (*fn. 14*) "all endeavors were used" Burnet, IV, 489.
144 (*fn. 14*) "made me the Tool" Wilkins, p. 147.
146 "William Kidd, hold up thy hand" All trial quotations from
      Howell, *passim*.
146 (*fn. 18*) "an old fellow" *Journal to Stella; Prose Works*
      (London: G. Bell and Sons, 1913), II, 205.
149 (*fn. 20*) "Robert Bradinham, Kidd's surgeon" *CSP*, 1700,
      no. 466.
149 (*fn. 20*) "an honest young man" *Hist. MSS. Com.*, VIII, 75.
149 (*fn. 20*) "is pretty home" *Hist. MSS. Com.*, VIII, 75.
155 "and at such place" Wilkins, p. 183.
156 "*infra fluxum*" Marsden, II, 263.
156 "he expressed abundance" Milligan, p. 163.
158 "no pirate at all" Philip Gosse, in the *Encyclopaedia Britan-
      nica*, 1953, XVII, 952.
158 "flimsey" Hinrichs, p. 139.
158 "precarious" Morris, p. 33.

Page
158 "the essential fact" Homer H. Cooper, "William Kidd, Gen-
      tleman," *American Mercury*, November, 1924, p. 337.
159 "If there was a French pass" Howell, p. 171.
161 "milk-and-water amateur" Brooks, p. 1.
161 "mesmeric revelation" Wilkins, pp. 290–1.

Rogers

Page
167 "By this means" Rogers, Introduction, ix.
167 "There never was any voyage" Callander, III. Quoted Little,
      45.
168 "a very honest" Rogers, p. 300.
169 (*fn. 4*) "'till he had prevailed" Cooke, Introduction.
169 (*fn. 4*) "did me the Honour" Rogers, Introduction, iii.
171 "Our Masts and Rigging" Rogers, p. 2.
171 "not 20 sailors" Rogers, p. 2.
171 "drank their can of Flip" Rogers, p. 5.
171 "crouded and pester'd Rogers, p. 7.
171 "Tinkers, Taylors" Rogers, p. 6.
171 "bring them to discipline" Rogers, p. 6.
171 "we might have exchang'd" Rogers, p. 7.
172 "all Hands drank" Rogers, p. 8.
172 "Now we begin to consider" Rogers, p. 8.
174 "Fine pleasant Weather" Rogers, p. 11.
174 "a good honest old Fellow" Rogers, p. 11.
175 "It was Mr. Vanbrugh's misfortune" Rogers, p. 14.
175 "dilatory Answers" Rogers, p. 15.
175 "Whereas there has been" Rogers, p. 17.
176 "proved of great use" Rogers, p. 17.
176 "We found" Rogers, p. 21.
177 "for the Good of the Voyage" Rogers, p. 173.
177 "continual Scenes" Rogers, p. 22.
178 "begging for God's sake" Cooke, I, 21.
179 "necessary for the Good" Rogers, p. 35.
179 "all manner of noisy" Rogers, p. 31.
180 "At parting" Rogers, p. 33.
180 "necessaries for our next" Rogers, p. 33.
180 "to a happy New Year" Rogers, p. 78.
181 "A little before six" Rogers, p. 78.
182 "We now account our selves" Rogers, p. 80.

Page
185 "to prevent men losing" Cooke, I, 121.
185 "by which we found" Cooke, I, 123.
185 "Our men begin to repine" Rogers, p. 106.
185 (*fn. 11*) "the Methods to prevent" Rogers, Introduction, xii.
185 (*fn. 11*) "this I have experienced" Lloyd, p. 127.
186 "She looks very pretty" Rogers, p. 107.
186 "I saw not" Cooke, I, 132.
187 "Imprim. All manner of Bedding" Rogers, p. 114.
188 "If all the foregoing" Rogers, p. 116.
189 "To my unspeakable Sorrow" Rogers, p. 117.
189 "About twelve" Rogers, p. 117.
190 "the briskest Spaniards" Cooke, I, 138.
190 "the best and soberest Man" Rogers, p. 118.
191 "I had rather be" Rogers, p. 122.
194 "They made a formidable Show" Rogers, p. 128.
194 "With a Handful" Rogers, Introduction, xiii.
195 "Some of their largest Gold Chains" Rogers, p. 131.
196 "A Man we had some Respect for" Rogers, p. 141.
196 "It's worse than Death" Rogers, p. 178.
197 "unfortunate Islands" Rogers, p. 153.
197 "the *Spaniards* Epidemick disease" Rogers, p. 178.
198 "Our men being very much fatigued" Rogers, p. 158.
198 "It's in vain" Rogers, p. 158.
198 "Puny mariners" Rogers, p. 179.
198 "We saluted each" Rogers, p. 162.
198 "ticketed with the Names" Rogers, p. 168.
199 "The Papists here" Rogers, p. 165.
199 "for Disputes about Plunder" Rogers, p. 173.
199 "healing Arguments" Rogers, p. 173.
199 "I long for a Reconciliation" Rogers, p. 174.
200 "A very agreeable Diversion" Rogers, p. 183.
200 "The young Padre" Rogers, p. 187.
201 "as big as a large Bear" etc. Rogers, p. 194.
201 (*fn. 17*) "a disconsolate black albatross" Shelvocke, p. 41.
201 (*fn. 17*) "I had been reading" etc. Wordsworth, p. 72.
202 "Each one is a strong castle" Schurz, p. 196.
203 "A Girl of Tawny Colour" Rogers, p. 204.
203 "We all looked very melancholy" Rogers, p. 212.
207 "To give the enemy their due" Cooke, I, 351.
208 "Twas our great Unhappiness" Rogers, p. 226.

Page
208 "utterly uncapable of the Office" Rogers, p. 226.
208 "his Temper is so violent" Rogers, p. 226.
209 "*Guam*, one of the *Ladrones Islands*" Rogers, p. 228.
209 "to keep those" Rogers, p. 263.
209 "His Room was more acceptable" Rogers, p. 262.
209 (*fn. 19*) "passed by us" Rogers, p. 269.
210 "you may immediately expect" Rogers, p. 264.
210 "I have known the men" Cooke, II, 29.
210 "one of them holding" Cooke, II, 44.
211 "a Bishop's Cap" Rogers, p. 281.
211 "We resolv'd to stay no longer" Rogers, p. 282.
212 "an ugly swelling place" Rogers, p. 300.
212 "out of the Noise" Rogers, p. 308.
213 "incens'd against us" Cooke, II, 100.
213 "Which ends our long" Rogers, p. 314.
213 "perishing for want of bread" Lloyd, p. 155.
214 "to keep to the Language" Rogers, p. 1.
214 (*fn. 21*) "a judicious use" Stanley, 141.
214 (*fn. 22*) "Mr. Ridpath for correcting" Powell, p. 125.
215 "The Wisdom of the Nation" Rogers, Dedication, p. v.
215 (*fn. 23*) "surviving Owners" Rogers, Dedication, iii.
216 "English inhabitants" Little, p. 173.
216 "ambitious to promote" Little, p. 174.
216 (*fn. 25*) "I might, perhaps" Quoted Little, p. 45.
217 "dangers, troubles" *CSP*, April 20, 1720, no. 47.
218 "Whereas it pleased" Public Records Office, London, C.O. 23, 14. f 225. Quoted Little, p. 221. Cf. also *CSP*, 1732, no. 310.

Epilogue

Page
221 "The privateers in our wars" Statham, p. 11.
222 "an infant" Paullin, p. 36.
222 "A short, easy and infallible" Allen, p. 50.
222 "God knows" Paine, p. 29.
224 "a social tete-a-tete" Coggeshall, p. 20.
226 "War is not at all" Book I, Chapter 4.

BIBLIOGRAPHY

ALLEN, GARDNER W. *A Naval History of the American Revolution.* 2 vols. Boston: Houghton Mifflin Co., 1913.

ANDERSON, BERN. *By Sea and River, The Naval History of the Civil War.* New York: Alfred A. Knopf, 1962.

ANDREWS, KENNETH R. *Elizabethan Privateering.* Cambridge: University of Cambridge Press, 1964.

ASHLEY, MAURICE. *England in the Seventeenth Century.* Baltimore: Penguin Books, 1963.

AUGUR, HELEN. *The Secret War of Independence.* New York: Duell, Sloan and Pearce, 1955. In Sources: Augur.

BANCROFT, HUBERT HOWE. *Works.* San Francisco: A. L. Bancroft and Co., 1883. In Sources: Bancroft.

BEIRNE, FRANCIS F. *The War of 1812.* Hamden, Connecticut: Archon Books, 1965.

BONNER, WILLARD HALLAM. *Pirate Laureate.* New Brunswick, New Jersey: Rutgers University Press, 1947.

BOWLES, T. G. *The Declaration of Paris of 1856.* London: Sampson Low, Marston and Co., 1900. In Sources: Bowles.

BROOKS, GRAHAM. *The Trial of Captain Kidd.* London: William Hodge and Co., 1930. In Sources: Brooks.

BURNET, GILBERT. *History of His Own Time.* Oxford: Oxford University Press, 1833. In Sources: Burnet.

BURNEY, JAMES. *History of the Buccaneers of America.* New York: W. W. Norton Co., 1950.

Calendar of State Papers, Colonial, 1661–1732. London.

CALLAGHAN, E. B. (ed.). *Documentary History of the State of New York.* Albany: Weed, Parsons and Co., 1850. In Sources: *Doc. Hist. N.Y.*

————. *Documents Relative to the Colonial History of the State of New York.* Albany: 1854. In Sources: *Docs. Rel. Col. Hist. N.Y.*

CALLANDER, JOHN. *Terra Australis Cognita.* 3 vols. Edinburgh: 1766–68.

Cambridge History of the British Empire. Vol. I. Cambridge: Cambridge University Press, 1960. In Sources: Cambridge.

CAMPBELL, WILLIAM W. *An Historical Sketch of Robin Hood and Captain Kidd.* New York: Charles Scribner, 1853.

CHAPMAN, CHARLES E. *A History of Spain.* New York: Free Press, 1965.

CLARK, G. N. *The Later Stuarts.* Oxford: Clarendon Press, 1934. In Sources: Clark.

COGGESHALL, GEORGE. *History of the American Privateers.* New York: 1856. In Sources: Coggeshall.

Complete Peerage. London: St. Catherine Press, 1910.

COOKE, EDWARD. *A Voyage to the South Sea, and Round the World.* 2 vols. London: 1712. In Sources: Cooke.

CORBETT, JULIAN S. *Drake and the Tudor Navy.* 2 vols. New York: Burt Franklin, 1899.

CROWNINSHIELD, B. B. *An Account of the Private Armed Ship "America" of Salem.* Historical Collections of the Essex Institute. Vol. 37.

CUNDALL, FRANK. *The Governors of Jamaica:* London: West India Committee, 1936.

———. *Historic Jamaica.* London: Institute of Jamaica, 1915.

———. *Studies in Jamaica History.* London: Institute of Jamaica, 1900.

DAMPIER, CAPT. WILLIAM. *Dampier's Voyages.* 2 vols. London: E. Grant Richards, 1906.

DEWHURST, KENNETH. *The Quicksilver Doctor.* Bristol: John Wright and Sons, 1957. In Sources: Dewhurst.

DOW, G. F., and EDMONDS, J. H. *The Pirates of the New England Coast, 1630–1730.* Salem, Massachusetts: Marine Research Society, 1923. In Sources: Dow-Edmonds.

EDWARDS, BRYAN. *A History Civil and Commercial of the British Colonies in the West Indies.* London: John Stockdale, 1819. In Sources: Edwards.

ERLEIGH, VISCOUNT. *The South Sea Bubble.* New York: G. P. Putnam's Sons, 1933.

ESQUEMELING, ALEXANDRE. *The Buccaneers of America.* London: George Routledge and Sons, 1923.

ESQUEMELING, JOHN. *The Buccaneers of America.* London: Swan Sonnenschein and Co., 1893. In Sources: Esquemeling.

FALCONER, WILLIAM. *A New Universal Dictionary of the Marine.* Revised by William Burney. London: T. Cadell and W. Davies, 1815.

FREEMAN, WILLIAM. *The Incredible Defoe*. London: Herbert Jenkins, 1950. In Sources: Freeman.

GAGE, THOMAS. *The English-American, His Travail by Sea and Land*. London: George Routledge and Sons, 1928. In Sources: Gage.

GARDNER, W. J. *History of Jamaica*. London: Elliot Stock, 1873. In Sources: Gardner.

GERHARD, PETER. *Pirates on the West Coast of New Spain*. Glendale, California: A. H. Clark Co., 1960.

GOSNELL, H. ALLEN. *Guns on the Western Waters*. Baton Rouge: Louisiana State University Press, 1949.

GOSSE, PHILIP. *The History of Piracy*. London: Longmans, Green and Co., 1932. In Sources: Gosse.

GREW, E. and M. S. *The Court of William III*. London: Mills and Boon, Ltd., 1910.

GREY, CHARLES. *Pirates of the Eastern Seas*. London: Sampson Low, Marston and Co., 1933.

GUTTRIDGE, G. H. *The Colonial Policy of William III in America and the West Indies*. Cambridge: University of Cambridge Press, 1922.

HAKLUYT, RICHARD. *Hakluyt's Voyages* (selected). Boston: Houghton Mifflin Co., 1929. In Sources: Hakluyt.

HANNAY, DAVID. *A Short History of the Royal Navy*. 2 vols. London: Methuen and Co., 1909.

HARING, C. H. *The Buccaneers in the West Indies in the XVII Century*. London: Methuen and Co., 1910.

———. *The Buccaneers in the West Indies in the XVII Century*. Hamden, Connecticut: Archon Books, 1966. In Sources: Haring.

———. *The Spanish Empire in America*. New York: Harcourt Brace and Co., 1963.

HILL, S. CHARLES. *Notes on Piracy in Eastern Waters*. Bombay: British India Press, 1923.

HINRICHS, DUNBAR MAURY. *The Fateful Voyage of Captain Kidd*. New York: Bookman Associates, 1955. In Sources: Hinrichs.

Historical Manuscript Commission Report, Duke of Portland. London, 1907. In Sources: *Hist. MSS. Com.*

HOWELL, T. B. *A Complete Collection of State Trials*. Vol. XIV. London: 1816. In Sources: Howell.

HURD, ARCHIBALD. *The Reign of the Pirates*. London: Heath, Cranton, 1925. In Sources: Hurd.

HUTTON, STANLEY. *Bristol and Its Famous Associations*. Bristol: J. W. Arrowsmith, 1907.

T

JAMES, G. P. R. *Letters Illustrative of the Reign of William III.* London: Henry Colburn, 1841. In Sources: James.

JAMESON, JOHN FRANKLIN. *Privateering and Piracy in the Colonial Period: Illustrative Documents.* New York: Macmillan Co., 1923. In Sources: Jameson.

JOHNSON, CAPT. CHARLES. *A General History of the Robberies and Murders of the Most Notorious Pirates.* London: George Routledge and Sons, 1932. In Sources: Johnson.

JOHNSON, ROSSITER. *A History of the War of 1812-'15* New York: Dodd, Mead and Co., 1882.

JONES, VIRGIL CARRINGTON. *The Civil War at Sea.* New York: Holt, Rinehart and Winston, 1960.

Journals of the House of Commons, 1803. In Sources: JHC.

KENDALL, CHARLES WYE. *Private Men of War.* London: Philip Allen and Co., 1931. In Sources: Kendall.

KNAPP, ANDREW, and BALDWIN, WILLIAM. *Newgate Calendar.* London, 1809.

LEDER, LAWRENCE H. *Robert Livingston and the Politics of Colonial New York.* Chapel Hill: University of North Carolina Press, 1961. In Sources: Leder.

LESLIE, CHARLES. *A New and Exact Account of Jamaica.* Edinburgh: R. Fleming, 1739. In Sources: Leslie.

LESLIE, ROBERT C. *Life Aboard a British Privateer.* London: Chapman and Hall, 1889.

LINDSAY, PHILIP. *The Great Buccaneer.* New York: Wilfred Funk, Inc., 1951. In Sources: Lindsay.

LITTLE, BRYAN. *Crusoe's Captain.* London: Odhams Press, Ltd., 1960. In Sources: Little.

LLOYD, CHRISTOPHER. *William Dampier.* London: Faber and Faber, 1966. In Sources: Lloyd.

LOWES, JOHN LIVINGSTON. *The Road to Xanadu.* Boston: Houghton, Mifflin Co., 1927.

MACAULAY, THOMAS BABINGTON. *History of England.* London: J. M. Dent and Sons, 1957. In Sources: Macaulay.

MALO, HENRI. *American Privateers at Dunkerque.* United States Naval Institute Proceedings, Vol. 37, No. 3, Whole No. 139.

MARSDEN, REGINALD G. *Documents Relating to Law and Custom of the Sea.* Navy Records Society, 1915–16. In Sources: Marsden.

MASEFIELD, JOHN. *On the Spanish Main.* London: Methuen and Co., 1925.

MEANS, PHILIP A. *The Spanish Main: Focus of Envy.* New York: Charles Scribner's Sons, 1935. In Sources: Means.

MEGROZ, R. L. *The Real Robinson Crusoe*. London: Cresset Press, 1939.

MILLIGAN, CLARENCE. *Captain William Kidd, Gentleman or Buccaneer?* Philadelphia: Dorrance and Co., 1932. In Sources: Milligan.

MONAGHAN, FRANK. *An Examination of the Reputation of Captain Kidd*. Proceedings of the New York State Historical Association XXXI. *New York History*, XIV, 1933.

MOORHOUSE, E. HALLAM. *Samuel Pepys*. London: Chapman and Hall, 1909. In Sources: Moorhouse.

MORRIS, RICHARD B. *Fair Trial*. New York: Alfred A. Knopf, 1952. In Sources: Morris.

OPPENHEIM, M. *A History of the Administration of the Royal Navy*, etc. London: John Lane, The Bodley Head, 1896. In Sources: Oppenheim.

OSGOOD, HERBERT L. *The American Colonies in the Eighteenth Century*. New York: Columbia University Press, 1924.

P. A. ESQ. (PHILIP AYRES). *The Voyages and Adventures of Capt. Barth Sharp and others in the South Seas*. London: 1684.

PAINE, RALPH D. *The Book of Buried Treasure*. London: William Heineman, 1911.

————. *The Old Merchant Marine*. New Haven: Yale University Press, 1919. In Sources: Paine.

PARRY, J. H., and SHERLOCK, P. M. *A Short History of the West Indies*. London: Macmillan Co., 1957.

PAULLIN, CHARLES OSCAR. *The Navy of the American Revolution*. Cleveland: Burrows Bros. Co., 1906. In Sources: Paullin.

PEPYS, SAMUEL. *The Diary of Samuel Pepys*. New York: Limited Editions Club, 1942. In Sources: Pepys.

PERRY, MILTON F. *Infernal Machines*. Baton Rouge: Louisiana State University Press, 1965.

PEYSTER, DE, FREDERIC. *The Life and Administration of Richard, Earl of Bellomont*. New York: New York Historical Society, 1879. In Sources: de Peyster.

PHILLIPS, J. LEOLINE. "Sir Henry Morgan, Buccaneer." Historical Sketches of Glamorgan. Vol. II. London: Western Mail, 1912.

POWELL, JOHN WILLIAM DAMER. *Bristol Privateers and Ships of War*. Bristol: J. W. Arrowsmith, 1930. In Sources: Powell.

PRATT, FLETCHER. *Civil War on Western Waters*. New York: Henry Holt and Co., 1956.

————. *The Heroic Years*. New York: Harrison Smith and Robert Haas, 1934.

PYLE, HOWARD. *Buccaneers and Marooners of America.* London: T. Fisher Unwin Co., 1897. In Sources: Pyle.

ROBB, NESCA A. *William of Orange.* London: William Heinemann, 1966.

ROBERTS, CLAYTON. *The Growth of Responsible Government in Stuart England.* Cambridge: University Press, 1966.

ROBERTS, W. ADOLPHE. *Sir Henry Morgan, Buccaneer and Governor.* New York: Covici, Friede, 1933. In Sources: Roberts.

ROBINSON, WILLIAM MORRISON, JR. *The Confederate Privateers.* New Haven: Yale University Press, 1928. In Sources: Robinson.

RODDIS, LOUIS H. "A Short History of Nautical Medicine." *Annals of Medical History.* Vol. III, No. 3, 3rd Series (May 1941), pp. 203–247.

ROGERS, CAPT. WOODES. *A Cruising Voyage Round the World.* Introduction and Notes by G. E. Manwaring. London: Cassell and Co., Ltd., 1928. In Sources: Rogers.

ROOSEVELT, THEODORE. *The Naval War of 1812.* New York: G. P. Putnam's Sons, 1882.

SCHURZ, WILLIAM LYTLE. *The Manila Galleon.* New York: E. P. Dutton Co., 1959. In Sources: Schurz.

SEITZ, DON C. *The Tryal of Capt. William Kidd.* New York: Rufus Rockwell Wilson, Inc., 1936.

SHELVOCKE, GEORGE. *A Privateer's Voyage Round the World.* New York: Jonathan Cape and Harrison Smith, 1930. In Sources: Shelvocke.

SLOANE, SIR HANS. *A Voyage to the Islands.* London: Vol. I, 1707; Vol. II, 1725. In Sources: Sloane.

SNIDER, C. H. J. *Under the Red Jack.* London: Martin Hopkinson and Co., 1928.

STANLEY, HENRY MORTON. *How I Found Livingstone.* London: Sampson Low, Marston, Low, and Searle, 1873. In Sources: Stanley.

STARK, FRANCIS R. *The Abolition of Privateering and the Declaration of Paris.* New York: 1897. In Sources: Stark.

STATHAM, COMMANDER E. P. *Privateers and Privateering.* London: Hutchinson and Co., 1910. In Sources: Statham.

STOCK, LEO FRANCIS. *Proceedings and Debates of the British Parliaments Respecting North America.* Vol. II (1689–1702). New York: Kraus Reprint Corporation, 1966.

STRONG, L. A. G. *Dr. Quicksilver.* London: Andrew Melrose, 1955.

SUTHERLAND, JAMES. *Defoe.* London: Methuen and Co., 1937.

TAYLOR, JOHN. *A Book About Bristol.* London: Houlston and Sons, 1872.

TREVELYAN, G. M. *England Under the Stuarts*. New York: Barnes and Noble, 1965.

VERRILL, A. HYATT. *The Real Story of the Pirate*. New York: D. Appleton and Co., 1923.

WARD, ESTELLE FRANCES. *Christopher Monck, Duke of Albemarle*. London: John Murray, 1915.

WILKINS, HAROLD T. *Captain Kidd and His Skeleton Island*. London: Cassell and Co., 1935. In Sources: Wilkins.

WILLIAMS, W. LLEWELYN. "Sir Henry Morgan, the Buccaneer," in *Transactions, The Honorable Society Cymmrodion*. London, 1905.

WORDSWORTH, WILLIAM. *Complete Poetical Works*. Boston: Houghton Mifflin Co., 1904. In Sources: Wordsworth.

WYCHERLEY, GEORGE. *Buccaneers of the Pacific*. Indianapolis: Bobbs-Merrill Co., 1928.

INDEX

Adams, John, 222

Adventure Galley, 148, 149; fitted out, 121; voyage to Indian Ocean, 121–26; fight with Portuguese, 126; falling to pieces, 129; plundered by Kidd's men, 130; burned, 130

Advice, 139, 139 n, 140, 141, 142, 145

Albemarle, Christopher Monck, 2nd Duke of, 85, 102–5, 106

Albemarle, Elizabeth, Duchess of, 102, 104

Albemarle, George Monck, 1st Duke of, 20, 49, 49 n, 59, 60, 67

Angel, 9

Anne, Queen, 4 37, 105 n, 154 n, 167

Anson, George, Lord, 213 n, 214

Antonio, 133–38

Archbould, Henry, 48

Arizabala, Don José de, 189, 190, 192

Arlington, Henry Bennet, Earl of, 49, 50, 67, 69, 86

Ascensión, 186, 197, 198, 199, 200

Assistance, 83, 104, 106

Augsburg, League of, 37

Avery, "Long John," 35–6, 36 n, 132

Ballard, Col., 103, 106

Ballet, John, 168, 177

Banister, Maj.-Gen. James, 85

Barlicorn, Richard, 149

Bath, William, 168, 179

Beeston, Col. William, 93, 94, 99, 99 n

Beginning, 186, 196

Begoña, 205–8, 207 n

Bellomont, Catherine, Lady, 135, 137

Bellomont, Richard Coote, Earl of, 122, 125, 132, 133 n, 157, 160; governor New England, 116; enlists Kidd backers, 117; signs articles, 119–20; invites Kidd to Boston, 134; arrests Kidd, 136–139; sends Kidd London, 139–145; attitude toward Crown witnesses, 149 n; recognizes validity of passes, 159

Berkeley, George, Lord, 85

Blackburne, Lancelot, 31 n

Blathwayt, William, 115

Bolton, Henry, 133, 138, 138 n

Bradinham, Robert, 149, 149 n, 150, 151, 153, 154, 157, 159

Bradley, Capt. Joseph, 74, 75

Bradley, Samuel, 112, 123 n, 133, 133 n

Browne, Richard, 61 n, 70, 80 n, 82 n

Buccaneers, 17, 44, 45; hunters, 21–23; take to sea, 24–25; early cruelties, 25; piety, 25–26; havens, 26–27; cross Darien, 30–32; last expedition, 32; necessary